# THE POWER OF PREGNANCY HELP

## *The First Fifty Years*

Dr. Peggy Hartshorn & Jor-El Godsey

Published by
Heartbeat International Publishing
5000 Arlington Centre Blvd.
Ste. 2277
Columbus, Ohio 43220

Manufactured in the United States of America, or in the United Kingdom when distributed elsewhere.

Scripture quotations are taken from the Revised Standard Version of the Bible, copyright © 1946, 1952, and 1971 the Division of Christian Education of the National Council of the Churches of Christ in the United States of America. Used by permission. All rights reserved.

Hartshorn, Peggy & Godsey, Jor-El
    *The Power of Pregnancy Help: The First Fifty Years*
    ISBN: 978-1-7377745-0-1
    eBook: 978-1-7377745-1-8

Cover design by: Andrea Trudden
Cover photo by: Heartbeat International
Copyediting and interior design: Claudia Volkman
Photo credits: Heartbeat International

# CONTENTS

# PREFACE

Through the lens of Heartbeat International, the world's largest network of pregnancy help organizations, this book tells the story of our movement: how it has grown into a mighty force for life around the world from tiny seeds planted over fifty years ago, what its scope is now, and where the Lord seems to be taking us!

At first this book was intended to simply be an update of the book I wrote for our 40th anniversary, *Foot Soldiers Armed with Love* (2011). Our president, Jor-El Godsey, and I would simply add information from the last ten years. But it was not to be that simple at all!

We ultimately determined that *Foot Soldiers Armed with Love* needs to "stand on its own" as it was written, and so it will continue to be available from Heartbeat Publishing. A very different book than this new one, it is more of a "memoir" about our founders (my heroes), my struggle to accept the leadership role for Heartbeat (how could I walk in their shoes?), and, once I became president in 1993, some of the key events in Heartbeat history during the next seventeen years as the Lord led me and our leadership team through a myriad of challenges and opportunities. In a sense, that book contains my personal testimony.

In *The Power of Pregnancy Help*, Jor-El and I tell our personal stories, but we also have collaborated to take a fresh look at the Heartbeat story within the history of the entire pregnancy help movement, including the fast-paced changes, growth, and impact of the last ten years.

One thing has not changed: this is still the story of how God has worked to bring help and hope to millions through ordinary people, the foot soldiers of the pregnancy help movement who place our trust in Him.

"Reader favorite" chapters of *Foot Soldiers Armed with Love*, those that tell the story of our three founders, Dr. John Hillabrand, Lore Maier, and Sister Paula Vandegaer, are included in this new book. But most of the other chapters are new. Some favorite historical pictures from *Foot Soldiers Armed with Love* appear here, but most photos are also new to this book.

Enjoy these amazing stories of what the Lord has accomplished over the last fifty years—and continues to accomplish today, through the pregnancy help movement!

—Peggy Hartshorn

# INTRODUCTION

## PEGGY'S STORY AS A FOOT SOLDIER

It was January 22, 1973—just another cold winter day in Columbus, Ohio. I had left our apartment and was driving north on High Street, the major north/south artery toward Ohio State University, where I was working on a graduate degree. My mind was on a meeting with my academic advisor, but I had the car radio on, vaguely listening to a program on NPR. Then the newscaster made an announcement that stunned me. The Supreme Court of the United States, ruling in a case called *Roe v. Wade*, had declared unconstitutional every one of the existing state laws that restricted abortion. A woman now had a "right to privacy" that covered a decision to have an abortion at any time during her pregnancy. In one fell swoop, they had declared unconstitutional every state law in our country that protected unborn children and their mothers from abortion! At first I could not believe my ears. Then I thought that as soon as I saw my husband (an attorney in his first year of practice), I would ask him to go to the law library and get a copy of the decision. Surely the radio had it wrong!

My mind raced back to my college years in California, the state that was among the four states to first liberalize their abortion laws in 1967. The ethics professor at our Catholic women's college warned our class in 1968, "Mark my words, in five years abortion will be legal all over the United States." I remembered a soft gasp of surprise and denial coming from the class at that time. Had that horrible prophesy come true? And had I not noticed what had been happening, preoccupied as I was with graduate school, my young marriage, the death of my father—all of which seemed to be the most important events in the world at that time?

If this news was correct, I *knew* I had to do something. For me, this was a never-to-be-forgotten day, seared into memory like other days in history when the United States suffered surprise attacks, December 7, 1941 (Pearl Harbor Day) or September 11, 2001 (the crumbling of the World Trade Center). For me, it was as dramatic a moment as when St. Paul got knocked off his horse.

I didn't fully realize then how that day would change my life, nor how God was already preparing me, and thousands of others, to become foot soldiers for Him in the battle for the sanctity of every person's life. I did not know then that I would be in this battle for most of my life, and that the battle was ultimately the battle of good versus evil. Nor did I know that the "army for life" that I would be joining, along with my husband, had been in formation well before January 22, 1973.

## From Home to San Francisco and Back: The Frog and the Water

Raised in a small town in Ohio, in a devout family with Catholic priests and nuns on my father's side and Protestant missionaries, church organists, and choir members on my mother's side, I went to college in the San Francisco Bay area in the mid-1960s. I saw, with amazement, billboards advertising abortion clinics being put up in 1967 after California legalized abortion. I had been shocked when our ethics professor predicted that within five years, abortion would become legal throughout our country.

But that was San Francisco, at the same place and time that the hippies were roaming the streets, experimenting with drugs, and singing "Make love, not war." On the nearby campus of the University of California at Berkeley, anti-Viet Nam war protesters were burning down buildings. During those years, we witnessed the assassinations of Martin Luther King Jr. and Bobbie Kennedy. The world seemed topsy-turvy.

When I returned to Ohio to marry my high school sweetheart, Mike, and attend graduate school, I was lulled into thinking that the world was being right-sided again. I had no idea that the sexual revolution of the sixties that I had watched unfolding in San Francisco was not an aberration. Instead, it was to become the "new normal" and, in fact, would be taken to extremes, which we see today, that I could not have imagined back then. This revolution was the culmination of a carefully orchestrated campaign, starting in 1921 with Margaret Sanger and the founding of Planned Parenthood (called the American Birth Control League), to change the sexual mores of the United States and of the world and to control the population (who should be born, to whom, and exactly when and where). In terms of sexual mores, their goal was to make sure that sexual intimacy was separated from a lifetime commitment to marriage, and especially separated from children. Since birth control has an inevitable failure rate, abortion became the "linchpin" of their plan.

Planned Parenthood eventually joined forces with Hugh Heffner and other purveyors of pornography to promote the idea that the purpose of sexual intimacy was solely for pleasure and recreation. They were masters at presenting this idea gradually. They "heated things up" ever so slowly at first so that many in the American public did not even notice it. The early *Playboy* magazines, once hidden behind retail counters, seem almost "innocent" compared to the disgusting pornography present today and readily accessible in our homes through the internet. College students burning bras in the sixties seem quaint compared to young children being victimized in sex trafficking and sexual exploitation today. Lesbians holding hands in the 1970s seem somewhat innocent compared to today's gay rights parades, so-called gay marriage, and now the jarring and unscientific but ever-more normalized idea of "gender fluidity." I could never have imagined in the 1960s that this is where it was all leading.

The generations that grew up in the sixties and later can be compared to the proverbial frog that was oblivious to the fact that the water he had been thrown into was intentionally being heated up ever so gradually. That frog eventually boiled to death. I have always felt extremely blessed that I was like the other frog. Coming from the healthy and normal pond that God designed for me, a strong Christian family that believed in and lived out God's design for life and love, I was thrown into hot water and jumped out!

That's why I reacted with shock and dismay on January 22, 1973. This was a call to action!

## First Steps into the Pro-Life Movement and Pregnancy Help

I soon found (from the phone book) that Columbus had a Right to Life group. I called and said, "What can I do to help?" The first president of Columbus Right to Life, economist Ed O'Boyle, and his wife, pediatrician Meade O'Boyle, took Mike and me under their wing, educating us on the issue and helping us find our place in the young pro-life movement that had actually begun to form during the mid-1960s in response to pro-abortion efforts. At that time, Planned Parenthood and their allies, especially the National Abortion Rights Action League (now NARAL Pro-Choice America), and the Religious Coalition for Abortion Rights (now Religious Coalition for Reproductive Choice) were leading the charge to legalize abortion state by state. These groups were also orchestrating just the right case to bring through the court system and eventually present before the US Supreme Court, and they found it in Texas. It was called *Roe v. Wade*.

I became active in right-to-life activities as soon as I could. This coincided with finishing my PhD in English literature and becoming an English and Humanities Professor at Franklin University in Columbus,

Ohio. I also became the volunteer education director of Columbus Right to Life. In addition to showing fetal development and abortion slides to any audience that would watch and listen, I was gathering people together to protest on January 22 each year and demonstrating (with our two adopted infants in a double stroller) in front of abortion clinics as they began to open in Columbus. Actually, we were doing the first "sidewalk counseling" and prayer vigils in front of abortion centers, although we didn't use those terms in those days. Soon I was also testifying in the Ohio legislature in an attempt to change the new law of the land and also working to elect pro-life candidates to office. This is what Right to Life did. It was the educational, legislative, and political arm and army of the pro-life movement.

Our call to action soon led to a call for even more personal involvement. People were calling the local Right to Life office, needing information for girls with crisis pregnancies, some of whom had been "thrown out" of their homes or abandoned by boyfriends because they refused to have an abortion. Ed and Meade were housing girls in their own home, and they asked if we would be willing to do the same.

In 1975, when Anne, the first of our twelve "girls," came to live with us in Columbus, little did we know that God was preparing us for a lifetime calling in the other arm of the pro-life movement—the service arm, or the "alternatives to abortion" movement. In fact, we also did not know that there was a relatively new organization called Alternatives to Abortion International or AAI (now Heartbeat International) based in Ohio and founded in 1971. In early 1978, at the first Ohio Right to Life Conference, held in Columbus, Mike and I would meet one of the founders of AAI, Lore Maier, and discover there was *another* entire army of pro-life foot soldiers being raised up by the Lord to provide help and support so no one would ever feel that abortion was their only alternative.

The discovery of AAI, now Heartbeat International, changed our own lives in ways we never could have imagined, as well as the lives of hundreds of thousands of other people who have also discovered this alternate army of foot soldiers, armed not with political action or speeches and debates, but with love. And this love has helped save and change millions of other lives over the last fifty years. That story is the subject of this book.

My husband and I felt called to start a pregnancy help center in Columbus, Ohio, inspired by the work of Lore Maier and that other army of prolife warriors and also by a call to commit to a "couple ministry" on our Marriage Encounter weekend in October of 1978. Mike and I attended our first AAI Academy (conference) in 1980, and we were "hooked"! We had a hotline installed in our bedroom in late 1980 (to make the phone book deadline for our hotline number), opened the doors of our first center, Pregnancy Distress Center (now called Pregnancy Decision Health Centers), on January 22, 1981, and became foot soldiers armed with love. I thought we would start the center and then go back to Right to Life, but that never happened. I was asked to join the AAI board at the end of 1986.

### Lessons in Leadership and Leadership Transition

One thing would lead to another, as often happens when you say "yes" to the Lord, and I eventually left my position as an English professor at Franklin University (where I taught full- or part-time for twenty years) and became the first full-time, salaried CEO (president) of AAI in 1993. At that time, we also changed our name to Heartbeat International.

The Lord put many people in my path and gave me many signs during these years. If you are interested in how I struggled with this call, how I finally said "yes," and then how the Lord led me step-by-step to realize that He really had prepared me all along for this leadership role, you can find that story in more detail in *Foot Soldiers Armed with Love,* available from Heartbeat International. In that book, first published in 2011, I realize that I tell Heartbeat's history almost as a personal memoir—my personal faith journey and leadership story is so intertwined with Heartbeat's early history! I heard it said recently that "God always gives those He loves lots of opportunities to learn to trust Him." That truth could sum up my life! Almost every event in my early years as president was an illustration of struggle, stepping out in faith with our leadership team of board members and staff, and then stepping back and watching with amazement at how the Lord multiplied our efforts, like He did with the loaves and fishes. (So that book is very different than *The Power of Pregnancy Help,* although it covers some of the same history.)

When you finally know you are on the path the Lord has set for you, and you know He is fully using your gifts, skills, and experiences to do His will, it is an exciting and powerful experience—even though it will be filled with challenges and obstacles. My job as Heartbeat president (1993–2015) was such an experience—it was more of a joy than a job. Even though it was sometimes exhausting, I loved it! Yet I always knew that someday that job and joy would come to an end. I prayed that I would know when the Lord would have me pass on the mantle of leadership; I did not want to be "early" or "late." At Heartbeat, we had seen too many instances when a leadership transition did not go well in one of our affiliated PHCs, for example, or in another national pro-life organization. Our Heartbeat board formed a Succession Committee around 2005, and we started reading literature on leadership transition, thinking through what the experts had to say on the subject. I was thankful for the information and wisdom we all gained by exploring the issue.

But when the time came, it was not any expert formula but rather listening to the promptings of the Holy Spirit that I believe helped us create a beautiful leadership transition. For that I thank our board at the time, especially our wise board chair Ken Clark, and Jor-El Godsey, our vice president, to whom I passed that mantle of leadership.

I began to discern that, in the unknown number of productive years I had remaining, God would have me try to accomplish what I had been pushing off my plate: more reflection about what the Lord had been teaching me, more writing, more mentoring, and more "passing on" to the next generation. But I also knew that He was not finished with me yet—and my call to Heartbeat's mission was as strong as ever! It was clear that Heartbeat needed a younger, faith-filled servant leader, one with a different skill set than I had brought twenty-three years earlier—skills more suited to the needs of the "times" and to this time in Heartbeat history, but also someone immersed in pregnancy help who could hit the ground running, so to speak.

It became clear that the Lord had already put this person in the leadership pipeline at Heartbeat almost ten years before—he was our vice president and my right hand, Jor-El Godsey. The board concurred 100 percent! Only much later did I learn that the timing of this leadership transition, while good for me, was not really ideal at all for Jor-El and his family. But, like the true servant leader he is, Jor-El trusted that it was the Lord's timing and said "yes" to the board's request. This turned out to be truly providential in many ways.

One of the most memorable experiences I have from my tenure at Heartbeat is the official "passing of the baton" at the Heartbeat International Conference in 2016. Jor-El preferred that I pass him a shepherd's crook, which I did, in a prayerful and beautiful experience. I have remained with Heartbeat as chair of our board, a position that I love. So, after forty-eight years, I am still a foot soldier. Why do I love my new hat (or helmet!)? A strong board is vital to achieving our goal of advancing effective, life-affirming pregnancy help around the world, plus I have the blessing of continuing to work with Jor-El, to see clearly how his leadership has allowed the Heartbeat Central team and the entire pregnancy help network to grow and bloom dramatically in the last five years! And it has been a joy to work with Jor-El in co-authoring this history of the power of pregnancy help through the lens of Heartbeat International from the earliest days of our founding in 1971 through the last five decades.

## A Hopeful Future

I am excited about the potential for the next decades of Heartbeat history! Over the past fifty years, millions of babies have been born who otherwise would have been aborted, and millions of mothers' (and fathers') lives have been changed for the better. But, in addition, our work has helped change Americans' views and choices related to abortion. The numbers and rates of abortion have dropped dramatically since their height in 1991, and so has the ratio of abortions to live births.

We are "winning" on abortion because we are changing the culture, one person and one family at a time. Abortion is a root cause (if not THE root cause) of the breakdown of the family. We not only reduce the number of abortions, but we also help women and families heal from the effects of abortion (and all the behaviors that people use to cover up their pain). I believe that God may be using our work to gradually return our American culture to one that values and respects each human life, honors God, and respects God's Plan for our Sexuality—that is, God, sexual intimacy, marriage between one man and one woman, unselfish love or self-gift, and children all go together. And what we model in America influences the world. Time will tell if this is what God is doing through the pregnancy help movement.

This army of foot soldiers armed with love, fifty years after it was first formed, is larger and stronger than ever, despite direct attacks and every conceivable obstacle that could be thrown in our path. This book contains the stories of some of these foot soldiers, powered by the love of the Lord. What could be more potent?

*Peggy's first step into the pro-life movement was with Right to Life in 1973. As President of Columbus Right to Life, she is with Mildred Jefferson, President of National Right to Life in 1977.*

*Peggy and Mike at the March for Life in Columbus, Ohio, with Katy in 1980.*

*Peggy and Mike, with their adopted children Katy and Tim, hosted pregnant mothers in their home for 13 years, experiencing, along with them, their range of feelings, wants, needs, and options.*

*The official passing of Heartbeat International leadership from Peggy to Jor-El at the 2016 Conference. With Jor-El, the Board that planned the transition (L to R): Chris Dattilo, Keith Armato, Cathy Clark, Ken Clark (chair), Peggy, Gary Thome, Jor-El Godsey, Pia de Solenni, Chuck Donovan, Sherry Wright, Derek McCoy.*

# INTRODUCTION

## JOR-EL'S STORY AS A FOOT SOLDIER

I first heard about something called a "pregnancy center" after having been arrested and put into a jail cell.

Not a normal place to hear about the precious Gospel-oriented ministry outreach that is pregnancy help. But jail it was in 1989. And that was my second jail experience!

### A Personal Matter

My journey into life-affirming pregnancy center outreach started not just with a lack of knowledge about this key part of the pro-life movement, but from being completely on the other side of the abortion issue.

I grew up near Fort Lauderdale, Florida, in a non-Christian home and as a product of public school. Sadly, neither equipped me with the moral clarity to righteously respond in the moment when I learned that my girlfriend was pregnant. Neither was I equipped with anywhere near the scientific reality of what was truly at the heart of the decision at hand—a whole, separate, unique human being.

To be clear, I failed both my girlfriend and my baby in that moment. I can't know what might have happened if I had found the courage to take a stance *for* our child, as both of us knew we were ill-prepared to care for a baby. Instead I defaulted to the selfish solution by encouraging and then facilitating the abortion of my own child. In those moments I would not have described myself with the label of pro-abortion or pro-choice, but my actions did. The tears shed in the wake of those moments quickly dried for me, and life returned to a semblance of normal. Of course, the relationship, as is all too common in the wake of abortion, did not survive much longer.

And yet, only a few years later, a new and very different relationship developed for me. Through a handful of providential incidences, I found myself opening my heart to a fully committed relationship with the God of the Bible, the Lord Jesus Christ, in 1986. In the months that followed, I began to learn of God by hearing and reading His Word, having been welcomed into the community of a warm, friendly, faith-filled local church. In this environment I began to understand God's true love for me—even the unconditional love He had for me while I was yet a sinner (see Romans 5:8).

It was in this very same church during a Sunday morning service that a visiting pastor delivered a message on the sanctity of human life. What he shared changed me in an instant. I remember that very moment, and always will.

"Abortion is not a social issue," the preacher said. Inside I recoiled at this because I had come to learn that it was very much a social issue. This was, after all, the late 1980s, and abortion had not only settled into the fabric of our social reality—it had become a common occurrence, with abortions climbing to the highest numbers ever. When a social structure such as American society permits by law more than a million abortions each year, it is certainly a "social issue."

But then the pastor added that "abortion is not a political issue." As a young adult I had paid scant attention to the national political scene, but even I knew that abortion was a persistent political hot button. This was the era of Ronald Reagan, being carried on by President George H.W. Bush and the messaging of the Moral Majority.

I frantically turned these two clearly false statements over in my mind, thinking that the pastor was missing it altogether. Had I been in a different church, I might have loudly objected to these statements. What I did not know in that moment is that I was being set up by the Holy Spirit.

"Abortion is a Gospel issue!" he thundered.

In that instant, that very moment, I *physically* felt the supernatural truth and the righteous power of his words. It was as if the scales over my eyes (or more correctly, my heart) fell away, and suddenly I was convicted to the core. Two powerful truths became crystal clear to me in that moment.

The first truth was that my sin was exposed fully for what it was. I had taken innocent blood, blood as innocent as that of Christ Himself on the Cross. Oddly, somehow I had been listening to the message in a detached way, as if it didn't apply to me but to someone else. Maybe to everyone else. But it *did* apply to me. Personally. And deeply.

## A Matter of Person

The second truth was that those who proclaim His Gospel must also champion these little ones that are being led to slaughter, *little one* meaning "a little person with the same God-given uniqueness as every other person." "Rescue those who are being taken away to death; hold back those who are stumbling to the slaughter" (Proverbs 24:11). Nowhere is this truer than of the little, defenseless unborn child whose life is "taken away" in the act of abortion.

When the preacher wrapped up his message, he did so with a call to get engaged immediately. Unlike most Sunday morning messages, this pastor was not waiting until we decided what, when, and how we might follow through with this message that morning.

In fact, he had prepared for that moment with handmade signs and invited us all to head directly to the nearest abortion clinic to picket and protest. With an overwhelming sense of conviction, I felt I could do nothing but join in that afternoon. We did not "Pass Go" or even stop for lunch. Instead we found ourselves, almost the whole of that little church, standing in front of the nearest abortion clinic declaring the unrighteousness of what happened there on a routine basis.

In truth, before stepping onto the sidewalk in front of it, I didn't even know such a clinic was so close to our church. In that hour we stood witnessing on the sidewalk, displaying in our signage and our somberness the seriousness of this "Gospel issue." And, for me, the vital importance of defending the unborn became clearer and clearer.

What I did not realize that day was that preacher was among the national leadership of Operation Rescue. In those days, Operation Rescue was known for protesting abortion clinics by peacefully and prayerfully blocking the entrance to them. They had already made national news with their protest events, called "rescues." They spread from the first one in upstate New York across the country, especially the Midwest, and they were planning to come to my own community in South Florida soon.

I would join them—more than once.

In a matter of weeks I had been transformed from pro-abortion to pro-life to pro-life activist. I got arrested for blocking entrance to the very type of clinic I had selfishly sought out just a few years earlier.

And it was the second of these arrests that landed me in jail, the county stockade to be exact, where I first heard about another type of pro-life activism: pregnancy help centers. Of course, this sounded warmer and more compassionate than the confrontational civil disobedience of blocking an abortion clinic.

Just a month or so later, I stepped into that little 800-square-foot pregnancy center I had learned about in jail. There I met Dottie Wobb, the newly appointed executive director tasked with opening the doors of a brand-new pregnancy help center of a new organization. What I saw was compelling—a place dedicated to helping women facing an unexpected pregnancy to never have to darken the door of the abortion clinic like the ones I had been seeking to block. Dottie showed me the "Counseling Room" and the "Material Aid" space and helped me understand how the whole thing was designed to walk with a woman through her journey and help her make a life-affirming choice.

My question "How can I help?" led to me connecting some tradesmen to the project to get their stalled construction to the next inspection point. That small part helped the pregnancy center get closer toward opening. To my surprise, I received a call and was invited to join the board of directors. Little did I know that this simple connection and small act of service would shape my future in a big way. I could not have understood then that my lifelong journey serving in pregnancy help had just begun.

## A Minority of Men

In our direct protests against clinics, there were always considerably more men than women, especially when the police began making arrests. But in the pregnancy help center, the vast majority involved were women. In those days, men were somewhat common as board members but little else—except as peripheral volunteers in construction, handiwork, and so on.

After all, "abortion is a women's issue," we're told. Abortion, or "reproductive rights," had become intertwined with the feminist movement. Since only women could get pregnant and thus have an abortion, only women could, and should, carry the conversation. Despite the fact that it was seven *men* in black robes that decided *Roe v. Wade* in favor of abortion as a constitutional "right," men were routinely silenced on the issue.

In 1976, just a few years after *Roe v. Wade*, during the *Planned Parenthood v. Danforth* case, the Supreme Court held that laws requiring "spousal consent" were unconstitutional. Men had no legal right to exercise "spousal veto power" in an abortion decision.

Yet abortion is not just a woman's issue. Every pregnancy involves a man, and for every abortion there is a man. Perhaps it's a man like me who wants the abortion. Or it might be a man who doesn't want it but is legally powerless to have any say. And some men are never told about the abortion—or even about the pregnancy, for that matter.

Sure, women experience the abortion directly. But men also feel the effects of aborting their child. And for those who can see beyond themselves, they also see the effects an abortion has on their partner.

Men, or at least pre-born baby boys, statistically represent about half of all abortions in the US. In other countries, it's actually pre-born girls that are targeted for termination because they are considered of lesser value than a baby boy whose work can enrich the family (i.e., India, China). In her book *Unnatural Selection: Choosing Boys Over Girls and the Consequences of a World Full of Men*, feminist Mara Hvistendahl writes begrudgingly, "After decades of fighting for a woman's right to choose the outcome of her own pregnancy . . . women are abusing that right."[1]

So it really comes as no surprise that the growth of the service side of the pro-life movement, the pregnancy help model of compassion and care of pregnant women, is largely borne by pro-life women.

As the arc of my involvement moved from board member governance to day-to-day staff member, I was certainly a minority. It was not uncommon for me to be the only male, or one of a very small percentage, at any meeting of pregnancy help staff and volunteers.

In fact, it led to a very special event.

All board members, by policy, were required to take the "Crisis Counseling Training" necessary for anyone volunteering to serve clients at the pregnancy center. As a man who had no expectation of ever needing to counsel a woman in a crisis pregnancy—namely because another policy didn't allow for males to counsel females alone—I was not especially interested. So I delayed until the very last opportunity a year later.

Yet it was in that training that I learned a great deal about how the crisis of an unexpected pregnancy can paralyze normal thinking,

---

1 Mara Hvistendahl, *Unnatural Selection: Choosing Boys Over Girls and the Consequences of a World Full of Men*, https://www.marahvistendahl.com/unnatural-selection.

shoving out all possible options until only one, abortion, remains. I also learned about the importance of listening actively. It was in listening that the keys for a life-affirming solution could be found.

Listening skills were augmented by breaking into pairs to practice passive versus active listening skills. The pairs in the room quickly formed, and a poor young lady named Karen—who was quite attractive and single—got stuck with me, one of the very few guys in the room. For most of that exercise, we sat back-to-back trying to explain a drawing the other couldn't see and had to duplicate. What resulted wasn't terribly accurate, but the point was to demonstrate how active communication is a great tool for clarifying the picture of someone in a crisis.

Over the next several months, I saw Karen at various pregnancy center activities—me in my board member role and Karen as a volunteer counselor. About a year after our first meeting at the training, she agreed to join me on our first date. One year later we stood at the altar and were married! (And we just recently celebrated our twenty-fifth anniversary.)

The board began to wrestle with the growth of our ministry. We served a densely populated area, and the need for more staff, and eventually more locations, was becoming apparent. We discerned it was time to add an executive administrator, a "number two" to the executive director, to focus on the business side and fundraising needs of our growing outreach. After a long search for just the right person, a curious set of "God-incidences" led me to say yes to being offered the position. I became the first male employee of our pregnancy center.

A few years later, a family move led to me to Colorado, where I stepped in to fill the role of the retiring executive director. Within just a few weeks of being the new ED, I traveled to the statewide Counselor's Conference where there was 187 women . . . and me. I know this because I counted!

## Changing States

I would travel to national conferences most years and walk into a roomful of women and only a few men. Some of these were national leaders, while very few were at local level leadership. At conferences the guys were easy to spot and connect with, and we created a fraternity of sorts. Several, like me, have become "lifers" in the life movement and are my good friends.

After seven years, my season of leadership in Colorado came to an unexpected close. Within days I providentially saw a posting for the position of vice president, Ministry Services, at Heartbeat International's headquarters in Columbus, Ohio. It had been my pleasure to meet Heartbeat's long-time president, Peggy Hartshorn, on more than one occasion. One of those was being part of the organizing force for a coalition of Colorado centers. Together we had drafted a charter and divided the state into regions. (There is a funny story about that involving this flat-land, Florida-raised kid drawing lines on the Colorado map without consideration of small details like Rocky Mountain ranges, snow-capped ridges, and sometimes impassable roadways.) Peggy, along with other national affiliation leaders, joined in signing our hopeful Colorado charter in a symbolic ceremony of unity and collaboration.

And now I found myself in a phone call with the legend herself during my first interview for the position. Peggy is perpetually gracious, warmly welcoming, and always a force for positivity. And she is also a PhD, a professor of English, and a wise veteran of pro-life ministry that could easily be intimidating if not for the aforementioned traits. While I believed my experiences and skill set equipped me for the job described in the posting, I was also keenly aware of the failings of my past. In that phone call I was open and candid, fully expecting my flaws to be disqualifying factors.

But I was wrong. Peggy and Beth Diemert, who was the outgoing leader of Heartbeat's Ministry Services team, did not see my flawed past that way. Instead they saw them as qualifiers for a ministry that needs overcomers—those who reconcile their past in such a way that they can use those experiences to minister to others with similar flaws or help them avoid those kinds of mistakes. By God's grace, in that phone call they melded the good with the bad to see something greater than the sum of its parts. That phone call led to an in-person interview in Ohio. In those days, every new staff person was interviewed by the entire Heartbeat staff. At that time this meant about a dozen staffers from the president (Peggy) all the way to the newest clerical assistant. I'm told there was a vote, and I was named the new vice president of Heartbeat International.

That meant moving from Colorado to Ohio in 2006. Our move from South Florida, where everyone likes to be in the winter, to Colorado, where everyone also likes to be in the winter, was quite the change. We loved Colorado. Ohio, on the other hand, was a place where most people are trying to escape to somewhere else during the winter. And I found myself in the heart of Buckeye Land in January, the heart of the winter! I surely didn't even know what a buckeye was back then, nor why this was an identity for every Ohioan as well as a rabid football identity. (A visitor to Columbus asked me once, "What is the religious make-up of Central Ohio?" The answer was easy: "Buckeye!")

The first week on the job I was whisked to Washington, DC, to take part in my very first March for Life. That same month I found myself seated around a leadership meeting table with many familiar faces I knew from a distance, having seen them on stage at the national conferences. While I was unfamiliar to them, they were known to me for their eloquence, commitment, and vision for life-affirming ministry.

The Bible says, "A [person's] gift makes room for him and brings him before great [people]" (Proverbs 18:16). To this day, I'm not sure exactly what gifts I have that this refers to, but I have certainly had the privilege of being before "great people." People in national leadership. People who faithfully lead their local pregnancy help center. People who invest their time, talent, and treasure in governance of life-affirming organizations. People who risk the wrath of this world to be seen as "foolish" for the work of the Kingdom.

Many of these are the women whom I work alongside, serve through my efforts, and celebrate in our shared mission.

One of those is Peggy Hartshorn. If I had to identify but a single benefit of joining and serving at Heartbeat, apart from the fulfillment of our mission, it is having the privilege to be mentored and led by her kind, faith-filled, Holy Spirit-anointed leadership. She is the definition of "servant leader" and has impacted countless lives, from those hosted in her home to the hotline conversations to the leadership of Heartbeat International and the global movement we serve.

On a plane ride back from our tenth trip together to DC for the March for Life, she asked if I would prayerfully consider the possibility of being her successor as president of Heartbeat International. This was not something I ever expected or sought in journeying to Ohio. The Lord knows this was not in my plans. It has been well said that "if you ever want to hear the Lord laugh, tell him your plans."

"Pro-life leadership," whether locally, nationally, or internationally, is never found in a booth at the job fair or in those tools that help you plot your ideal career. But through prayer and Providence, stick-to-itiveness and sacrifice, faith and flaws, in 2016 the board appointed me as only the second president in the history of Heartbeat International. Not since the leadership of Dr. John Hillabrand in the founding of the organization had a man led this special, enduring work. While Peggy left the day-to-day role, she accepted the mantle of board chairperson and continues to be a vital part of Heartbeat International to this day.

Decades after that first small conference I attended, men are still in the minority among active staff and volunteers of pregnancy help organizations. Fortunately, though, the ratio has improved significantly from being .006 percent of that Counselors Conference I attended. At the Heartbeat International Annual Conferences, we consistently have more than 10 percent men on hand. Most, like I was, are executive directors who are able to help a local pregnancy help organization precisely because there is a developed staff of women. A small one-man pregnancy help organization really needs to be a one-woman shop, if at all.

On a number of occasions, seasoned women leaders in the movement have approached me and thanked me for being an integral part of this portion of the pro-life arena. Far too many men have been poor examples of abandoning, or even pressuring, women to abort. I was that man too. But by God's grace I have the honor and privilege of standing with other pro-life men and a bevy of wonderful women in this work. Each of us has been called to champion life in the caring and compassionate outreach that is pregnancy help.

This is a women's issue. And it is a man's issue. Because it is, and forever will be, a human issue.

*Jor-El with his wife Karen and family.*

*Jor-El's pro-life journey from "Rescue South Florida" in front of an abortion clinic, to volunteering with wife Karen at a Florida PHC, to Heartbeat Vice President (at the March for Life).*

*Jor-El as Vice President of Ministry Services, with his team in 2008. (Betty McDowell, on his right, serves now as his Vice President of Ministry Services, and Molly Hoepfner, second from left, is Event Specialist.)*

# CHAPTER 1

# THE ARMY TODAY AND HOW IT ROSE UP

## Jor-El Godsey and Peggy Hartshorn

*"I would rather feel compassion than know the meaning of it."*
SAINT THOMAS AQUINAS

Compassion is the hallmark of the modern pregnancy help movement. Every woman should be loved and supported in her pregnancy. As Aquinas reminds us, compassion is something most keenly felt and necessarily experienced. And every year at least two million women and men are served in and through compassionate, grassroots pregnancy help efforts.

Two million served in one year is a lot. And that is just in the US alone, according to the latest pregnancy center report by the Charlotte Lozier Institute (2019).

Today, just into its second half century, pregnancy help outreach is a key constant amidst the larger, "up and down" accomplishments of the pro-life movement.

Despite abortion clinics' multibillion revenue being more than quadruple the donation-based revenue of local pregnancy help center locations, there are more than five PHCs for every one abortion clinic. The continuing proliferation of pregnancy help outreach is recognized as a major contributor to the decade's long decline (since 1990) of the number of abortions (down 46 percent), the rate of abortion (down 97 percent), and the ratio of abortions to live births (down 43 percent) in the United States.

## Spectrum of Soldiers

While it's easy to count building and mobile units, maternity homes, and hotline numbers, it is most important to recognize that the backbone of pregnancy help is its people, the foot soldiers in the battle for life, armed with love.

The best alternative to abortion is another person. Nowhere is this demonstrated more clearly than in the spectrum of people who fill out the "ranks" of the army that is the pregnancy help community. Most are volunteers, but many are full- and part-time paid staff. Many serve clients directly, face-to-face, while a sizeable number work "behind the scenes" with administrative matters, board governance, clerical needs, maintenance musts, and fundraising efforts. It is estimated that 70,000 workers currently serve in pregnancy centers in the US, eight in ten of them volunteers.

Not unsurprisingly, many, like myself, have their own personal abortion story. Each of these feels deeply the importance of providing meaningful alternatives so that someone else will have the chance to make a different decision than they did. The remainder of the community, who were preserved from their own abortion experience, empathetically identify with the difficulty of an unintended, unexpected pregnancy. Everyone, abortion story or no, feels the intense need to make sure no woman feels so alone, or so coerced, that they think the only option available to them is to terminate the life within.

An increasing number are licensed and certified professionals, especially from healthcare and related fields, with advanced degrees and specialized training. While physicians most often volunteer to be medical directors and also to read ultrasounds, the ranks of pregnancy help organizations (PHOs) have swelled in the last two decades with nurses and sonographers. They bring their own knowledge, experience, training, and medical acumen to bear in the compassionate work that is pregnancy help outreach. Healthcare help that has flowed into the movement adds rich elements to the relational model of care.

Our most recent Pregnancy Help Organization Salary Survey shows 60 percent of the respondents occupying key staff positions have college degrees. Among executive directors, this rose to more than 70 percent with college degrees and nearly 20 percent holding post-graduate degrees. Academic credentials bolster the sense of calling to this critical pro-life outreach.

A pro-life ethic is not uniquely Christian. Yet the pregnancy help movement, and its grassroots founding and flourishing, can be attributed to its embrace by the Christian community. Life-affirming churches of all stripes have been the source of manpower that has sustained the pregnancy help model apart from fluctuations in the economy and variations in politics. Preserving and protecting the sanctity of life is a clear biblical value that easily connects to the mission and vision of pregnancy help.

Francis Schaeffer, one of the best know Evangelical voices of the twentieth century, famously noted, "Every abortion clinic should have a sign out front that says, 'Open by permission of the local church.'" Indeed, every pregnancy center and maternity home should have a similar one that says, "Open by the compassionate commitment of local church pastors and parishioners." Churches, or at least church people, are the backbone of the ministry that reaches two million every year. This includes Catholics, Evangelicals, Orthodox, and all who respond to the biblical imperative to "rescue those being taken away to death" (Proverbs 24:11).

Indeed, James 1:27 captures, at least allegorically, the heart of the

Christian who serves in the pregnancy help movement. "Religion that is pure and undefiled before God and the Father is this: to care for orphans and widows in their affliction." Our modern culture effectively creates widows by leaving them alone or with no hope in their unintended pregnancy. The unborn are every bit the orphan, being left helpless and without a voice.

Across the spectrum of soldiers in this loving army are those who feel called to step into the "valley of decision," where life and death are in the balance, and champion the Gift of Life and the Giver of Life.

## Different Sizes and Shapes

Today, the physical locations of the pregnancy help movement reveal its consistent growth and adaptation, from the concrete sidewalk to the clinic exam room to virtual consultations. In the early days, these fledgling nonprofits, with very limited resources, established themselves in spare church offices, a small vacant home, or a maybe a small storefront space in a traffic-friendly mini-mall. Some of the very first centers operated out of the office of a friendly doctor who was willing to order the pregnancy test done at a nearby lab (there were no quick pregnancy tests in those very early days). These offices might be filled with donated furnishings, a mismatched blend of homestyle extras and business office castoffs.

As the ministry of pregnancy help has matured, many pregnancy help centers now operate out of specialized spaces that were designed and built from the ground up to capably organize medical and consultation services to minister to the surrounding community. It is the mark of an especially matured ministry and generous community that allows a nonprofit to purchase land and build the ideal location to maximize ministry needs.

With nearly 80 percent of pregnancy help centers (PHCs) providing medical services, such as ultrasound and STD/STI testing, many occupy office settings in the midst of the same medical office building that houses doctors and dentists or pediatricians and podiatrists. These are familiar surroundings, natural habitats even, for the many licensed medical professionals who populate pregnancy help today. Somehow, these types of buildings have a similar, unmistakable medical building scent!

Confidentiality of our client and patient files is a core value in pregnancy help (as it is with all health and counseling professionals). We all work hard to keep client information secure and confidential. But no client files are more secure than those kept in the vault a former bank in Greeley, Colorado! A few years ago, a Heartbeat International affiliate, the Pregnancy Resource Center, relocated to the updated former bank building on a busy intersection. The general contractor was able to relocate the bank's existing massive movable filing cabinets into the bank's empty vault. Now PRC can lock their client files behind eight inches of solid steel!

Some centers that once rented and converted homes into cozy ministry centers now own properties that have been further developed. In some cases, ownership involves a multi-unit property with space for branded programs or perhaps other tenants that provide monthly income.

To focus on attracting a familiar demographic, the inviting smell of coffee and a comfy place to connect has been the goal of several pregnancy help centers. Borrowing the earthy coffee shop motif blended with some decent brew has been an excellent way to connect with clients, especially in campus-oriented locations.

Mobile units—RVs and the like, with ultrasound tech on board—represent owned ministry assets that carry vital pregnancy help to underserved areas where no brick-and-mortar locations exist. More than a hundred of these rolling clinics traverse the byways and physically extend our outreach for greater accessibility to the community.

Possibly most striking is the transformation of former abortion clinics, previously dedicated to profiting from pregnant moms and the demise of their unborn. More than two-thirds of the abortion clinics existing in 1990 have since closed their doors. Some of these buildings and offices have been purchased, reclaimed, and redeemed for life-giving work that serves moms, supports life, and results in the rescue of many babies. From Chattanooga, Tennessee, to Hialeah, Florida, to La Puente, California, to College Station, Texas, there are dozens of pregnancy help centers that stand as a testament to the optimistic tenacity of pro-life members of these communities.

The modern pregnancy help movement resides in high-rises and healthcare centers, standalone buildings, storefronts, and still in homelike settings and on church property. We serve millions through in-person interaction and heartfelt hotline calls. We fulfill the mission through myriad places and people, all oriented toward compassionate care and life-saving ministry.

## Diverse Methodology

The arc of the last fifty years has focused the compassion arm of the pro-life movement almost singularly on growing and expanding the work of pregnancy help centers, those specific places that present a harbor of hope and a hand to help, either in the form of brick-and-mortar or a mobile unit that rolls on wheels to various locations. Both have core programs that include compassionate counseling (peer and sometimes professional) and often medical services such as ultrasound. PHCs with these kinds of services number nearly three thousand in the US and another fifteen hundred in the rest of the world.

But pregnancy help is the mission, a pregnancy center is only a method.

Pregnancy help also includes extended care like that found in four hundred pro-life housing ministries dedicated to helping moms through their season of maternity. Almost all of these homes help mom and baby beyond birth with holistic care and services oriented toward solid, sustainable life skills. (Maternity housing efforts are not unique to pregnancy help ministries, as some governments and social service organizations seek to fulfill this critical need with various housing arrangements in first- and third-world countries.)

A more recent development comes through the promise and potential of technology, and its adoption was thrust upon our whole movement by the 2020 global pandemic. Helplines manned by pro-life volunteers preceded the creation of the first stand-alone pregnancy center, but the idea of virtual client care is a far more recent reality spawned by the rise of internet connectivity and the personalizing power of the smartphone. Videoconferencing such as Skype empowered early virtual pregnancy help ministry pioneers. With Apple's FaceTime and later Zoom, video connection tools have become an extension of face-to-face relationship-based ministry. This extends help far beyond the brick-and-mortar of the pregnancy help center, or even the mileage reach of the mobile unit.

Along with "new school" technologies is the continued presence of pregnancy help on sidewalks outside of abortion clinics. Whether in front of the entrance to a private physician's abortion practice or a government-run hospital, the best "last chance" to engage the abortion-bound woman is right where she has to go to get one. Fading is the vitriolic protester presence, instead replaced by calm, welcoming advocates who step onto the sidewalk with the mindset to pray peacefully and love unconditionally. In essence, they are the pregnancy center on the sidewalk, without walls, without protection from the elements, but with the same heart and hope for mother and baby.

All of these various and diverse methods work best in concert together. Both virtual outreach and sidewalk advocates will usually need the services that require a brick-and-mortar home base like the pregnancy help center. The PHC's intervention effort soon yields to extended care needs that can include housing and life skills development. Together they can be a pathway for an unexpected pregnancy to become a gift of adoption to a childless family facilitated by a courageous mom, a pathway for couple or family unification, or a pathway of support for a single mother.

The key PHC services, reported by our Heartbeat affiliates in the US and shown in the following chart, gives a clear picture of the programs that are present in addition to the common pregnancy tests, peer counseling, and material services:

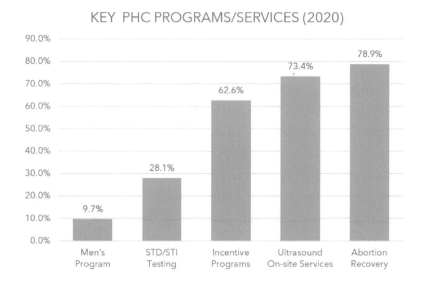

KEY PHC PROGRAMS/SERVICES (2020)

Indeed, the best alternative to abortion is another person.

## More Effective

The heart of the modern pregnancy help has maintained the same core compassion for life since the waning days of vinyl albums and black-and-white television. That core compassion has stayed true even as the movement and the methods have been enhanced by innovation, experience, technology, and tenure.

We reach more women at-risk—those who are abortion-minded and abortion-vulnerable—than ever before. Not only do we reach more, but we serve them better with more focused services (such as ultrasound) integrated into evergreen relational counseling components. This translates into more consistent life-affirming outcomes and long-term impact into future generations.

The "army" of caring, compassionate advocates for life that comprise the pregnancy help movement continues to reach further and rescue more.

## How the Army Rose Up

Heartbeat was founded by an ob-gyn who was at what would normally be considered retirement age, a refugee from Nazi Germany, and a young Catholic nun who had recently become a licensed social worker. Two were from an aging industrial city on the Great Lakes, Toledo, Ohio, and the other was from the fast-growing city of Los Angeles in the Golden State of California. God used ordinary people, with seemingly extraordinary amounts of foresight, passion, courage, and faith, to begin this great work. This describes our founders and many others who worked alongside them.

Dr. John Hillabrand, Mrs. Lore Maier, and Sister Paula Vandegaer give the founding date of Heartbeat as November 13, 1971, at the first constitutional meeting in Chicago, held at the O'Hare Inn adjacent to O'Hare Airport. Present at the meeting were some of the founders of the approximately sixty help centers and hotlines that were in existence in North America at that time. They saw the need for an affiliation body or an "umbrella group" to help unite and develop this growing movement of pregnancy help and life-giving alternatives to abortion.

While we are called Heartbeat International now, at this meeting we were first named Alternatives to Abortion Incorporated and nick-named AAI, and so we were called during the first twenty years of our history. Thus, fifty years ago we became the first network of diverse alternatives to abortion services (pregnancy help centers, pregnancy help medical clinics, maternity homes, and adoption agencies) founded in the United States.

But the story of our founding goes back, at least, to the late 1960s. Heartbeat is truly a movement of the Lord, and how do you date the first motions or "trembling" that eventually becomes so strong that it is felt, cannot be ignored, and must even be given a constitution and a name?

The entire pro-life movement started in the 1960s when it became clear that there were forces pushing for legalized abortion in every state, and Heartbeat's story is part of that bigger one. Colorado, California, Oregon, and North Carolina were the first to liberalize their laws in 1967, allowing abortion for "hard cases" such as mental disability of either child or mother, rape, or incest. In 1970, New York allowed abortion on demand up to the twenty-fourth week of pregnancy, and similar laws were passed in Alaska, Hawaii, and Washington State. Many people who had never been "touched" directly by abortion, but who were pro-life and pro-family because of both instinct and deeply held religious beliefs, abhorred these developments. Forces organized to counter the efforts to liberalize abortion laws, and they met with great success. Before January 22, 1973, thirty-one states still allowed abortion only to save the life of the mother.

Some people were wise enough to understand completely the well-organized and strategic forces behind the drive to legalize abortion (see Introduction). Our founders were among this prescient and wise group. They fully understood the attack on human life and its profound effects on not only individuals but on our entire culture and the values underpinning it. They knew that a "safety net" for women and babies was needed.

So they began in the late 1960s to develop services such as hotlines and counseling for women in their own communities so these women would never feel forced into abortion because they thought they had no other alternative.

The first freestanding pregnancy center was founded in 1968 by Louise Summerhill in Toronto, Canada, and called Birthright. Other people in Canada were inspired to follow her example, and she soon developed a charter for new Birthright-named centers to follow. Birthright opened an office in Atlanta, Georgia, in 1969. (For this pioneering work, Heartbeat International recognized Birthright International with one of our Legacy Awards; see Appendix II.)

In North America, the first independent life-affirming pregnancy help service (outside of professional social service agencies) that can be identified was a hotline founded in 1971 in Los Angeles, California, and called Lifeline (as part of the Right to Life League of Southern California). Also in 1971, Dr. John Hillabrand, assisted by his nurse Esther Applegate, began operating a pregnancy help center and soon moved it to the same building as his medical office in Toledo, Ohio. It was called Heartbeat of Toledo. (Both Right to Life League and Heartbeat of Toledo are also recipients of our Legacy Award; see Appendix II.)

Some of the pioneers knew each other, but most were generally unaware of the existence of the others (remember, this was before the internet!) until they met in Washington, DC, in early 1971. Monsignor James McHugh, a priest who headed the Family Life department of the United States Conference of Catholic Bishops and had an overview of what was happening, called a meeting of these pioneers, and sixty people attended. Among them were Dr. John Hillabrand, Lore Maier, and Sister Paula Vandegaer. Most of the original sixty pioneers were Catholic, but they did not think of their work as "denominational"; they thought of it as "humanitarian." (Msgr. McHugh also held two meetings in Washington for political and legislative pro-life activists well before January 22, 1973, and thirty-five states were represented. He used the name "National Right to Life," but gave this name to Dr. J.C. Willke and others when they eventually formed that nonprofit corporation.)

Out of that first meeting in Washington DC, in early 1971, a follow-up one in Toronto (where it was proposed that all centers take the name of Birthright and adopt the Birthright charter), and a mailed-in survey of participants, a new vision was birthed. It was to create a federation of independent alternatives to abortion service providers, quite different from one another, based in the United States but also networking with those outside our country who were developing pregnancy help services. This led quickly to our founding and the constitutional meeting of AAI held that same year in November, in Chicago.

But the story of our founding and foundations is more than one of dates and events during the birth of the entire pro-life movement; it is a story of real and fascinating people with vision, values, and beliefs that are still an essential part of who Heartbeat is today.

*Pregnancy Help is found on sidewalks, in storefronts, in closed abortion clinics, on corners, in former homes, next to abortion clinics, on wheels, in former banks, in churches, in adoption agencies, next to college campuses, online and on the phone, outside abortion clinics, in maternity housing.*

*Heartbeat International staff at the 50th Birthday Celebration Conference in 2021 (43 of the 101 full and part time staff of "Heartbeat Central"). Executive Team: Jor-El Godsey, President (3rd row, far left); Tony Gruber, Controller (3rd row, 4th from left); Betty McDowell, Vice President of Ministry Services (3rd row, 8th from left); Danielle White, General Counsel (2nd row, 3rd from left); Cindi Boston-Bilotta, Vice President of Advancement (2nd row, 5th from right).*

*Heartbeat International board at the 50th Birthday Celebration Conference in 2021. (1st row, left to right) Keith Armato, Sherry Wright, Jor-El Godsey, Shiney Daniel, Peggy Hartshorn, Ann Laird, Alejandro Bermúdez. (2nd row, left to right) Doug Grane, Chris Humphrey, Zeke Swift, John Wootton, Joe Dattilo, Chuck Donovan. Not pictured: Ron Blake and Gary Thome.*

# CHAPTER 2

# OUR MEDICAL ROOTS:
# JOHN HILLABRAND, MD (1908–1992)

### Peggy Hartshorn

Dr. John Hillabrand was born over a century ago. "Dr. John," as I and most others knew him, had been in medical practice for thirty-seven years before the founding of AAI in 1971. He received his medical degree from the University of Michigan in 1934. He did residencies in Obstetrics and Gynecology at St. Vincent's Hospital in Toledo, Ohio, at Boston Lying-in Hospital, Boston, Massachusetts, and at the Illinois Research Hospital in Chicago. He started private practice in Toledo in 1938, served four years in the US Navy Medical Corps during World War II, and returned to Toledo in 1946 where he served the community until his reluctant retirement at age eighty-two.

Dr. John was an obstetrician and gynecologist in solo practice who had a personal care for each of his patients and loved delivering babies. As a doctor and a Catholic, his respect for human life was a natural part of him. For him, healing was both a physical and a spiritual calling.

I heard him say more than once, "I have delivered eight thousand babies and never lost a mother." When I first heard him make that statement, after I had already become a part of the pro-life movement,

I was sure he was going to finish the sentence with "never lost a baby." But his respect for life and his desire to protect and guard it extended not only to babies but also, of course, to their mothers. And, in fact, to mothers and babies equally and at the same time because he considered both to be his patients.

This was an essential perspective that Dr. John brought to AAI and that is still part of Heartbeat International today. We are both mother- and baby-centered. We do even more than "save babies." We save lives in a life-changing way, both for mothers and babies and for others in the family circle as well. As our story proceeds and AAI matures into Heartbeat International, this will be even more evident.

Dr. John spoke up publicly and became active when he saw his patients, either mothers or babies, in jeopardy. He saw the effects of the early doses of the birth control pill, whose high estrogen levels led to many deaths from blood clots. He became an expert witness in court cases relating to the pill in the 1960s, and he was also an expert witness in appellate court cases of women who were severely injured by or died from "safe, legal" abortions after 1973. He was a consulting expert at annual meetings of the American Trial Lawyers Association in Dallas and in New York City.

He also understood, from a scientific and moral perspective, that human life begins at conception. So, when the drive began to legalize abortion, he testified in state legislatures and in Washington, DC, on when human life begins and on what abortion actually consists of: the destruction of human life.

At a small event in a private home for Heartbeat International about ten years ago, one of the guests was Bob Marshall, a state representative in Virginia. When he realized that Heartbeat was the same organization that was started by Dr. John, he was eager to tell me his story. As a recent college graduate in 1970, he was hired as a legislative aide in Congress and was witness to the first hearings in our nation's capital on the question "When does human life begin?" He remembered Dr. John Hillabrand's persuasive testimony that human life begins at conception and must be respected and protected, and he told me how powerful Dr. John's debating skills were as he demolished the vacuous arguments of pro-abortion proponents in Congress. Representative Marshall then offered to send me copies of Dr. John's congressional testimonies that he had kept in his office files all these years.

What a blessing it was for me to meet someone, so unexpectedly, who was as touched personally by Dr. John as I have been. If only our country had made truth, for which Dr. John was such a good witness, the basis for our laws and court decisions at that time, how much death and suffering would have been prevented!

An outstanding practitioner in his field, Dr. Hillabrand was board-certified, a member of the American College of Surgeons and International College of Surgeons, and a member of fourteen other medical academies and societies. He was a founding fellow of the American College of Obstetricians and Gynecologists, but his convictions caused him to resign in 1973, in protest of their pro-abortion position.

Dr. John naturally brought professionalism, an emphasis on collegiality, and high standards into the foundation of AAI. This emphasis was prevalent in all the early meetings and conferences (called Academies) of AAI and in all of his AAI communications, and it has become a core value of Heartbeat International.

Our terminology has changed; we called our movement back then the EPS movement, standing for Emergency Pregnancy Services. Today we call it the pregnancy help movement. But we were then and still are today an association of independent affiliates (providing a wide range of services that are "alternatives to abortion") who respect one another, learn from one another, and desire to do our work in a spirit of collegiality and entrepreneurialism, both challenging and collaborating with one another. We were then and are now grassroots and bottom up, not top down.

For example, this is what Dr. John wrote, in his elegant and somewhat formal style, in an invitation to the third annual AAI Academy in 1974. It is addressed to "My Dear Friends in Service":

To state that the EPS movement is glorious, humanitarian, and unprecedented, has become a veritable cliché. Yet it is none the less true. It remains exciting, venturesome and rewarding. It is a grassroots movement by its very nature. It will never be a "trickle down" establishment where all the brains, inspiration, know-how, and initiative are at the top. Every registrant is in fact a rich repository whose duty is to share earned experience with others who stand to profit therefrom.

Dr. Hillabrand was a humble man, and he was always learning, as well as giving of his time and experience. With such a busy professional life, it is hard to imagine how he had the energy to start three of the very first national and international pro-life organizations that are still among the strongest and most influential pro-life groups. As well as being a co-founder of AAI, now Heartbeat International, he was also a founding member of Americans United for Life (also started in 1971), and he served as chairman of its executive committee. He was program co-chairman of the first international pro-life meeting held in New York City in 1967, and he was active in four subsequent international meetings until the National Right to Life Committee was formed and grassroots support was developed (he also helped found Ohio Right to Life in 1968).

In his own medical practice, Dr. John saw many women with unexpected, even "crisis" pregnancies. When abortion became legal in a few states, even before January 22, 1973, it was an option that women began to ask about, many feeling pressured to seek out abortion as the new "safe, legal" alternative.

Dr. John's long-time nurse and office manager, Esther Applegate, told me that many of his patients brought in nieces and friends who needed help and support. He would see them in his practice and then refer them to existing community services, but there were more girls and women in need than he and his office nurse could personally handle, especially with the care and attention he wanted them to have.

Esther said, "He knew abortion was around the corner," and he knew that a bigger safety net was needed.

So he decided to open another office close to his medical practice and call it "Heartbeat of Toledo." It was one of only a handful of pregnancy help services in the country, and it opened its doors in 1971. Esther Applegate, who moved between the medical office of Dr. Hillabrand and the new pregnancy center, soon located in the same building, helped girls and women in both locations. She remembers Dr. John's excitement and sense of humor on the opening day of this pioneering pregnancy center. Esther told me with a smile, "He called on the phone the first day and tested us by saying, 'My daughter is pregnant and considering abortion; where can I take her?' But I recognized his voice!"

In the same year that Heartbeat of Toledo, Ohio, opened its doors, Dr. John attended that legendary meeting of sixty pregnancy help pioneers in Washington, DC, and was one of the three visionaries (with Lore Maier and Sister Paula Vandegaer) who founded AAI. At the constitutional meeting in Chicago later that year, which officially brought AAI into existence, he was elected treasurer of the new organization. Dr. John served in leadership on the AAI board through our transition to Heartbeat International, starting in 1990.

He always presided over our annual Academies, seeming to be our "guiding spirit" on the ground, as the Holy Spirit was in the eternal realm. Dr. John also continued to contribute his medical and scholarly expertise to our publications and bring his peers into our movement. But he was forced to retire from medicine and volunteerism in the early 1990s when he suffered a small stroke, and he passed into the next world in 1992. His papers and extensive library have a home at Franciscan University in Ohio.

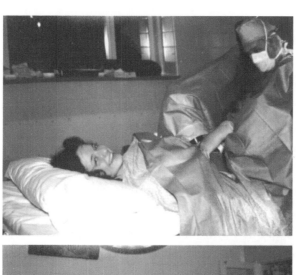

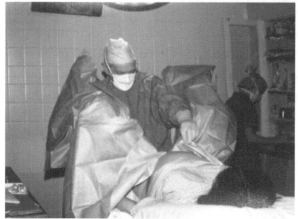

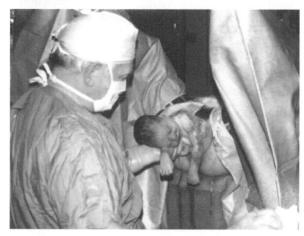

*Dr. John often said, "I have delivered 8,000 babies and never lost a mother." This always reminded us that both mothers and babies were his patients and were our focus in pregnancy help. It also reminded listeners that, with good medical care, mothers' lives can be preserved without resorting to abortion.*

*At the time Dr. John founded AAI, he was at the height of his professional prestige, a member of 16 medical academies and societies and founding fellow of the American Society of Obstetricians and Gynecologists. He resigned from that Society in 1973 in protest of their pro-abortion position.*

*Dr. John, with "old world" charm and wit, was the regular Master of Ceremonies at the AAI Academies (Conferences). In 1978, Dr. John introduces Phyllis Schlafly, founder of Eagle Forum that helped defeat the Equal Rights Amendment that could have enshrined feminist-favored "rights" (such as abortion) in the Constitution.*

# CHAPTER 3

# OUR HUMANITARIAN ROOTS:
# LORE MAIER (1923–2004)

## Peggy Hartshorn

Mrs. Eleanore Maier, whom most people called Lore (pronounced Laura), was born in Germany in 1923 and barely lived through the Hitler era. She immigrated to the United States in 1951 and became a citizen in 1957. She called herself the sole survivor of Nazi Germany among her family of six. She has a fascinating and courageous story that helps explain her passion for the sanctity of human life and why she devoted so much of her life to serving mothers and babies and to the development of AAI, now Heartbeat International.

Lore was a ten-year-old student at the Lyceum of St. Thérèse in her native Leobschütz, Germany (in Upper Silesia, now part of Poland), in 1934, when Hitler came to power. In an interview published in the *Catholic Chronicle*, May 20, 1983, Lore recounted many of the details of those years. At her school, crucifixes and religious pictures were removed. "You could see their eerie outlines on the walls," she recalled. Pictures of Hitler youth leaders were hung. The curriculum was changed and lay teachers replaced the nuns one by one, until only two were left to mop the floors. Although Lore's father, a World War I cavalry officer, opposed the Nazis, she was forced to join the Hitler youth groups. "If you were a child who wasn't a Hitler supporter . . . you were often excluded from games and relationships with your peers." And police observers were everywhere.

She eventually followed her dream to study acting at the university, and she joined a community theater group in Danzig (where she took roles of heroic women, including Joan of Arc). But in 1944, the Russians began a final assault, and she was in the path of the violence and chaos that accompanied the collapse of Nazi Germany. She had left Danzig at age twenty-one and returned to Leobschütz to be with her mother and try to save what was left of her family. Her father had died, and her brother (conscripted into the German navy) had frozen to death in the waters off Finland after his submarine was torpedoed. Within a couple months of Lore's return to her hometown, her mother died. In February 1945, she was able to get her pregnant sister out of Germany to have her baby, in relative safety, in Prague. Thus, Lore's own sister and her nephew were the first of many mothers and babies that Lore saved.

Lore recalled that when it was imminent that the Russians would come, refugees were fleeing the war and arriving in her city from Hungary, Romania, Russia, and elsewhere. "Women in open trucks clutched babies that had frozen to death," and prisoners freed from concentration camps arrived in the city. "There were long columns of gray-faced skeletons," she recalled. (Leobschütz is not far from one of the most notorious death camps, Auschwitz, in Poland, and it is close to what was then the border of Czechoslovakia). Lore brought some of the refugees into her family home, and she refused to leave.

Leobschütz changed hands between the Germans and the Russians five times. Finally, bombs were falling day and night, and her house collapsed around her. She made it outside to find "human bodies and horse carcasses everywhere." She ran to the local hospital and volunteered with the Red Cross, helping wounded war victims and refugees of many nationalities. She eventually helped evacuate the city as the Russian army took over.

Thus began a harrowing three-month journey. Lore, sometimes walking with bleeding feet, sometimes hiding and traveling in trucks or other vehicles, wandered with large groups of other refugees, with almost no food, out of Germany and through Czech territory (where the Czechs were welcoming the Russians). German nationals were being shot (sometimes by Czechs, sometimes by Russians). With the help of one German who spoke Czech, at one point she saved her life by posing as a Red Cross nurse on Czech business, using the only Czech word she knew, "Welcome."

Lore was interred in three different forced labor camps, operated by Czechs, where the prisoners had almost nothing to eat but thistles in the fields. "We were like goats; we picked the ground clean," she said. Conditions were so terrible that many died around her. Despite the threat that those who fled would be shot, she planned her escape. One rainy night, she hid in the women's latrine until 11:00 p.m., and then slid on her stomach under the barbed wire of the camp. She eventually made her way into Bavaria, where "it was like coming out of hell," she said. "There were fields and people. Two American soldiers gave me my first American passport."

Lore stayed in post-war Bavaria and threw herself into humanitarian work. She worked with the United National Relief and Rehabilitation Administration, aiding concentration camp victims. Then, for two years she worked for the Spruchkammer (Court of Justice), where she was a court reporter for the German government trials of Nazi war criminals. From 1949–1951, she was executive secretary of the Government Water Division in Munich, Germany.

Lore immigrated to the United States in 1951 and married Frederick Karl Maier, a United States citizen, in 1952. I understand that they met in the United States, but returned to Germany for their marriage, then settled in Toledo, Ohio, where Mr. Maier owned a steel company. Lore became a citizen in 1957.

Lore said, in the interview from 1983, that her wartime experience left her with little bitterness. Rather, she said, it left her with a passionate interest in life and its protection. Her inspirational speeches and articles, published in some of the first pro-life publications, focus on the danger of violent solutions to perceived social problems, the intrinsic value of every human life, and the fact that, at least in the United States, we have the power to choose life, not death. Not only in each personal case of abortion, but as a nation we can change our laws to protect life.

Although I met Lore at an Ohio Right to Life Convention in Columbus, Ohio, in 1978, an event that radically changed my direction in the pro-life movement (see Introduction), I never knew the details of her past until I read them many years later from clippings in the AAI files. In my eyes, she was always a beautiful, elegant lady from the generation of my parents, the World War II or "Greatest Generation," who was a highly motivational and eloquent writer and speaker. I can vouch that she had no bitterness; she was a very hopeful and inspirational leader who focused not on the past but only on a positive vision of the present and future. She often pointed out that in the United States people have the freedom (unlike in Nazi Germany) to make changes in the law, to recognize the sanctity of life of each person, and to engage in humanitarian service that could overcome the tide of abortion and disrespect for human life.

Later I would come to realize that more was needed than humanitarian service and changes in the law. By the time I became Heartbeat International president in 1993, it was clear that the damage caused by abortion on demand in our country over the twenty years since 1973—and caused worldwide by the lack of respect for human life—needed not only political and humanitarian action but also a cultural and spiritual "cure." This led to changes implemented as AAI became Heartbeat International in the 1990s. But that is the subject of a subsequent chapter in our history.

From our own experience since 1973, we recognized the effects of the lack of respect for human life not only on the victims, but also on our society as a whole. Even before *Roe v. Wade*, however, Lore warned us of what would happen to our culture (because she saw what had happened in Nazi Germany). Here are some of her words from an article in *Marriage and Family Newsletter*, April 1971, a publication with international subscriptions, edited by John E. Harrington. Lore's article, published along with letters from readers in London, Rome, Brazil, Canada, and the Philippines, was headlined "If We Are Not Pro-Life, We Are Against Our Own Survival."

I lived comparatively close to Auschwitz, the concentration camp most infamous for the extermination of innocent prisoners. My townspeople never knew what was going on in there during the war. Whispers had been heard toward the end of the war, but the whole bitter truth did not come out until the prisoners were liberated and streamed in long columns through the streets of my little hometown in their ragged uniforms. Their faces were numb and their spirit was gone in spite of their new freedom. Even in those victims who survived, the dehumanizing impact of destruction and cruelty was apparent. From the foregoing it is clear that inhuman behavior takes its toll not only from the victim, but also from the oppressor, as well as from those who stand by idly or helplessly in silent acquiescence.

And so it is with abortion. The victim loses every time. The abortionist becomes emotionally detached and insensitive to the value of human life. The bystander, even though initially interested and concerned, may tire of the controversy and succumb to the semantic gymnastics and clever subterfuge of the proponents. Unknowingly, indifference gradually takes over to the point of complete apathy. The mother, because of her particular role may suffer in one or all of these areas. Yet it is the mother who determines the fate of man. She holds society together or causes it to crumble, because she is the pillar, the mother of all men. . . .

If we choose abortion, we will pay the highest price. Abortion is worse than war, worse than any inhumanities of any dictatorship, because it erodes the moral fabric of society . . . Abortion not only takes a far greater toll of innocent life, but it degrades the abortion collaborators to the lowest level of cruelty and immorality. . . . Our efforts to push back the tide of abortion will be the measure of our character and will determine for us and for all posterity the kind of world in which we shall live.

If we are not pro-life, we are against our own survival!

How did this refugee from Nazi Germany go from being the immigrant wife of a successful Toledo businessman to a pioneer in the pro-life movement and a key ally of Dr. Hillabrand? Dr. John knew Mr. and Mrs. Maier; Lore was one of his patients, whom he called Frau Maier. Esther Applegate recalls that Lore was widowed in 1967, after only fifteen years of marriage. She was childless, and, distraught and grieving, she entered into a period of depression. Dr. Hillabrand, needing help with his many pro-life endeavors and knowing Frau Maier's history and her organizational skills, said to her, "Do I have a job for you!"

So Lore was "called" through another person who perceived her gifts and sensed that God might have a role for her. That is the story of most of us involved in this great work! The rest, as they say, is history. Lore was the co-founder with Dr. John of that early pregnancy center, Heartbeat of Toledo, and at one time was its executive director. She was one of the sixty people present in Washington, DC, when the idea of a networking body or federation for the emerging centers was birthed. And she became the first executive director of AAI, chosen for this role at the constitutional meeting in Chicago in 1971.

In the 1970s, a formative decade for the entire pro-life movement, Lore was also a board member (for over ten years) of AUL, Americans United for Life, in Chicago. She was a co-founder and vice president of PLAN (Protect Life in All Nations), a world federation of international,

national, regional, and professional pro-life organizations and foundations (started in Washington, DC, in 1978). She also joined the Advisory Board of American Life Lobby (now American Life League), in Washington, DC. Her strong belief in collaboration and unity, reflected in the founding vision of AAI and in her role with these other organizations is still a core value of Heartbeat International.

Like Dr. John, Lore seemed to be a ball of energy and worked countless hours, all on a volunteer basis, to lay the foundations for several pro-life organizations, especially for AAI. As I look at the records from her tenure as executive director of AAI, whose first office was set up in Toledo, Ohio, I am amazed at the amount of work she produced with only a small cadre of equally passionate volunteers.

This was the era when electric typewriters were in vogue and Xerox technology was not widespread. Multiple copies of things were generally made from dittoes (with smeary purple ink) or mimeograph. Thousands of pieces of paper are in the files from this period, including many carbon copies and lists that were painstakingly typed, retyped, and corrected (presumably drafted from index cards that were then alphabetized to help organize the hundreds of contacts that were being made around the world). There are hundreds, perhaps thousands, of personal letters composed and responded to from throughout the United States and around the world.

The first list of life-affirming pregnancy help in existence (called the *Directory*, now called the *Heartbeat International Worldwide Directory*), was developed by Lore and given to board members in 1972. Distributed on mimeographed sheets of paper, it contained 103 entries, including all the locations where pregnancy help was known to exist in the United States, plus a few in Canada and one in New Zealand, including individual names of contacts that were interested in starting centers.

Our 2021 Worldwide Directory contains 6,942 entries in 114 countries. It is developed using the latest in database technology, available on the worldwide web and updated regularly. When I think of the work that Lore and her volunteers did to keep track of this fast-growing movement with the now-primitive tools available, it is truly amazing!

Lore retired as the AAI executive director in 1982, but she remained a vital force in the organization—always present, always inspirational—at the annual Academy (Conference), and she continued to serve on the board through our transitional period in the early 1990s. When we celebrated Heartbeat's 25th Anniversary at our Conference in 1996, we honored her with one of our inaugural Servant Leader Awards. She was unable to attend in person, but she read me her greetings over the phone, which I delivered to the attendees. I recently found her handwritten greeting in an old AAI file. Her message encapsulates the passion of her vision for our work and her attitude of service and acceptance of each person, no matter their imperfections or situation:

> From the start our goal has been to make help available to every girl or woman distressed by pregnancy—a truly universal appeal that knows no boundaries to origin, country, religion, education, political persuasion, or social standing—simply to be called humanitarian. These twenty-five years can only be considered a first step in a far reaching and never ending journey for Life. Consider yourselves the torchbearers who in time will pass on to others that come after us the glorious task of working to preserve and protect the lives of mothers and babies. Always remember to be truly helpful to a person in distress and not to expect too much at the start, to be patient and to be kind. To be tolerant of the human condition regarding various aspects of life requires us to understanding, resourceful, humble and respectful. With this attitude in your hearts—your efforts will not fail! Thank you all for your outstanding commitment! Our generation and future generations will benefit greatly because of you!

*Lore in her role as AAI Executive Director and speaker at an early AAI Academy (Conference).*

*Lore and her younger sister in Germany in peaceful times. Lore, at age 22, helped her pregnant sister escape to Prague during the chaos at the end of the Hitler regime. Thus her only living relatives were the first mother and baby she saved.*

*Lore receives an award of appreciation for her volunteer leadership as Executive Director, at the 7th AAI Academy in 1978, from Dr. William Lynch, Vice Chairman of the AAI Board.*

*Lore as a young woman.*

# CHAPTER 4

## OUR ROOTS IN THE DIGNITY OF WOMEN: SISTER PAULA VANDEGAER, SSS (1939–2021)

### Peggy Hartshorn

Our third co-founder, Sister Paula, a member of the Academy of Clinical Social Workers and a licensed clinical social worker in the state of California, tirelessly answered—for fifty years—the pro-life call that she responded to as a young member of the religious order Sisters of Social Service. Sister Paula retired from pro-life work only this year, due to health reasons, stepping down from the presidency of International Life Services, based in Los Angeles (which she founded in 1985 after leaving AAI leadership). Only months before she passed from this life, she was able to send a heartfelt video message to our conference in celebration of Heartbeat's 50th birthday. It can truly be said of her: she fought the good fight; she finished the race; she kept the faith.

She was honored in person at the 40th Anniversary Conference of Heartbeat International in 2011 with the first of Heartbeat International's Legacy Awards. This is the description of the award:

Heartbeat International Legacy Awards recognize people and organizations whose contributions represent a major and lasting impact in the pregnancy help movement, affecting generations to come.

The legacy Sister Paula left to us is not only her unwavering commitment but also her influence on our founding principles and values, teaching resources, and professional standards.

Sister Paula created the first counseling manual in our field, even before AAI was founded. She applied the principles of professional counseling and social work to a brand new mission: crisis pregnancy "counseling" done by laypeople providing alternatives to abortion. Sister Paula's original manual and her widespread trainings throughout the country resulted in the fact that, as Sister sometimes smilingly pointed out, there are parts of her early manual in almost every current pregnancy help training manual used today! However, in the late 1960s, when Sister took on this task, the field of crisis intervention for women was relatively new, and crisis phone lines were not common (early "crisis counseling" was done on groundbreaking suicide prevention hotlines). Moreover, a general standard of the profession of social work is "client self-determination"—that is, the client must ultimately make her own choices. How does a Christian person in this new field of crisis counseling for pregnant women who could now choose abortion reconcile this professional standard with our conviction that the choice of abortion is not a good or ethical choice either for the woman or for her baby?

Sister Paula's pioneering manual and training articles (later published in the AAI journal called *Heartbeat* magazine) emphasized treating every woman who comes to us with a crisis pregnancy (or after abortion) with unconditional respect and love. She, a person created by God, must be the center of our attention and concern (not the occasion for a "lecture" from us or a debate on the pros and cons of abortion). Sister Paula always emphasized the importance of listening carefully to each woman's story and treating her in a loving, caring, nonjudgmental way—the importance of discovering who she is, affirming her, and helping her discern the best choice for her baby and herself, based on who God created her to be as a woman. (Or as Sister might say, the "psychology" of who she is as a woman and the difference between what abortion and motherhood will mean to her as a woman). Sister also emphasized that, while the woman will ultimately make the final decision on whether or not to have an abortion, she deserves complete information on abortion and its risks as well as complete information on the development of her baby.

How did Sister Paula Vandegaer come to leave such a legacy to our movement? Well, like anyone who has received a "call" on their lives, because she said "yes" to the Lord, Sister's life took shape very differently from what she had originally planned. In fact, when I interviewed Sister Paula for our 40th Anniversary video and Legacy Award, she laughingly told me, "Three things I never wanted to be were a nun, a writer, or a teacher. And I became all three!"

Sister took her vows as a member of the Sisters of Social Service as a young girl in 1959. She then earned a bachelor's degree in psychology from Immaculate Heart College in Los Angeles in 1962, and then went on for a master's in social work from the Catholic University of American in Washington, DC, specializing in psychiatric casework. She returned to Los Angeles and began working as a caseworker for the Catholic Welfare Bureau, where from 1966–1968 she did general counseling of a wide variety of clients. The Lord began to specifically prepare her for what lay ahead when she became a supervisor and case worker in the Natural Parent Department of Holy Family Services in Los Angeles, an adoption and pregnancy counseling agency specializing in counseling unwed mothers and fathers.

At that time, the Catholic Church, especially Catholic Social Service Agencies, were in the forefront of providing professional social work services related to crisis pregnancies, and they operated many homes for unwed mothers and many adoption agencies across the country. Catholic Social Service Agencies are still numerous and handle some related cases;

however, the demand for maternity homes, especially large ones with related adoption agencies, has all but disappeared in the United States due to the widespread promotion of abortion and the fact that unwed motherhood is no longer considered a stigma. In a sense, our volunteer-based pregnancy help movement, using lay "counselors" and other client advocates, and now nurses and other medical personnel, has largely replaced these formal social services for those facing a crisis pregnancy. And Sister Paula gave laypeople the tools, early in our movement, to help women in a professional, loving and caring way.

Pro-abortion proponents began efforts to change the abortion law in California (and other states) in the mid-1960s. A loose coalition of pro-life people of various professions got together to fight this legislation and to lobby against the bill in the California legislature in 1968, and they called themselves the Right to Life League (believed to be the first pro-life group to organize in the United States and use the name "right to life," and one of the first to offer pregnancy help services). The group was in contact with another member of the Sisters of Social Service, Sister Rosemary Markum, who urged Sister Paula to get involved.

The California law passed, despite their efforts, and was signed by Governor Ronald Reagan, who later said it was the one decision he regretted about his record as California's governor; he said he was misled by the "hard cases" arguments related to rape, incest, and life of the mother. But once abortion became legal in California, it was clear that a safety net was needed for women, and pro-life people had to be trained to talk to women and help them choose alternatives to abortion.

For example, the very first pro-life pregnancy hotline came into existence on May 5, 1971, in Whittier, California, through the efforts of Margaret Nemecek, as an outreach of the Right to Life League of Southern California (the group founded in 1968 to battle attempts to liberalize abortion laws). Sister Paula, then a board member of the Right to Life League, was asked to train the first hotline workers—who were members of Margaret's daughter's Girl Scout troop!

Sister Paula gathered together four social workers from Catholic Social Services (which has always had a policy that their counselors do not refer for abortions), and they met every two weeks for three months to develop that first training manual. The Right to Life League began doing pregnancy tests at the Whittier center soon after that, and the League became one of the first affiliates of AAI when we were formed in 1971 with leadership from Sister Paula.

On a personal note, it is amazing for me to realize that I (an "Ohio girl") was in college for four years in California at this same time (see Introduction). I saw the billboards advertising abortion services going up, and I was shocked and appalled. I had no idea until many years later that the pro-life movement was also developing in that state at that very same time, or that someday I would be carrying on the work of one of the California founders of this movement, Sister Paula Vandegaer.

Sister Paula first met Dr. John and Lore at that 1971 meeting in Washington, DC, and at the follow-up meeting in Toronto. She recalls that the three of them and others sat up until 2:00 a.m. debating whether a franchise model (such as a Birthright), as was proposed, would work in the United States, where a variety of diverse service models were already being used. Sister says that, after that meeting, Dr. John and Lore Maier, who had been appointed to help organize efforts in the United States, sent out a questionnaire to all the US groups in attendance. The overwhelming desire was for a federation model of independent service providers, not a franchise model.

According to Sister, Lore and Dr. John worked very quickly after that to develop this new organization, their work culminating in the "constitutional" meeting in November 1971 in Chicago, and the naming of this new group AAI. Sister Paula could not make it to Chicago for this first meeting, but she came to the second board meeting in early 1972 and was promptly elected secretary of AAI. At that meeting, Lore distributed that first Directory, the list of centers  and contact persons interested in starting a center in the United States (103 entries).

At that point, Sister Paula became the "right-hand person" to Lore Maier. Lore promptly wrote a manual called *Suggested Guidelines for Establishing Pro-Life Emergency Pregnancy Service (EPS) Centers.* Along with Sister's *Pregnancy Counseling Manual*, people with a passion for the mission had everything they needed to get going! Sister recalled, "It was so exciting to see all the energy—the Holy Spirit was moving throughout the land, and all before 1973! Once we had the manuals, from then on it went like crazy—centers were starting at a rate of two per week! The movement was so rapid, so incredible. I was traveling all over to give trainings, from New York to Hawaii. Our feeling was, for God's sake, get them going."

Like most of us who have come later into this same movement, Sister Paula found out that God does not call the equipped; he equips the called. To show His power and build our faith, He asked her to step out of the "comfort zone" of professional counseling and depend on Him. She told me an amazing story of how, at a crucial point in our history, the Lord provided her with a vision, making it perfectly clear that the vision was from Him, and then brought her the help and tools she needed to make that vision a reality.

Lore needed more help in the Toledo office and asked Sister to move there and assist her. However, Sister had a role in her religious order and could not leave California. She saw that she could help Lore by taking over the newsletter. It consisted of mimeographed sheets that were sent out monthly to all centers and other contacts. But she also knew that the newsletter needed a major upgrade; in fact, she realized that it could and should be an informative and professional journal or magazine for our field. (Right to Life had just begun their newsletter, the first and only one for pro-life at that time.) Sister was trained how to counsel, but she knew nothing about writing and publishing a magazine. Yet she thought that this was exactly what God wanted her to do!

God gave her several unmistakable signs as a confirmation. First, one of the younger Sisters of Social Service said that her brother, the former editor of his college newspaper, wanted a job in publishing and was willing (for a small salary) to edit and publish the magazine for them. Sister knew she would have to raise some money. After a meeting, she was putting some dishes away and chatting with those present. She began to share the vision. One woman gave her five thousand dollars, and a priest gave her a thousand dollars. She did a phone-a-thon soon after and quickly raised all the funds she would need for the first year!

The younger Sister's brother designed a brochure for Sister Paula to use in selling the idea to the AAI board, but he left a hole in the brochure for a picture to be added later. He went on vacation, leaving Sister to fill that hole. Sister remembers walking down a hallway, thinking and praying, "God, I don't know how to write; I know nothing about printing; I know nothing about all of this—I am a social worker!"

Sister soon ran into an old friend named Kathy Hochderffer, an artist, who knew nothing about the idea of the magazine or how inadequate Sister was feeling. Kathy mentioned to Sister Paula that she recently had a dream about her. In her dream, Kathy and another artist friend were in a room with Sister Paula, who was pacing back and forth. Kathy told Sister Paula, in the dream, "Sit down and stop worrying. We are laying out the magazine for you."

When Sister recovered somewhat from her shock in hearing Kathy's dream, she asked Kathy if she knew who the other person was in the dream. Kathy said that it was Karen, who had painted with her many years ago. Karen had been raped as a girl, and her mother had forced her to have an abortion. She became so distraught over the abortion that, many years later, she shot herself in the head.

Dumbfounded, Sister was finally able to tell Kathy about her vision for the magazine to help the fledgling alternatives to abortion movement, and about the urgency of the brochure with the hole in it! Kathy immediately offered to help, but she confessed that she had no idea what to draw for that brochure. It would have to be a key image to convey the vision. Sister asked Kathy to pray about it overnight.

The next day Kathy returned with a sketch of a pregnant girl, leaning against a tree in a dark forest, but there were rays of light was filtering through the darkness. At her feet there was the bare hint of sticks fallen in the form of a cross. It seemed inspired! This was the picture that filled the "hole" in the brochure. Sister took this to the board meeting in Pittsburgh in 1977, and the board approved the idea of the magazine, as well as the founding of the West Coast office of AAI (Sister Paula's office), where the magazine would be published.

The Lord used Sister Paula and *Heartbeat* magazine to help bring about the phenomenal growth and development of the pregnancy help movement. And, given the central role of Karen in Kathy's dream and perhaps in the inspiration for the girl in the woods, it is fitting that *Heartbeat* magazine published the first research in the entire pro-life movement suggesting the existence of post-abortion syndrome (in a study from Japan). It is also fitting that the movement Sister Paula helped found also birthed many of the first abortion recovery programs; 79 percent of current Heartbeat affiliates now have such programs as part of their core services.

But that is not the end of the story of how the Lord confirmed Sister's mission. At a subsequent AAI Academy, the keynote speaker was Archbishop Elko. He told them about an experience he had had many years ago on a train in Europe. A young man came into his compartment and said, "You're a priest, aren't you? I hate the Church." The man then spent the rest of his time in the compartment sketching on a pad. When he came to his stop, he tore the drawing off the pad and gave it to the Bishop. It was a picture of a young woman in a forest, leaning against a tree, but there was no light. Departing the train, the young man said, "That's why I hate the Church—the Church puts you in dark places and does not show you a way out!" Sister Paula said that the Bishop's message to the audience was this: "You, in the pro-life pregnancy help movement, are the light in the forest, and YOU show women the way out!"

Sister shared with me how awed she was that God had put together a woman who committed suicide many years before (after an abortion) and an archbishop to help her see that He was in charge and would provide not only the vision, but the means to make it a reality! She is also grateful that the Lord sent Kathy to her. Kathy was called into the pro-life movement on the day that she shared her dream with Sister Paula in 1977. She continued to partner with Sister Paula, first as the editor of *Heartbeat* magazine and then as the executive director of International Life Services.

Sister told me this story while we were sitting in her International Life Services office in Los Angeles. She was sitting very close to the drawing of the girl in the forest, with the light shining through the trees and the suggestion of the cross at her feet; a smaller version was on her desk, and a larger one was the only decoration on the wall. She saw this "lesson" every day: we in the pregnancy help movement are the Church, the Body of Christ, and the Church does bring light in the darkness.

I feel fortunate that I was among the thousands of others trained by Sister Paula year after year at the AAI Academies, through the 1980s, and I used her training and articles in *Heartbeat* magazine to guide my "counseling" with pregnancy center clients. Two of her key writings at that time for me were "Helping a Sexually Active Woman to Say 'NO'" and "The Guidance of the Spirit in Our Counseling." I used to take these two articles into the room with me while I waited for the results of the client's pregnancy test (this was before centers began "self-testing" and before we had medical clinics), and I read them over and over to give me insight and courage before I went out again to talk to the client.

This was in the early 1980s. When a client had a negative pregnancy test (60 percent of our tests were negative), it was tempting to simply give her the results and let her go, because our main purpose was to provide a safety net if the client had a positive test and was considering abortion. What to say to a girl or woman who was not pregnant at that point? We did not refer her for contraceptives, and amazingly, we did not talk much about sexually transmitted diseases because there were basically only two that we knew of, and they could be cured by antibiotics. (Imagine the days before we even knew about HIV/ AIDS! It was in 1981 that researchers in San Francisco made note of a new and deadly illness among the gay population in San Francisco.)

Feminism was at its height, and I expected most girls and women to laugh at me if I suggested simply practicing abstinence until marriage, especially at our pregnancy center office at the campus of The Ohio State University (where students sometimes came in with spiked hair, sprayed pink or purple, bizarre makeup, and other attempts to show their rebellion from traditional norms and standards).

But Sister's articles gave me the courage to present my client with a new vision of herself and her gift of sexuality and ask her to consider a new way of life that was in keeping with the woman God created her to be. I'm sure I am not the only pregnancy center volunteer who was so affected by Sister's writings. My growing commitment to this vision of true womanhood eventually led to the development of the Sexual Integrity Program for Heartbeat International, to be discussed at the proper time in this history.

After Sister Paula left Heartbeat leadership in 1985 and founded International Life Services in Los Angeles, she continued producing *Living World* magazine, which contained excellent articles on all areas of pro-life, from abortion to euthanasia. Kathy Hochderffer, who first dreamed and then sketched the picture of the girl in the forest, remained Sister's "right hand," and served as executive director of International Life Services. In 2000, Sister wrote a textbook, *Introduction to Pregnancy Counseling*, with twelve supporting videos to teach counseling skills. Since 1967 she was involved in the formation of over one hundred pregnancy centers. Sister also founded a program called Volunteers for Life, a group who live in community for one year and dedicate themselves to service agencies in the Los Angeles area.

Sister Paula's emphasis on the dignity of the woman (from her psychological perspective) corresponded to Dr. Hillabrand's emphasis on caring for the woman (from his medical perspective), and these corresponded with Lore Maier's passion for the dignity of every human person (from her humanitarian and experiential perspective). Underlying all these perspectives was the Christian faith of each of our founders, an essential part of who they were and how they viewed the world and those in it. This was true of all the pioneers in the pro-life movement. Christianity was so integral to who they were that, paradoxically, they did not talk or write about it as explicitly as you might expect. This changed later in our movement, something that we will discuss as our history continues into the 1980s and 1990s.

It was the unity in our pregnancy help movement—the welcoming of all Christians and the diversity of pregnancy help within Heartbeat International—that formed the emphasis of Sister Paula's message on the occasion of Heartbeat's 2021 conference celebrating our 50th birthday. Sister's final message to the movement she had helped found and lead for fifty years were words of thanksgiving for what the Lord has accomplished:

> We formed a union—fifty years ago—that has endured to this day. Thanks be to God. Some of our centers are Evangelical or Catholic, or they're both, and they're strong. Our centers are strong today because of our identity. And so, thanks be to Heartbeat . . . you have been there, Heartbeat, all along, to unite us, to keep us all together, to train us all, and to help us get along with one another. Thanks be to God.

*Sister Paula trained volunteers to answer the first-ever pregnancy help hotline, started in 1971 in Whittier, California, as part of the Right to Life League of Southern California.*

*Hanging in Sister Paula's office is this drawing of the pregnant girl with rays of light shining through a dark woods. It was the "sign"— from a dream about a real woman who committed suicide after an abortion— that convinced Sister to start Heartbeat magazine to provide foundational training for the movement (pp. 67–68).*

*Sister Paula founded Hearteat Magazine in 1978 which published cutting edge research (such as the first study of trauma after abortion in Japan) and articles on culture, family life, population control, adolescent development, international abortion, and more. The magazine, which was published for nearly 10 years, also covered AAI events and developments.*

*Sister Paula, center front, with a pioneering group of pregnancy help volunteers.*

*Sister Paula and Peggy at the 1994 Heartbeat International Conference, and Sister Paula receiving the first Heartbeat Legacy Award at the 2011 Heartbeat Conference.*

# CHAPTER 5

## LASTING FOUNDATIONS FOR THE MOVEMENT

### Peggy Hartshorn

Each of our three co-founders, Dr. John Hillabrand, Lore Maier, and Sister Paula Vandegaer, brought special gifts to the establishment of AAI, and they incorporated into our work the values, purposes, and principles that characterized not only AAI's first twenty years, but also have become the foundation for the growth and development of Heartbeat International over the last thirty years. In the previous three chapters we have tried to capture some of their special gifts and the life experiences and expertise that have left clear marks on the pregnancy help movement both then and now.

The name *founders* carries with it the concept that these first leaders laid down the foundations for the organization they started, Alternative to Abortion International. And today, that organization, now Heartbeat International, is indeed built on those foundations. However, our founders believed, and Heartbeat believes today, that they were building for the entire pregnancy help movement, then and now—not just for those that became or would become official affiliates. Anyone who provided life-affirming pregnancy help was and is welcome, all learn and contribute, all work together to advance the mission of saving and changing lives. So, the foundations were built and are maintained now for the entire pregnancy help movement.

This chapter will highlight, one by one, those values and principles that have stood the test of time and characterize not only Heartbeat International today but the pregnancy help movement as a whole.

### Always More Than Saving Babies

All three of our co-founders had a view of our work that encompassed more than saving babies. Those who describe the mission of pregnancy help centers as "saving babies" are only describing a part of our founders' vision and mission and part of the movement's vision today.

Our founders focused on both mother and baby, and, in fact, on the family and the entire culture. They saw that we were involved in this work to serve women in need and help them so they could save their babies, but also (especially in the work of Sister Paula) that we were in a position to help women understand their true womanhood. Dr. John and Lore's writings and talks also show that they viewed an attack on the sanctity of human life in the womb as an attack on society as a whole and on all humanity that would have profound ramifications. Lore tried to warn of the effect of abortion not only on women themselves and the family, but also on the perpetrators (the abortionists), and even on those who merely stood by and observed (the general public).

The first logo that was chosen for AAI, used in the very first communications in early 1972, was called "Hearts of Gold." It is not a baby, nor is it a mother and child. The logo features two larger gold hearts (with some lines and markings, the result of life's scars, experience, maturity, and wisdom) surrounding a tiny, unmarked, pure golden heart that represents the innocent human child. The logo shows that we need to protect, shelter, and nurture that child, born and unborn. The hearts of gold represent the family as God intended it. With the family relationships disrupted and in need of healing, the larger, sheltering hearts could be those of us in this movement protecting the child. Heartbeat's logo has changed to the "Heart of the Future," but Heartbeat International still features our "Hearts of Gold" on our premier Legacy Award since God's plan for the family is still at the heart of our mission.

One of the amazing things about the early AAI Academies (Conferences) was the diversity of expertise represented in the "Faculty" or conference presenters. To help the emerging centers with program development were marriage and family experts, psychologists, psychiatrists, counselors, doctors and nurses (with expertise on pregnancy and maternity care, fetal development, labor and delivery, nursing, sexual transmitted diseases, infertility, and more), early childhood education experts, researchers, social workers, mothers, fathers, and more.

Programs developing then within the first centers (despite the early term EPS or Emergency Pregnancy Services) and first maternity homes were focused not just on the crisis intervention needed for women coming in for a pregnancy test, but on parenting and family unification. For the "negative test client," programs were developing to help her understand the risks of sexual intimacy outside of marriage. Centers were developing referral networks in their own community and finding like-minded potential partners who could amplify these messages—for example, in schools and in the culture at large.

Today, if you attend a Heartbeat International Conference or any other gathering of pregnancy help organizations around the world, you will find the same. We are about much more than saving babies. Our foundation stones are motherhood, fatherhood, healthy families, and a pro-family culture.

## Collegiality and Entrepreneurialism

One of the primary values that our founders imbedded into Heartbeat International and into our entire movement is collegiality. Collegiality involves collaboration, respect for different ways of arriving at the same end, and encouragement for the sharing of ideas among peers. Entrepreneurialism involves experimentation, creativity, new ways of doing things, and learning along the way. With both values, models for successful operations and programs often come from the "bottom up" rather than the "top down."

This is first reflected in the original language used to describe AAI as a "federation" of independent providers of alternatives to abortion services. Affiliates are not all franchises of a particular model (although some may be). Our founders sometimes described AAI as a "trade association" for those called into the same work. This is true of Heartbeat International today, and thus we describe it as an "association" for those engaged in life affirming service who voluntarily affiliate with one another under the banner of Heartbeat International.

AAI was founded in the US as an alternative to the franchise model Birthright that existed already in Canada. AAI welcomed Birthright centers to affiliate with AAI, and many of them did throughout the 1970s and 1980s. Likewise today, Heartbeat International welcomes independent organizations as affiliates, but also organizations that are part of a franchised network either in the US (such as Thrive or Birthchoice) or overseas (such as the CAMs branded centers in Latin America and the CAVs under MPV, *Movimento per la Vita*, in Italy).

The value of collegiality, with an aim to constantly share, learn, and improve, has always been reflected in the annual training conference, called the AAI Academy by our founders and now the Annual Heartbeat International Conference. Every year, for fifty years, pregnancy help organizations, affiliates of Heartbeat or not, have a place to come together to teach and learn from one another. Presentations are given primarily by our affiliates who, today, respond to a "request for proposals" and offer to provide a workshop that highlights an innovative program or project.

For twenty years of our history, the AAI Academies were hosted and planned almost entirely by individual affiliated organizations. Each year, one of the affiliates offered to host the Academy in their home city, plan the program with some help from the central office, design the conference brochure, and handle all the local arrangements for conference attendees.

I have attended almost every conference since my first in 1980, and I can attest to the quality of those gatherings, planned and hosted by local centers (then) or featuring the work of local affiliates (today) in a spirit of collegiality. Today, expert planning, coordination, communications, and leadership is provided by Heartbeat Central. But the competence of our experts "on the ground"—pregnancy help service providers—make our annual conferences premier educational, training, and networking events for the entire pregnancy help movement.

Attendees, presenters, and exhibitors need not be official affiliates of Heartbeat International. Our conferences (and other training opportunities) are open to life-affirming pregnancy help organizations and individuals called into our work.

A typical Heartbeat Conference now may unite over a thousand people from nearly thirty countries, representing over three hundred organizations, providing various tracks of training with more than eighty workshops and more than one hundred presenters. What a cornucopia of educational and relationship-building opportunities!

Heartbeat International has remained, in many ways, a "bottom up" organization since our founding, not a "top down" one. At Heartbeat Central we don't claim to know what is best for every organization and in every community around the world. There have always been individual leaders and some organizations in our pregnancy help movement who have made their reputations by arguing that there is one "best" way of doing business and delivering services (and it is their way). They are tilting off the foundation, so to speak. As a movement, we want to hear, see, learn, and evaluate what they say and do, nevertheless. But these "outliers" are generally few and far between, and sometimes, if it becomes clear that their method is not best for all, they eventually lose influence.

## Principles and Service

Other core values that make up our foundation are expressed in Heartbeat's affiliation principles (which must be agreed to upon affiliation or re-affiliation). The original six were adopted early on by AAI. The first five of those, listed below, are nearly identical to the five Heartbeat affiliation principles today. (The original sixth principle was this: "AAI takes no position on religious, political, or family planning issues." Since it could be argued that abortion itself was indeed a religious, political, and family planning issue, and we did take a position on abortion, we dropped that principle in 1993.)

- AAI affiliates propose and offer through education, action, and creative services, alternatives to abortion, and thereby provide more positive choices for the woman distressed by pregnancy.
- AAI affiliates shall not discriminate regarding race, creed, color, national origin, age, or marital status.
- Services of AAI affiliates are personal and confidential.
- AAI is nonjudgmental.
- AAI affiliates shall not advise, provide, or refer for abortion or abortifacients.

Heartbeat Principles of Affiliation today:

- Heartbeat affiliates propose and offer, through education and creative services, positive choices for the woman challenged by pregnancy.
- Heartbeat affiliates shall prefer and promote the value and

place of sexual intimacy, children, and family building within marriage between one man and one woman.

- Heartbeat affiliates' services are personal, confidential, and nonjudgmental.

- Heartbeat affiliates shall not discriminate in their services on the basis of race, creed, color, national origin, age, or marital status.

- Heartbeat affiliates shall not advise, provide, or refer for abortion, abortifacients, or contraceptives.

Note that Heartbeat's second Affiliation Principle was not reflected in the original five of AAI. It was added to clarify the stronger stance of Heartbeat on what we call "God's Plan for Our Sexuality," part of the reframing of our Christian core. The fifth principle was amended to include "contraceptives" in 2019. The reasoning behind both of these changes is discussed in chapter 7.

These affiliation principles, going back to our founders, have been a major influence on the entire pregnancy help movement. For example, they inspired the core affiliation principles for new pregnancy help organizations that started in the 1990s, including the National Institute of Family and Life Advocates (NIFLA), founded by Tom Glessner.

In 1995, Heartbeat, NIFLA, and Care Net met to discuss an "ethical code of practice" for pregnancy help centers, especially as it related to how we care for the women and others that the Lord sends to us. We started with the affiliation principles of Heartbeat International and worked from there to develop a list of principles that we called "Our Commitment of Care." This was signed onto in 2001 by all the existing affiliation groups except Birthright (which agreed with the standards but declined to sign on, pointing to a requirement in their charter). The signatory groups agreed to promulgate "Our Commitment of Care" among the centers that were part of their networks and make them a standard for affiliation.

As our relationships with these organizations continued to grow, it became clear that we agreed not only on standards that related to how we cared for the client, but also on common operational standards that related to governance, fundraising, and medical services (pertinent laws and medical standards of care). In 2009, Heartbeat International proposed that additional standards be added to "Our Commitment of Care," and we arranged for input from all the original signatories and other pertinent partners. The updated document, called "Our Commitment of Care and Competence" has been signed onto by thirteen national organizations that provide affiliation, training, or resources for pregnancy help centers and clinics, with the continuing exception of Birthright (see Appendix V).

When there are wild accusations made by those who want to close us down (see chapter 10) that pregnancy help ministries are, by their very nature, coercive, misleading, or even harmful to women, we can point to "Our Commitment of Care and Competence," our statement of ethical principles, which is posted in client care offices throughout the country.

The foundation for such principles, and for their collegial adoption by our entire movement, goes back to AAI and the values and first two decades of the history of our movement.

## Nondenominational

Finally, our three co-founders were Catholic, but they were adamant, like all early pro-life leaders, that the movement not become solely a Catholic one. In fact, our opponents tried to characterize the pro-life movement as such, to cause it to become "marginalized" and viewed as simply a reaction from a minority religious group that took their marching orders from celibate men in Rome. I personally heard these charges when I became a speaker for Right to Life in 1973. As AAI history shows (see chapter 1), the Catholic hierarchy prodded the laity to get organized (as the meetings called by Monsignor McHugh demonstrate), but the official Catholic Church wanted only to be a catalyst for a broader movement of the Christian church, the Body of Christ.

Catholic pro-life pioneers were very eager to get all Christians involved and into leadership, as the example of Care Net illustrates. A recent article on the founding of the Evangelical pro-life organization originally called Christian Action Council (CAC), now Care Net, indicates that it was Catholic prompting and funding that launched their efforts. The article was written by Robert Case, the first executive director of CAC. The organization had been founded by Harold O.J. Brown in 1975, a professor at Trinity Evangelical Divinity School in Deerfield, Illinois. Robert Cole points out that while "the new council drew its members from the evangelical ranks, it drew its funding from the ad hoc Committee in Defense of Life . . . a Roman Catholic creation."

CAC first focused its mission on being "a conservative Christian political advocacy group," and Cole explains how difficult it was to get Protestant denominations involved in the 1970s. The second CAC executive director, Rev. Curtis Young, moved CAC from political advocacy toward "a counseling and care ministry." At one point, CAC contacted AAI and asked for help and advice on starting pregnancy centers with an Evangelical statement of faith. The AAI board invited Curt Young to serve on the board and learn everything he could from AAI. He did serve in 1981 and 1982, and CAC "planted" their first Evangelical center in Baltimore in 1981. CAC now goes by the name of Care Net and focuses its mission on pregnancy help centers, characterized by an Evangelical Statement of Faith.

Some Evangelicals deployed a "church-sponsored" pregnancy help model. The first of these was alongside the Edgewood Baptist Church in Columbus, Georgia, spearheaded by Pastor Andy Merritt in the early 1980s. He established a dedicated outreach, "Pregnancy Center Ministry," as a specific program of the church. Moreover, Pastor Andy traveled the country to help inspire and assist nearly 500

Evangelical pregnancy centers throughout the nation. The pregnancy help ministry at Edgewood Baptist became comprehensive, and eventually the church even established an independent Christian adoption agency to further help the mothers and babies they served. For his contribution to our movement, Heartbeat honored Pastor Andy with our Legacy Award (posthumously) in 2021.

Our founders adopted the terms "nondenominational and nonsectarian" to describe the nature of AAI and the centers that were part of our network. The meaning of these terms and how they apply to the centers themselves and to the services provided to centers were never totally defined. Some affiliates interpreted them to mean (as I did, when my husband and I started our center in Columbus, Ohio, and affiliated with AAI) that our center was not part of one denomination and would welcome all Christians to join us in this work. Another term to describe this would be "ecumenical." Our center also knew that when we attended AAI Academies, we would meet Christians involved in the same work from many different denominations.

Some centers, however, interpreted the terms as meaning that it was inappropriate to "proselytize" or try to convert clients to our own beliefs. Others still thought that these terms meant that AAI affiliates should not describe our organizations as "Christian" per se (nor as Catholic, Baptist, etc.), nor should we provide materials with a specific Christian message if we wanted to remain "nondenominational and nonsectarian." The lack of clarity on how to interpret these key terms led to great diversity among affiliates on how they viewed their identities: as a Christian organizations or as secular organizations (run by Christian people).

Throughout our history, the terms "nondenominational and nonsectarian" have helped create a very diverse group of Christians and Christian ministries within the entire pregnancy help movement. In that sense, these descriptions are foundational.

But when we became Heartbeat International, we clarified our identity as being "Christ-centered." How that happened and how it affected everything from our conferences to our training materials is the subject of chapter 7.

## Unity

Lore Maier was fond of saying, "There can never be too many pregnancy help centers. There can never be any competition among us." So-called "healthy competition" can have the effect of making us stronger and more effective, of course, but unhealthy competition brings out the worst in people and organizations. Lore and our other founders were the first people to intentionally spread the vision of forming a variety of independent pregnancy help centers across the US and around the world. They traveled extensively at their own expense, offering services and affiliation with AAI but realizing that not all centers would find a "home" in AAI. Materials and training were available to any center, regardless of affiliation. By the time AAI became Heartbeat International in 1992, the value of unity was an essential part of our identity. We never were and never should be in competition with any other part of the compassion arm of the pro-life movement.

For me personally, disunity among Christians is especially distressing because I believe it deeply pains Our Lord. He emphasized His desire that we remain as one on the night before He suffered and died for our sins (disunity among Christian brothers and sisters being among those sins): "I do not pray for these only, but also for those who believe in me through their word, that they may all be one; even as you, Father, are in me, and I in you, that they also may be in us, so that the world may believe that you have sent me" (John 17:20–21). This unity, Jesus tells us, is necessary in order for the world to believe in Him.

The unity we want to model among Christians within Heartbeat International has been noted above and will be discussed further in this book, but what about the place of pregnancy help in the pro-life movement? And does the fact that there are so many pregnancy help organizations now (about three thousand in the US alone!) or that there are hundreds of pro-life groups (at the local, state, and national levels) mean that "we should all just get together"? Interestingly, as our founder profiles make clear, Dr. Hillabrand (and Lore Maier to a more limited degree) was a founder or on the governing or advisory boards of several other pro-life groups, including the legislative and political group Americans United for Life, or AUL, also founded in 1971. Obviously, they believed that there could be different missions but an essential unity of purpose.

Why are there so many individual pregnancy help centers and so many other pro-life groups? As an "insider" in the pro-life movement, here are my thoughts. First, there are many different strategies that have proven effective within the overall pro-life mission in the US. Here is a "stab" at articulating that overall mission: to promote the value of the sanctity of every human life in our culture, and especially, since abortion is the most horrendous and widespread attack on innocent human life, to reduce the number of abortions and eventually eliminate abortion as a legal option here and around the world. Another all-inclusive way of stating the overall mission has come into widespread use: to turn from a Culture of Death and create a Culture of Life. (This wording was first used by St. John Paul II in his 1994 encyclical, The Gospel of Life, or *Evangelium Vitae*.)

Strategies related to the broad anti-abortion mission have sometimes been divided into two types. The first type consists of strategies that attack the supply side, the availability of abortion: pass laws restricting, limiting, regulating, and eventually outlawing all abortion, enforce strict licensing on abortion clinics, uncover abuses and get abortionists out of business, boycott businesses that give money to pro-abortion organizations, and take our tax dollars away from Planned Parenthood, which owns the largest chain of abortion clinics in the US and funds abortion around the world, and more.

The second type involves strategies that reduce the demand for abortion, such as educational strategies that inform the general public about what abortion is and its effects on babies, women, the entire family, and culture. Other strategies that reduce demand are those that provide a myriad of incentives so that women choose to have their babies, provide help and support so that women do not feel that abortion is their only alternative, make ultrasound available so both mothers and fathers can bond with their babies while they are in the womb, and more. According to this thinking, the pregnancy help movement would be one of the "strategies" attacking the demand side of abortion.

Pro-life organizations have emerged to take up each one of the above strategies. No country in the world except the United States, with its entrepreneurialism and "can do" attitude, with its guarantee of freedom of speech, its system of local, state, and federal laws, its judicial system, its tradition of philanthropy, predominant Judeo-Christian culture (for the time being!), and its myriad of Christian churches, could generate the large number of pro-life organizations and individuals who feel called into this movement. Pro-life people in other countries are astounded at the pro-life activity and diversity in the US. This is a good thing!

This diversity and overlapping of efforts may appear to be counterproductive; however, it may in fact be the kind of energy and dynamism that is the mark of workings of the Holy Spirit! The pro-life movement cannot be stamped out—there are simply too many of us, moving in too many directions. Eliminate some, and others will immediately take their place. One will fall, but others will jump in to raise the flag and march on. The disunity that many perceive in the movement is sometimes, no doubt, the work of the Devil, but it may also be the protection of God.

Moreover, there is much more coordination and collaboration that takes place among the many organizations in our movement than most people realize. This includes regularly scheduled meetings of national leaders and multiple attempts through the years to develop overarching strategic plans.

There have always been and still are some organizations or individual leaders who are "lone rangers" and ride alone, so to speak, refusing to join coalitions or work together with fellow leaders or groups. And there are others who, for a while, seem to convince enough people that their unique approach or service is the "only way to go." They create division and confusion temporarily, but generally the truth emerges that no one person or approach is perfect, that we need to humbly continue to grow and learn together to become an effective network of care. The value of unity and collaboration has been deeply embedded in our movement since the beginning, and it remains there.

## Worldwide Scope

Another vision of our founders has become essential to who Heartbeat International is today and still impacts the entire pregnancy help movement: their international vision. Almost immediately after the name AAI was adopted (Alternatives to Abortion Incorporated), Lore and Dr. John proposed that the initials AAI represent a new name, Alternatives to Abortion International. The board finally officially approved this change in 1974.

Lore in particular had a strong international vision, coming as she did from Europe and speaking several languages. Remember, too, that she was a German teenager at the time of the holocaust, and she saw firsthand the effects of the devaluing of human life in her own homeland. Her correspondence files show that she was exchanging letters during the first few years of our history with contacts from all over the world, urging them to start pregnancy help centers and keeping track of the nascent movement worldwide.

The first Directory of service providers consisted of mimeographed sheets of paper, distributed by Lore to the Board in 1972. It had 103 entries (some were names of people planning to start pregnancy help services). In the list were a few centers in Canada (Birthrights) and one in New Zealand. The official AAI Directory of centers around the world, dated July 20, 1976, shows nine official affiliates outside the US, having been sent certificates of affiliation: three in Canada (Hamilton and Sudbury, Ontario, and Winnipeg, Manitoba); and one each on Auckland, New Zealand; Amsterdam, The Netherlands; Bogota, Colombia; Everard Park, South Australia; Bern, Switzerland; and Port-Au-Prince, Haiti.

Meanwhile, Lore had developed a World Council, an advisory board consisting of pro-life leaders in at least twenty other countries. During Lore's tenure as executive director, she and Dr. John took many trips to other continents, at their personal expense, to share the vision and consult with the growing network. Through the first twenty years of our history, the numbers of pregnancy help service providers opening around the world continued to increase dramatically, and AAI tried to keep track of the existence of all of them (whether or not they formally affiliated) through the regularly updated Worldwide Directory.

International representatives often joined the early AAI boards, the first one being Pierre Prineau from Bogota, Colombia. Daniel Overduin from Australia joined the board in 1977. When I joined the AAI board in 1986, Bente Hansen from Norway was a fellow member. AAI board minutes from 1977 indicate that AAI was aware of 782 centers in the US and 1,350 foreign centers ("centers" at that point were often in the very beginning stage of formation and sometimes listed by the name of the "founder").

When AAI became Heartbeat International, our international outreach continued, and chapter 14 tells the story of that amazing growth. The Heartbeat International World Council began functioning again officially in 2019 with representatives from our eight international affiliation partners, groups whose members are joint members of Heartbeat International. These networks function in the following countries or regions of the world: Canada, Italy, Spain, Mexico and

Latin America, Israel, Africa, South Africa, Australia, and Southeast Asia. Heartbeat International has affiliates in over sixty-nine countries.

The vision to reach around the globe with pregnancy help has become part of the entire pregnancy help movement. Many centers overseas are started through formal and informal outreach by those who know about American pregnancy centers and feel led to start one or more outside the USA. This includes missionaries, ex-patriots, service men and women, even former "foreign students" who were helped by pregnancy centers while they were studying in the US! Individual pregnancy help centers, inspired by the Holy Spirit and sometimes by a fortuitous personal contact (perhaps in business or as a result of travel) have started and support centers in other countries. All of this has added up to 4,093 listings in the US and 2,849 in 113 other countries in our 2021 Worldwide Directory where pregnancy help service providers are available today!

## Personal Involvement, Compassion, Armed with Love

Our founders helped motivate and raise up thousands of people around the world, mostly volunteers. Their primary tool or "weapon" for saving and changing lives was love, presented to clients in the form of personal involvement with them in their struggles. If you divide the pro-life movement into various arms (legislative, political, educational, activist, service), we are the service or compassion arm of the movement.

*Anti-abortion* does not fully describe our compassion mission. *Pro-life*, in the traditional sense of the word, does describe us: we not only protect and defend the physical life of the unborn, but also the life and health (physical, emotional, psychological, and spiritual) of the mother and family, and we do this in a Christ-centered way. God is love, and love is our way, the "weapon" we are armed with in this battle to defend and protect. We act with compassion, which means to "feel with" another, to enter into their suffering, and to minister to them through and with the love of Christ.

In a sense, our pioneers were fortunate in that they were not confused into thinking that there was a magic formula—some special set of steps, specific pictures or video, or even a tool like ultrasound—that they could use to help the mother and save her baby's life. The only thing they had was love!

We have a lot of wonderful tools today, but they don't work very well unless they are used with the personal touch, the personal involvement and love of one person shared with another. This takes time and sacrifice of self on the part of the person doing the loving. Human nature has not changed. God created us with a deep need to love and be loved, and most people in need, when treated with love, respond with love. Our call to love remains, even if we don't receive love back.

That this was modeled by our founders and became a hallmark of AAI was evident when Heartbeat was contacted right before our anniversary in 2011 by one of Dr. Hillabrand and Lore Maier's original clients from the 1970s. We had placed an invitation on our website for people to share their stories with us. Imagine our shock when the first person to communicate her story was Raena, who met Dr. John and Lore at Heartbeat of Toledo, Ohio, when she was sixteen and pregnant.

Raena told us that she has never forgotten the love and care that Dr. John and Lore gave her. She remembered that their original pregnancy help center was called Heartbeat of Toledo. She was thinking of them one night, wishing she could "give back" some of what they gave her, so she Googled "Heartbeat" and found Heartbeat International! Here is Raena's original message to us about the love she received, a love that saved not just one baby, but two:

In 1975 I found myself pregnant and alone. My father was a Baptist minister and connected me with Dr. John Hillabrand in Toledo, Ohio. He and Lore Maier counseled me and convinced me to have the baby, and Dr. Hillabrand became my obstetrician. I was close to eight months pregnant and had just had my first Lamaze class. One day I began to have terrible pains in my back. Dr. Hillabrand told me to meet him at his office. He announced, "We are having a baby!" I was five centimeters dilated, so he told us to get to the hospital. I was in the hospital about one and a half hours when he took me into the delivery room. He delivered my daughter slowly and gently. I wanted to keep her more than anything. I held her, and fed her, and she smiled at me. I knew I couldn't provide for her or give her more than love, and she needed much more than that. [On that] chilly March day, my parents and I went to the church, and on the altar, we dedicated her to God and to his keeping. Then we took her to the Lutheran Social Services, and I placed her for adoption.

After that I was so distraught and sad. . . . I finished high school and went to a year of college. I then followed my parents to Rhode Island, where my father had taken a new church. By the age of twenty-three, I had become an alcoholic. I was homeless, sleeping in the city park with my clothes in a bus station locker. By the grace of God I got sober. [After] about two weeks of sobriety, I was raped. I was so hysterical and out of my mind that I went into a rehabilitation center. . . . They must have noticed something, because they made me take a pregnancy test. The results showed that I was pregnant, and it could only be from the rape.

This time everyone insisted [that] I had to have an abortion, that there was no way I could have the baby. Dr. Hillabrand and Lore Maier had a profound effect on me and made my dilemma of what to do with the growing fetus inside of me extremely difficult. I was praying and meditating on my bunk bed at the center, and two men in white came into my mind. They told me that I was going to have another girl and that she was a gift from God. . . . They gave me her name and said that she had come just for me and that I would keep her and raise her as my own. She is twenty-six now and a beautiful ray of light in this world. She just got her MSW degree, and she majored in policy and homelessness.

The daughter I placed for adoption is thirty-four now and found me fourteen years ago. She has wonderful adoptive parents and had a very good upbringing. She and I are very close and speak several times a month. She is so much like me and my other daughter that it is uncanny. I will always be grateful to Dr. John Hillabrand and Lore Maier for their deep belief in the value of Life and for inspiring that quality in me.

When I called Raena and eventually met her in person, she told me that her two daughters, neither born in ideal circumstances, "light up a room" when they enter! Both of them are involved in professions that "give back," and she cannot imagine the world without them. She confirmed that neither Dr. John nor Lore ever knew that the love they showed her when she was sixteen and pregnant with Shannon had also saved Briena.

Raena said that her father often dropped her off at Dr. John's office for a medical appointment, and then she would help Lore in the nearby AAI administrative office. Lore put her arm around Raena at one point, told her about her harrowing experiences in Nazi Germany, assured her that God had protected her, and told Raena that He would protect her as well. Raena told me this was the message she remembered when she realized she was pregnant as a result of the rape: "If Lore had the courage and faith to go on, I can too. And God will help me."

I talked to Raena again as we prepared to celebrate the 50th anniversary of Heartbeat International. She immediately began talking about Dr. John and Lore, calling their work with her "priceless." Raena now has four grandchildren! Both Shannon and Briena are in helping professions—social work and mental health.

Raena recently led a community effort to open an emergency shelter and a day resource center for the homeless, which was completed in 2020. She says she is called to service and is waiting for where God will call her next. She had the opportunity to share her adoption choice with a homeless pregnant woman about six months ago, and the woman followed in Raena's steps and chose adoption for her daughter.

This emphasis on real love, compassion, and life-giving care for another person permeates the writings and teachings of our founders and early role models, as the essence of what pregnancy help offers to the world, one person at a time. Most likely, every foot soldier in the world would agree that love is what we share, and the more we give it away, the more it increases.

Dr. John, for example, in a presentation on AAI ethical values and goals delivered at the 1977 AAI Academy in Pittsburgh, contrasts the love we provide in pregnancy help with the selfish kind of "l-u-v" that had been ushered into our thinking during the sexual revolution, especially in the 1960s (in slogans such as "Make luv not war!"). Here is the encouragement for our mission that Dr. John offers:

> Our goal, very simply put, is to reach as many as we possibly can, and with provident good fortune, to reach every individual who is in need. In this manner, the ripple effect can reach all of humanity. By lighting "one little candle" enough times, the world can be changed. Love (l-o-v-e) can supplant luv (l-u-v). We, you and I, can be the better for having tried, even should we fail. But, failure is not actually in the book in these endeavors, for these candles of love are never extinguished and do carry their impact wherever employed. Ours are not the problems; ours are only the opportunities. With truth and right as our guide, we will not, we cannot fail.

In chapter 7, you will learn how this emphasis on love, from our very founders, led to two of the new rebuilding blocks when AAI went through our reframing as Heartbeat International in the third decade of our history: *The L.O.V.E. Approach* and "God's Plan for Our Sexuality."

*AAI and our movement today emphasize life-saving love—for women, families, and babies. AAI's principles of service inspired the movement's Commitment of Care and Competence (Appendix V). Raena (left, with her baby and family in the 1970s) says Dr. John's and Lore's love saved both of her children from abortion (her second baby they never knew about!), see pp. 91–94. Nearly fifty years later, Chelsea (right) found that same kind of love at Compassion Care Center and chose life for Taelynn.*

*AAI's emphasis on collegiality, grassroots response, and entrepreneurialism is also foundational to the pregnancy help movement. The resulting creativity and its impact are recognized with our Legacy Award (Appendix II). Dinah Monahan pioneered the widely used "Earn While You Learn" program in the PHCs and maternity home she founded, including the first Apache Reservation PHC. Andy Merritt pioneered the first Evangelical church-sponsored PHC (1981), complete with an adoption agency.*

AAI's emphasis on Christian unity is also foundational to the movement. Sister Deidre Byrne, Little Sisters of the Sacred Hearts, retired US Army Colonel and physician in the Abortion Pill Rescue Network, and Bishop J. Alan Neal, international missionary and pro-life advocate, whose Agape Christian Faith Center is in Germany, exemplified this unity as keynote speakers at the Heartbeat Conference in 2021.

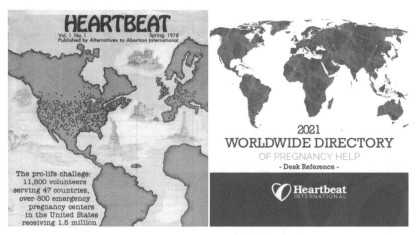

AAI's missional objective to make known all life-affirming pregnancy help around the world, as reflected in an early issue of Heartbeat magazine and in our current Worldwide Directory, is foundational to our movement's passion for expanding pregnancy help (chapters 11 and 14). The printed 2021 Directory lists 4,093 locations in the US and 2,849 in 113 other countries!

# CHAPTER 6

## TRANSITIONING AND REFRAMING

### Peggy Hartshorn

By 1985, our three founders were no longer actively involved in the management and programming of AAI, although Dr. John and Lore were still on the AAI board. Two physical moves of the headquarters and two executive directors were short-lived. From 1986 through 1992, the organization was entering into a period of decline and then transition. This is a somewhat predictable stage in the life cycle of an organization once the initial period of rapid growth and development—fueled by the passion of the founders—comes to an end. AAI's momentum could not be sustained, and a leadership succession plan had not been intentionally developed and implemented.

Heartbeat now teaches about these predictable stages in the life of an organization, but this is something I had no knowledge of while I was living through them with AAI and Heartbeat. Let me clarify: I say I lived through these stages because I became an AAI board member in 1986, I stayed on the board through this period, and then I became the first full-time paid staff member of the newly named Heartbeat International in 1993. I only read about these stages of organizational development later, and looking back, I can see that our organization could have been a "case study." The stages are sometimes designated as imagine and inspire, found and frame, produce and sustain, and review and renew.

If review and renew does not take place when needed (when the organization is not sustaining), an organization can go into decline and dissolution. We are thankful that going into the dissolution stage was not God's plan for AAI! Instead, God gave us the opportunity to review and renew all the wonderful "foundations stones" of AAI, then refound and reframe. This period of reframing extended from about 1993 into the early 2000s. With His guidance and grace, we have been producing and sustaining since then (as I hope this history illustrates).

The story of our transition period from my perspective, including my call from the Lord to leave my full-time position as a university professor in Columbus, Ohio, and a volunteer in pregnancy help to become Heartbeat's first president, is very personal. It involves ups and downs, signs and graces from the Lord, and many dear people He put in place to help me see His plan for me and for Heartbeat. It was confusing along the way, and I struggled with what the Lord would have me do for two agonizing years. But once I said "yes" and took my first baby steps as Heartbeat president in 1993, the confusion was over, and I knew He had me where He wanted me and that He would accomplish His purpose—despite the fact that I felt totally unequipped. And He was faithful! This chapter will summarize a few bits of my personal story during the leadership transition from our founders, but you can read all the details, if you want, in the first edition of Heartbeat's history, published in 2011, *Foot Soldiers Armed with Love: A Memoir of Heartbeat International's First Forty Years*.

In this chapter and the next, the focus is primarily on the once strong "building blocks" of the AAI foundation that needed to be repaired, replaced, or restored so that new framing could be added and the structure itself would be stronger than ever.

## Key Events in the Leadership Transition from AAI to Heartbeat

Lore Maier announced her resignation as executive director in 1982, and Elinor Martin, founder of an excellent center and maternity home in White Plains, New York, was appointed as (volunteer) executive director of AAI in 1983. She moved the administrative office from Toledo, Ohio, to White Plains. Sister Paula resigned in 1985, the West Coast office was closed, and Sister Paula then founded International Life Services. Dr. John and Lore were both aging, but they continued to care deeply about the organization and the movement, and they stayed on the board through 1990.

Between 1985–1990, during these changes in leadership, the normal AAI services for affiliates continued: an annual Academy (organized by one of the affiliates), the annual Worldwide Directory, and *Heartbeat* magazine (the publication of which was taken over by an affiliate in Michigan). Unfortunately, Elinor Martin died suddenly, but the central office stayed in New York, held together by her administrative assistant. The AAI affiliate in Columbus, Ohio, where I served as chairman of the board, would have been somewhat unaware of the changes in leadership except that we had offered to plan and host the 1986 Academy. After the conference, in the fall of 1986, I was asked to join the AAI board, and it was only at that time that I understood the transition we were experiencing.

In late 1988, Judy Peterson, the leader of a maternity home in Orlando called BETA (which started as a Birthright center), assumed the position of chairman of the AAI board, and Judy's right-hand person in Orlando became the executive director. Judy's new vision involved major changes for AAI, including eliminating the Directory, de-emphasizing our international mission, changing our name to WHEF (Women's Health and Education Foundation), and making *Heartbeat* magazine a publication for young mothers, supported by advertising. The board members did not accept the new vision, however. Instead, we remained committed to the vision of our founders, and Judy resigned in late 1989.

Board members held an emergency meeting at which several members resigned due to age, family health problems, or general discouragement, leaving only five of us: our founders Lore and Dr. John, a member from Norway (not present), Carol McMahon, director of the Genesis maternity home in Pittsburgh, and myself. Lore and Dr. John insisted that they could only take advisory roles on the board. Carol was hosting the AAI Annual Academy in 1990, so she could not assume additional duties. Her husband died of a heart attack soon after, and she ended up having to resign from the board altogether.

I was the sole remaining board member who was in any position to take on leadership. I could not believe that the Lord would want AAI to simply cease to exist, having worked so powerfully through this organization for so many years. My respect for Dr. John and Lore and my passion for our mission would not allow me to do nothing, so I offered to assume the role of acting chairman of the board. I said I would "keep things going" by temporarily moving the central office to Columbus and by trying to build up the board membership so we could eventually find an executive director and move forward.

I came home and called our previous offices in Orlando and White Plains to have our assets sent to Columbus. Orlando informed me that all AAI had there was bookkeeping records, which they promptly sent to me. White Plains informed me that there had been a fire at the AAI office and everything was destroyed. We had about seven thousand dollars in our bank account, primarily from sales of our Directory and affiliation fees.

With almost no assets, I asked our Columbus pregnancy center executive director in early spring of 1990 to allow AAI to open our administrative office in a large, walk-in closet at one of our client offices. My husband and I had a big wooden desk that we moved into the closet, I had a phone installed, and I bought a used, five-drawer Steelcase file cabinet and a computer. That was the beginning of our Columbus Heartbeat International headquarters, still at this point operated entirely by volunteers.

I also called Dr. John and Lore to tell them about the lack of records from Orlando and White Plains. To my shock and delight, Lore informed me that she had only sent copies of all the AAI materials to White Plains, so she had, intact, all of the records from our founding through her resignation, plus all the publications and board records up to 1990! She and Dr. John invited me to come to Toledo to pick them up.

Although I didn't fully realize it at the time, this would be my last visit with our founders and my heroes and mentors, Dr. John and Lore. Dr. John had experienced a slight stoke. Although it was a quick blackout and he returned to normal, he was distraught that his physician had told him he must retire from his medical practice and not risk another incident that could result in harm to one of his dear patients. He was in the process of dismantling his large medical library and gave me two of his books. Lore presented me with several cartons of records, including all correspondence (many with notes and letters in her own handwriting), financial records, publications, and AAI board minutes from the beginning. Lore and Dr. John helped me load the materials into the trunk of my car. What a treasure from our founders and the early history of the pro-life movement in the US and around the world!

## Key Step in Reframing: Making the Decision to Act

In 1990, when I set up the AAI headquarters in Columbus and committed to rebuilding the AAI board, I was acting almost out of "instinct"—I knew that a nonprofit organization needed not only an office, but a strong board and an executive director. For nearly two years I thought one of my jobs was to find a full time executive director who would eventually develop the staff we needed to serve our affiliates and the pregnancy help movement. Meanwhile, the board members and I, with some key volunteers, kept the core AAI programs going. We were a "working board" for sure.

The event that finally motivated me and other board members to act more decisively was our annual board meeting in 1992, scheduled in conjunction with our Annual Conference. It was just two days after Bill Clinton had been elected. After eight years under Ronald Reagan and four under George Bush, the election of Bill Clinton was a shock. Our board thought we would never again have a pro-life president and that we would make no further progress toward a Human Life Amendment or the overturning of *Roe v. Wade*. Clinton's election also came on the heels of the *Planned Parenthood v. Casey* decision by the Supreme Court, also in 1992, that some thought should have overturned *Roe v. Wade* but instead reaffirmed the woman's "right to choose." Our meeting was glum.

In hindsight, we know that God used those events in 1992 to reactivate the pro-life movement as a whole, not just AAI. Our board decided at that meeting that the alternative to abortion part of the pro-life movement had to "kick into gear" if we were to save lives and advance the sanctity of human life in our world—and that meant us.

God used the words of a pregnancy center director at that same conference, Carol Aronis, to convict me that I was supposed to step out in faith, relying on Him, and become the full-time leader of AAI. I was to devote my energies to rebuilding the pregnancy center network so the compassion arm of the pro-life movement could take a leadership role in saving and changing lives and advancing the dignity of every human life. And so, after additional months of soul-searching, I took the position that I had promised to find someone else to fill, and I became the first full-time staff member of the organization. (Because we had no fundraising in place, my first paycheck was actually about three years later!)

In partnership with our board, I concentrated my attention and energy on what I now can name the reframing phase of Heartbeat International's history. Looking back, it becomes clear that our reframing phase continued throughout the third decade of our history, the 1990s and to the mid-2000s. Here are the major "building blocks" we used to rework and refashion Heartbeat International on the foundations built so well by our AAI founders.

## Wise Governing Board

Once we committed at the 1992 annual meeting to "step up to the plate" in the face of the challenges we anticipated under the Clinton administration and beyond, a strong board was even more important. Because of my experience as chair of the board of our local center since 1980, I knew that a strong governing board is essential to the growth and health of an organization. With all the major decisions that were ahead, we needed wise, skilled, and experienced counsel on our board. As Proverbs 15:22 says: "Without counsel plans go wrong, but with many advisers they succeed."

In fact, three of our original Heartbeat board members served for twelve consecutive years without a break: my husband Mike, an attorney and businessman; Anne Pierson from Loving and Caring; and Janet Trenda, a pregnancy center founder from California, who became the board chair after me. Heartbeat later honored them as "foundational board members."

They and other board members gave gifts of time, talent, and treasure to help Heartbeat grow and develop. A list of Heartbeat International and AAI board members for our first fifty years is in Appendix III. These people have been core volunteers, prayer partners, and discerning decision makers (or "governors") for Heartbeat.

An effective governing board is one of the hallmarks of Heartbeat International today, and we devote a great deal of time and effort to keep our board strong and engaged in good governance. Heartbeat considers a strong governing board led by an active chairperson as one of the two crucial "spheres of influence" in nonprofit organizational structure. The other sphere of influence is the staff, led by an effective CEO (or president or executive director). These spheres must work together in harmony if the organization is to prosper and the mission is to be fulfilled.

## Our New Name

One of our key decisions in the reframing process was to change our name from AAI to Heartbeat International. This was a difficult and emotional decision since Alternatives to Abortion International had been our name for over twenty years. "Alternatives to abortion" had become the generic term in public use for the services we provided, much like the corporate name Kleenex is commonly used as a generic name for tissues. The Yellow Pages, for example, used the headings "Alternatives to Abortion" to contrast with the heading "Abortion Services." However, several people, including experts in communications and public relations, told me that we needed to get the word *abortion* out of our name because it polarizes people and has bad connotations.

The board considered new names for over a year, but none on the list seemed right. Finally, I had what seemed like a revelation. None of the names we were considering connected us to our foundation, AAI. I suggested that we take the name Heartbeat, a name connected with us from our very first newsletter in 1972, the name of several of our early centers, and the name of our groundbreaking periodical, *Heartbeat* magazine. I called Sister Paula, and she had no objection. So, we officially became Heartbeat International. It had to have been an inspiration of the Holy Spirit because no one ever since has suggested that we change our name (again). Its significance is understood immediately in any language around the world, and in the words of one of our dear supporters, "Heartbeat is the heartbeat of God."

## Central Coordination and Leadership: "Heartbeat Central"

When it was clear that I was being called to take leadership of Heartbeat in a full-time staff role rather than from a board position, I thought the title president was better than executive director (since I had never been an executive or a CEO). I knew that a full-time leader who was building a qualified and competent staff was essential if we were to carry out the goals originally set by our founders and still affirmed by our board.

Remember, AAI had only had volunteer leadership through the first two decades of our history (with an occasional paid "secretary" in the national headquarters). Most of the services to affiliates were provided by Sister Paula in the West Coast office and Lore Maier in the Toledo office, who had tremendous help from Dr. Hillabrand's nurse Esther Applegate. A handful of experienced directors and founders of AAI affiliates around the country were available to answer questions and mentor new directors and leaders on an informal basis. They were members of a volunteer group called "regional directors" that was never fully developed. Actually, an all-volunteer leadership was not uncommon in nonprofit organizations during the 1970s and 1980s (and it was a requirement in the charter of Birthright centers). Another name sometimes used for nonprofit organizations was "voluntary organizations."

The original goals established by our founders for AAI services to the network were brilliant and comprehensive. In fact, they are still central to Heartbeat International services today, almost fifty years after they were laid out in the first AAI manual. Here they are:

- Training resources
- A regular newsletter
- Consultation and training on-site
- An annual conference to share ideas and programs
- A directory of all existing pregnancy help services worldwide
- A toll-free number to help connect women in need with a pregnancy center

As the network grew, it became more and more difficult to achieve these goals—these promises to our affiliates—solely with an all-volunteer central office. When I became president, we kept the same goals of our founders, but I was committed to building a staff to carry out the work at an even higher level of excellence. We committed to building what we now call "Heartbeat Central," the central office or headquarters of our network where we fulfill our responsibilities to our affiliates and serve the entire pregnancy help movement. The foot soldiers on the ground deserve the best training, help, and support we can possibly provide them—to lighten their loads as they carry out the mission we are all called to.

The sixth goal, a toll-free national number, is the only one we did not tackle immediately. The achievement of this goal helps Heartbeat reach and rescue even more people than ever before and connect them to our network of care. The story of Option Line is the subject of chapter 12.

The first staff member I hired was Judy Schell, a nurse who had written to me a letter from Eastern Europe while I was acting chair of the board. She was working with a Catholic missions group, trying to start a pregnancy center there. I was ashamed that Heartbeat, during that transition period, could offer her prayers and emotional support but no practical help. Judy had returned to her home in Pennsylvania by the time I became Heartbeat president. I asked her to be my "right hand" in developing the central office and fulfilling our commitment to our affiliates. She agreed to help raise donations to cover her salary (mainly just enough to pay off her college loans) and she had "room and board" at Mike's and my home.

Judy and I contacted the approximately 250 centers that had paid AAI twenty-five dollars in any of the previous three years, the cost of annual affiliation and a free Directory. Based on our new service plan and benefits, about one hundred of those centers agreed to pay one hundred dollars for an annual affiliation. They were the first official affiliates of Heartbeat International. Judy stayed for two years before she married her fiancé and moved to New Jersey. She and her husband,

Tom, now have four wonderful grown-up children, and all of them are still key supporters of Heartbeat International.

The "rest of the story" is that God has continued to provide Heartbeat with exceptional working partners on the staff who have always been the right people for the right time. They each have a story of how they came and what they have uniquely contributed to our mission. I wish I could tell you every story!

Three key staff members sent to us by the Lord in this reframing stage of our history—all of whom are still with us—include Beth Diemert, our Ministry Services director from 1998–2005 (and now back full-time again on our staff), Betty McDowell, who worked with PHCs as a consultant on-site (but joined our staff in 2004 and is now vice president of Ministry Services), and Jor-El Godsey, who became our Ministry Services director in 2006 and is now Heartbeat president.

As our network has grown and our services and programs have increased to meet the needs of people around the world, our staff has grown by leaps and bounds. We now have over 2,900 affiliates in over sixty-nine countries, and many of our services are provided not only to them but to anyone in the pregnancy help movement. In 2021, we have just over one hundred people on staff, including full- and part-time staff members and those working on a contract basis.

The original goals of our founders have been "built out" through the last thirty years by talented and devoted Heartbeat staff members, most of whom have years, if not decades, of experience as foot soldiers themselves.

Let's just look at the first goal, "Training Resources"—which, under AAI, consisted of two manuals (Lore's on operations and Sister Paula's on "Counseling") and quarterly issues of *Heartbeat* magazine focusing on top-notch articles on client counseling. Today, Heartbeat has an Academy that includes a wealth of printed training manuals (not only on client care and programs, but also on governance, legal issues, medical issues, center management, and more). The Academy also provides online training (full courses and over 220 webinars) that has served over seven thousand students, with six thousand people actively learning at the present time. Updates for people in various leadership positions within our network (who serve as board members, directors, development directors, and client services personnel) are sent regularly via digital publications such as *On the Leader Board, Heart and Home, Take Heart, Medical Matters, Sexual Integrity Communique,* and more. As a result of excellent training resources, Heartbeat today can provide an LAS (Life Affirming Specialist) certification, as well as CEUs for nurses who are key staff members of the PHCs that provide ultrasound and other medical services.

Heartbeat Central has been a crucial addition to our AAI foundation.

## Exemplary Servant Leadership

We were blessed with fine leaders who laid the foundation for Heartbeat International, as shown in the three chapters that profile each of our founders. In our reframing stage, we put a name to the kind of leadership they displayed—Servant Leadership—and we set that forth as a core value for Heartbeat International.

We invited as many of that founding generation as we could (early AAI board members and founding center directors) to our 25th Birthday Celebration at our annual conferences in Chicago in 1996. Several were able to attend, including Sister Paula. To honor them, we inaugurated our Servant Leader Award. All of these heroes could lead effectively, build a team, and get results. Yet each also had a great humility and modesty and put others ahead of self. Service to others is what they were all about.

Lore Maier could not be with us in Chicago, but she wrote a statement that she dictated to me over the phone. I shared it with all the attendees when we bestowed on her the Servant Leader Award. Recently, while updating our history, I found a sheet of paper from a yellow tablet in some old files that contained Lore's statement in her own handwriting, the statement she read to me over the phone. Here are Lore's remarks, and they illustrate both her visionary leadership but also her desire to model humble service to others:

> From the start our goal has been to make help available to every girl or woman distressed by pregnancy—a truly universal appeal that knows no boundaries to origin, country, religion, education, political persuasion, or social standing—simply to be called humanitarian.
>
> These twenty-five years can only be considered *a first step* in a far-reaching and never ending journey for life. Consider yourselves the torchbearers who in time will pass on to others that come after us the glorious task of working to preserve and protect the lives of mothers and babies.
>
> Always remember to be truly helpful . . . and not to expect too much at the start, to be patient and to be kind. To be tolerant of the human condition regarding various aspects of life requires us to be understanding, resourceful, humble, and respectful. With this attitude in your hearts—your efforts will not fail!
>
> Thank you for your outstanding commitment! Our generation and future generations will benefit greatly because of you.
>
> With faith in all your endeavors—appreciation and love,
>
> Lore Maier

Heartbeat has given Servant Leader Awards at each annual international conference since our founding generation received them in 1996. Today, as we give the awards, we call to mind our real role model, Jesus, the greatest of all servant leaders. Although He was Lord and God of all, He washed the feet of His disciples. When He did that, He specifically asked us to do the same: "If I then, your Lord and Teacher, have washed your feet, you also ought to wash one another's feet. For I have given you an example, that you also should do as I have done to you" (John13:14–15).

## Formal Collaborations

Unity is a value embedded in our foundation, as we discussed in the previous chapter. In our reframing period, we moved from unity as a value to unity as demonstrated in more formal collaborative projects. When I first became Heartbeat president in 1993, our network needed more legal training, especially since we had been coming under more and more blatant attacks (see chapter 10) from pro-abortion groups since the mid-1980s. A pregnancy center director introduced me to Tom Glessner, who started NIFLA that same year to focus on the legal needs of pregnancy help centers. NIFLA did not have a vision to provide the range of services that Heartbeat was providing our affiliates, so we decided to "join forces" and encourage our centers to jointly affiliate with both Heartbeat and NIFLA. Tom joined the founding Heartbeat board, and I became a member of the founding NIFLA board. Our collaboration lasted for many years, and hundreds of pregnancy help centers are still joint affiliates of Heartbeat and NIFLA.

We were among the original signatories in 2001 for the Commitment of Care that described the ethical standards of practice for the entire pregnancy help movement, and Heartbeat proposed the revision that became the Commitment of Care and Competence in 2009 and an amendment in 2019, as discussed in chapter 5.

Heartbeat International was also a founding member of the Leadership Alliance of Pregnancy Care Organizations (LAPCO) that unites the national organizations that are part of the compassion arm of the movement. The thirteen founding organizations met on January 8, 2000, with a prayer leader and intercessor, and decided to continue as a formal collaboration. The LAPCO mission is this: "We exist to glorify God by joining in prayer and worship, discerning God's will, promoting and guarding unity, discussing, and developing collaborative relationships among leaders of national pregnancy care ministries." LAPCO still meets yearly for two days. The first day is devoted to prayer and the second day to business.

Nothing like our Leadership Alliance exists in any other part of the pro-life movement. I believe that the Lord has truly blessed the pregnancy help movement through the years in part because of our desire to be united, as He would have us be. I believe that our emphasis on a full day of prayer each time we meet is the key to working together cooperatively and collaboratively, despite our differences in mission, strategy, and methods.

The close relationships we have built have led to some strategic joint efforts. For a period, Care Net and Heartbeat International published joint legal manuals and medical manuals, and our most impactful collaboration was during the first ten years of Option Line's history, the subject of chapter 12. Collaboration has remained a powerful part of Heartbeat's culture as will be discussed in subsequent chapters.

We demonstrate that we are better together.

The reframing processes described in this chapter relate primarily to the structure and organization of Heartbeat. The next chapter will focus on the most important part of our reframing, the core of who Heartbeat is and what we reflect to the world: our Christian identity.

*Heartbeat's reframing period included greatly expanding our original training resources. The first "AAI Manual" on operating a pregnancy help center was one booklet. Heartbeat now provides on-site training, multiple conferences, a wide variety of printed manuals, hundreds of on-line webinars, podcasts, and complete courses. New center directors (above) peruse the choices at a Heartbeat Pregnancy Help Institute.*

*Office of first Heartbeat President, 1993. Note the lack of technology except for two telephones, one for incoming and one for outgoing calls!*

*"Heartbeat Central," with paid staff to serve our affiliates, was a crucial step in reframing. By 1998, we had grown from one staff member to 7, pictured here with one of our volunteers. Virginia Cline (far left) and Beth Diemert (second from right) are part of the Heartbeat team today—101 full and part time staff!*

*Another crucial step in our reframing period was redeveloping a strong Governing Board. Many of these early governing Board members served 12 years (L to R, front): Mary Weyrich, Janet Trenda (first Board chair after Peggy), Peggy, John Tabor, Anne Pierson. (L to R, back): Maria Suarez Hamm, Pat Hunter, Mike Hartshorn, John Ensor.*

*Reframing included a more pro-active approach to our worldwide mission by providing networking and training opportunities to international leaders through Conference scholarships. The first group, in 1999, with Peggy (center) and Beth Diemert (right) are from England, Romania, Mexico, Australia, Ireland, France, Sweden, and Zambia (not pictured).*

*Reframing included more formal collaborations. Rev. Curtis Young, second ED of Christian Action Council (Care Net) at the 1994 Conference. Heartbeat worked with Curt, Focus on the Family, and other national pregnancy help organizations on marketing, adoption and other projects.*

*Reframing included focusing on the leadership qualities that Heartbeat models. The first Servant Leader Awards are presented to members of our founding generation in 1996. (L to R): Dr. Frank and Alice Brown, Annette and Tom Krycinski, Dr. Margaret White, Anne Pierson, Sister Paula Vandegaer, and Dr. Herb Ratner.*

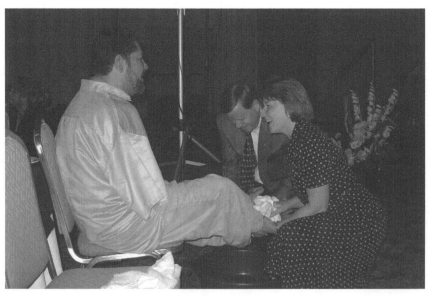

*Inspired by Jesus's example of Servant Leadership, washing the feet of His disciples, attendees at the 2000 conference washed each other's feet. Peggy and Mike Hartshorn serve musician Tony Melendez, who, born without arms, plays the guitar with his feet.*

# CHAPTER 7

## REFRAMING: OUR CHRISTIAN CORE

### Peggy Hartshorn

The most important reframing decision we made when we transitioned from AAI to Heartbeat International was to describe Heartbeat explicitly as a Christian organization, with God's love at our core, and to make sure that our Christian core was embedded deeply and was clear to our entire network.

The word *core* comes from the Latin word for *heart: cor.* The heart, of course, literally refers to the organ inside the human body that pumps our blood. But even in ancient times, the heart stood for so much more than a physical organ at the center of our bodies. A search of dictionaries online gives a massive number of meanings and connotations. The meanings that capture what I mean by Heartbeat's Christian core are *center, life,* and *love.*

I believe it was an inspiration of the Holy Spirit that both our founders and reframers adopted the heart for use in our publications, logo, and eventually in our name itself. The heart (both the word and the symbol) was in the forefront from the very beginning of our history, and it remains so today and for the future. Our current logo is named the Heart of the Future!

But how to briefly describe the love that is the center of Heartbeat—our pro-life mission, method, and culture?

The core of Heartbeat's culture could be described as an effort to live out the two greatest commandments—love the Lord your God with your whole heart, mind, and strength, and love your neighbor as yourself—especially in our mission of pregnancy help, but also with one another and within our organizations. This understanding of how profound our core really is has deepened through the years, especially in the decade of our reframing in the 1990s, and that is the story of this chapter.

## Heartbeat as a Christian Association

AAI was never explicitly called a "Christian organization." The terms used to describe it, up to our reframing period, were "humanitarian" or "nondenominational and nonsectarian," which had led to a variety of interpretations from affiliates. These ranged from "I guess we can describe ourselves as a Christian ministry, but not a Baptist, or Catholic, or Presbyterian one" to "We cannot have anything in our center or our programs that would hint that we are Christians—it might turn away clients or make them believe we are forcing our views on them." There were different opinions on whether sharing the Gospel could or should be part of the mission of pregnancy help.

AAI was, from the beginning, an outreach of and by Christian people. (There was only one Jewish woman I ever met within Heartbeat, and she headed an agency staffed primarily by Catholics.) Sister Paula, in her talk at our 25th Anniversary Conference in 1996, used the term "first wave" to describe the Catholics that had been the predominant force in the early years of the pro-life movement, and the term "second wave" to describe the Evangelical Christians and other Protestants who began to enter the movement in the late seventies and early eighties, motivated in large part by Francis Schaeffer and Dr. C. Everett Koop, who toured the country in 1979, showing the galvanizing pro-life film *Whatever Happened to the Human Race?*

One of the effects of this influx of the "second wave" was that centers with an explicitly Evangelical statement of faith were intentionally developed by the Christian Action Council, later renamed Care Net, with help from AAI and especially with financial support from Catholics (chapter 5). Another effect was that Evangelical Christians were volunteering in large numbers in some of the original AAI centers. This had happened at the center I helped found in Columbus, Ohio. So, when I became president of Heartbeat, I had personally worked closely with both Catholics and Evangelicals at our center for ten years, and I loved it. There were always challenges, but solving the issues as they arose and understanding one another's beliefs and perspectives brought great rewards.

As we reframed the new Heartbeat International, we wanted it to be clear that we were still the "big umbrella" envisioned by our founders in the early 1970s that welcomed many models and forms of pregnancy help ministries. They could be primarily composed of Catholics, or of Evangelicals, or of Orthodox Christians, or they could be mixed. They could have a purpose of explicitly *sharing* Christ with clients, as some did, or they could see their role primarily as *being* Christ to their clients through serving them in their hour of need, as others did.

They could be inspired and led by the biblical command to "go into all the world and preach the gospel to the whole creation" (Mark 16:15), as many of the "second wave" centers were. Or they could be inspired by Jesus' words, "Truly, I say to you, as you did it to one of the least of these my brethren, you did it to me" (Matthew 25:40), as many of the "first wave" centers were. Some centers at that time adopted their statement of faith from the National Association of Evangelicals, some had adopted the Apostle's Creed or Nicene Creed, and some had developed a statement of faith through discussions among Christians of various denominations that were working in their center.

Since our founding in 1971, the culture had dramatically changed, and client needs had changed too. Then, it could be presumed that the culture was basically a Judeo-Christian one, and that this would be reflected in the programs and values of most community-based organizations. By the 1990s, however, this was no longer to be expected. Charitable organizations were distancing themselves from explicit Christianity. It was becoming "politically incorrect" to make one's Christianity public. Of course, our American culture has become even more hostile to Christianity since then, and there are many nonprofit organizations that are explicitly anti-Christian.

I wrote an article in our first newsletter after I became president in 1993, announcing that Heartbeat would be "an interdenominational Christian association" of life-affirming service providers. I dropped "nondenominational and nonsectarian" and "humanitarian" from our vocabulary. I was not then, and am not now, totally happy with the "new" word choice, since many churches do not see themselves as "denominations," and sometimes the term "Christian" is thought to refer to primarily "born-again Christian," and some do not think of it as including Catholic Christians (this was especially true in 1993). The term "ecumenical" did not seem a good one either, since to many Catholics at the time the term connoted something that was "lukewarm." Recently the term "ecumenical" is beginning to have more positive connotations. Today, we often refer to Heartbeat as a "Christ-centered association" of life-affirming service providers, which seems the best way of describing what we know as "better together."

As Heartbeat president, I also found the eloquent and inspirational document "Evangelicals and Catholics Together," initiated by Chuck Colson of Prison Fellowship and Father Richard John Neuhaus of the Institute on Religion and Public Life. Published on March 29, 1994, it was signed by thirty-nine scholars and Christian leaders whose names and reputations are still well known, including Rev. Pat Robertson, Dr. Richard Land, Dr. Bill Bright, Dr. Os Guinness, Rev. Avery Dulles, John Cardinal O'Connor, George Weigel, and Michael Novak. Over the years, they issued other joint statements worthy of note.

The authors made a clear list of the basic Christian beliefs on which Evangelicals and Catholics agree, and a list of those issues ("doctrine, worship, practice, and piety") where we "continue to search together—through study, discussion, and prayer—for a better understanding of one another's convictions and a more adequate comprehension of the truth of God in Christ." They then urged strong Christians to work together, or "contend together," in the modern world that so opposes Christ. The statement specifically discussed the importance of Evangelicals and Catholics working together on the issue of abortion, calling abortion "the leading edge of an encroaching culture of death," and it specifically commends the pregnancy help center movement and our efforts for the sake of the unborn, mothers, and fathers.

Its conclusion I still find inspiring. It matched then (and still does now) our passion within Heartbeat for Christians to work together in the hostile world in which we live (which has become ever more hostile since 1994), transcending our theological differences in order to most effectively carry out our mission as Christians to "share the Good News":

> We do not know, we cannot know, what the Lord of history has in store for the Third Millennium. It may be the springtime of world missions and great Christian expansion. It may be the way of the cross marked by persecution and apparent marginalization. In different places and times, it will likely be both. Or it may be that Our Lord will return tomorrow. We do know that his promise is sure, that we are enlisted for the duration, and that we are in this together. We do know that we must affirm and hope and search and contend and witness together, for we belong not to ourselves but to him who has purchased us by the blood of the cross. We do know that this is a time of opportunity—and, if of opportunity, then of responsibility—for Evangelicals and Catholics to be Christians together in a way that helps prepare the world for the coming of him to whom belongs the kingdom, the power, and the glory forever. Amen.

This document has been the basis for a workshop that is sometimes presented at Heartbeat Conferences and is still popular today in our online Academy, since Evangelicals and Catholics continue to be drawn into our pregnancy help movement, and we continue to "contend together" in a world that is becoming more and more hostile to Christians and our worldview.

## Officially Documenting Our Christian Identity

Heartbeat and the majority of our early affiliates were incorporated for "charitable purposes" when they became nonprofit organizations in their states and when they applied to the IRS for a status that would allow gifts to be tax-deductible. The IRS gives this coveted status (501c3) to organizations that can show charitable, religious, and/or educational purposes. During our reframing period, Heartbeat amended our articles of incorporation and notified the IRS that we added "religious purposes" to "charitable purposes." We advise that our affiliates do the same. This gives us the most protection possible in asserting our right to be exempt from federal, state, and local laws that threaten our freedom of speech and freedom of religion.

More recently, Heartbeat adopted the Nicene Creed as our statement of faith for our own board and staff. While we are still the "big umbrella" that I described earlier and our affiliates have autonomy in how they handle this issue within their own organizations, today we strongly advise our affiliates to make their Christian identity as clear as possible in their bylaws and in all policies and procedures, due to the current attacks on our freedom of speech and religion, even the recent efforts to force us to refer for abortions. (These attacks will be discussed more fully in chapter 10).

We are prepared to defend our right to be a faith-based nonprofit organization that lives out the biblically based values at the core of our vision, mission, and programs.

Our explicitly Christian identity is clear today in all of our training materials and communications, and it is on display in beautiful ways at our annual conferences. But it started with baby steps. At the 1994 conference in Columbus, Ohio, we added an interdenominational prayer service to our full program of general sessions and workshops. In 1995, at the Pittsburgh conference, we added a daily time of praise and worship, now a favorite at all of our conferences. Most often we had an Evangelical worship team, but when we were in Pittsburgh in 2002, we invited a praise and worship team from Franciscan University in Steubenville, a Catholic college nearby. I expected that the participants would not notice the "difference"—and I was right!

After the first couple of years of great praise and worship sessions, Catholic attendees asked if we might consider adding early morning Mass at the hotel, which we did. A few years later, they requested a special time available for confessions. Would our Protestant brothers and sisters accept these changes, we wondered? They did. After many years, these options have become the expectation, and more and more people who attend our conferences, both Protestants, Catholics, and Orthodox, comment positively on the spiritual "wealth" available.

It's hard to believe that at one time we worried that these changes might fatally disrupt our hard-fought unity, coming as we did from many expressions of Christianity and many deeply held religious beliefs, traditions, and styles of prayer and worship. The Devil would have loved to create disunity and harm our movement, but the Lord has protected us and even strengthened our unity as a result!

## At the Core: The L.O.V.E. Approach

Heartbeat's Christ-centered orientation was demonstrated clearly with the publication of our first training manual. When I began answering phone calls at Heartbeat Central from our affiliates, one thing I heard over and over again was, "We need a volunteer training manual."

I looked everywhere for a general "counselor" training manual that would meet the needs of our diverse group of affiliates, but I could not find one. I met two other leaders in our movement who were working on training manuals, but they did not have a vision for writing a manual that would meet the needs of both Catholic and Evangelical volunteer "counselors" (who filled the US centers) as well as counselors in other countries, some with radically different cultures. So I decided to start working on the new training manual that many of our affiliates had requested. I had been training the volunteers and staff at our local PHC, Pregnancy Decision Health Centers, and other centers in central Ohio. The system I had developed over that ten-year period eventually became *The L.O.V.E. Approach*, with the first edition published in 1994.

Clearly biblically based, *The L.O.V.E. Approach* takes its inspiration first of all from the parable of the sower in Matthew 13:3–8, since we are planting seeds in our work and it's the Lord who really brings the fruit. Second, it takes its inspiration from chapter 13 of St. Paul's first letter to the Corinthians, sometimes called St. Paul's hymn to love, which describes the source of the love we share with the people we serve, God Himself, and the loving approach we take with them. L.O.V.E. stands for Listen and Learn, Open Options, Vision and Value, and Extend and Empower.

I became convinced, during my own experience with clients, that we must "always be prepared to make a defense to anyone who calls [us] to account for the hope that is in [us], yet do it with gentleness and reverence" (1 Peter 3:15). The Vision and Value step of *The L.O.V.E. Approach* clearly answers the question, from the Heartbeat perspective, of whether sharing the Gospel can or should be part of our mission. The V Step proposes the opportunity to share with our clients explicitly that they are special and valuable because they are made in the image of God, and they are loved so much that they have also been redeemed by Him. Regardless of what they have done, they can be forgiven and have a relationship, through Jesus, with the God who made and loves them so much. This is a new vision of self and a new vision of God for many of our clients.

*The L.O.V.E. Approach* advises that we be open to the leading of the Holy Spirit as to when it is appropriate to share this Good News. The woman in front of us has, of course, come to us for a specific need, and we are there to meet her need (for a pregnancy test, for information, for help with deciding among options, for knowing how far along she is in the pregnancy, for support, and more). She may not be ready for this message about the love of the Lord, or she may not be ready for the full sharing of it, especially the first time we meet her. But we are always "planting the seed" and reflecting the love of Christ to her just by who we are and the light of the Lord that shines through us.

Love is also the method of our approach to the client, as in St. Paul's beautiful description:

> *If I speak in the tongues of men and of angels, but have not love, I am a noisy gong or a clanging cymbal. And if I have prophetic powers, and understand all mysteries and all knowledge, and if I have all faith, so as to remove mountains, but have not love, I am nothing. If I give away all I have, and if I deliver my body to be burned, but have not love, I gain nothing. Love is patient and kind; love is not jealous or boastful; it is not arrogant or rude. Love does not insist on its own way; it is not irritable or resentful; it does not rejoice at wrong, but rejoices in the right. Love bears all things, believes all things, hopes all things, endures all things. Love never ends. (I Cor.13:1-8)*

I truly believe that *The L.O.V.E. Approach* was an inspiration from the Lord. It has stood the test of time (revised editions have been published in 2005, 2011, and 2021), and it has been adapted for all kinds of service models now in existence in our movement (counseling, medical, residential, adoption agency, abortion recovery, and more). It has also been proven to be culturally adaptable and "universal" in many ways. It is used in centers that have primarily Protestant or Catholic staff and volunteers, in those that are denominational, such as Baptist centers, or in those that are mixed. It is used well in cities, small towns, and rural areas—and by all ethnic groups.

It is widely used around the world, and Heartbeat has provided special licenses for its use in Africa, Asia, Latin America, and Australia. It has been translated into Spanish, and it has also been adopted in Italy (as *The 5 A's*). It is the first training course to become available when Heartbeat launched our online Academy in 2010. *The L.O.V.E. Approach* is the basis for training of all our Option Line staff and is used by them to communicate—via phone, email, live chat—with about 1,100 people per day, many of whom are at risk for abortion. The approach has helped save and change thousands, perhaps millions, of lives.

*The L.O.V.E. Approach* has become part of Heartbeat culture, a major addition to the foundation of AAI as described in the previous chapter. Because it is respectful, loving, relationship building, and affirming, and because it is helpful in sorting out options and moving forward in unity, we try to make it the way we communicate with one another on the staff, on our board, with our supporters, with our affiliates, and with all the other foot soldiers we communicate with daily.

Those of us who know the four steps realize that it "works" with any person we want to form or build a relationship with—in our family, with our friends, and in our church, ministry, or community. Heartbeat Publishing in 2020 issued a version of the four steps for everyone: *The L.O.V.E. Approach: 4 Proven Steps to Transforming Relationships in Your Family, Church, and Community.*

## At the Core: God's Plan for Our Sexuality

When I was first introduced to the pregnancy help world at the AAI Conference in 1980, I was amazed at the scope of pregnancy help issues being presented. Some speakers and programs focused on prevention issues such as sexual abstinence until marriage; others on support such as childbirth classes; others on crisis intervention and abortion alternatives; others on long-term care such as housing; others on healing after abortion and abuse; others on natural family planning and fatherhood and motherhood issues; still others on psychological needs and counseling approaches, and more! There were pastors and priests in attendance, married couples and single people, religious sisters, international participants, and many academics and professionals from a wide variety of fields of study and practice. Maybe you have had the same somewhat mind-boggling experience when you attended your first Heartbeat Conference!

Somehow, we all knew then that there was something in common that united us in our passion for life-affirming pregnancy help (besides being in favor of alternatives to abortion), something that was broader than the issue of abortion and more specific than the fact that we were all Christians. It was the issue of the family and the place of sexual expression within marriage.

I believe the Lord helped me to articulate this when I made it the subject of my keynote address to the 1999 Heartbeat International Conference. I called it "God's Plan for Our Sexuality." I believe it is part of the new vision and value we have the opportunity to share with every person the Lord sends to us.

I shared, in this 1999 keynote, that part of the core of our call in the pregnancy help movement is not only to save babies and women from abortion, but also to share this vision of God's plan for our sexuality whenever we can. The core around which all of the diverse groups and programs in the pregnancy help movement (prevention, crisis intervention, support, healing) are united is right here, in God's plan for our sexuality. God is using all of us to help put that plan back in place, to reconstitute it in this world today where it has almost been destroyed by the Devil through the destruction of our sexual mores.

Heartbeat defines "God's Plan for Our Sexuality" this way. There are five things that go together: sexual intimacy, marriage between one man and one woman, children, selfless love (or self-gift), and God. If we remove one or more of these five from God's equation, we have most of the societal and family-related ills of our time. For example:

- Marriage without selfless love, or without God, and often without children, leads to loveless, godless, material-driven partnerships that easily end in divorce.
- Sexual intimacy without marriage leads to cohabitation, fatherlessness, and children raised in one-parent families with all their attendant problems.
- Sexual intimacy without selfless love and marriage leads to STIs, STDs, promiscuity, prostitution, human trafficking, and objectifying of people.
- Sexual intimacy between people of the same sex or transgendered individuals leads to higher rates of STDs, STIs, broken relationships, and other problems we are just beginning to understand.
- Sexual intimacy predicated on eliminating children leads to abortion, abortion trauma, lack of trust between men and women, and broken relationships.

In fact, if you think about it, most social and personal problems today can be connected to not living out God's Plan for Our Sexuality and trying to cover the resulting pain with drugs, alcohol, and other addictive behaviors, along with destructive behaviors like domestic violence and child abuse.

In editions of *The L.O.V.E. Approach* since 1999, the Vision and Value step has been expanded to include offering the new vision of God's Plan for Our Sexuality, not the "equation" above, but more specifically, the vision of the dignity of women. We introduce women to a new vision of who they have been created to be by God—their female sexuality, their gift of femininity, and their gift of fertility (that is so endangered by the lifestyle they are leading). Once they grasp the true nature of their femininity, not only will their own lives be transformed, but these women will help rebuild the family.

## Sexual Integrity Program and Fertility as a Gift

The most comprehensive explanation of this vision of true femininity in Heartbeat resources today is in our Sexual Integrity Program. It was originally developed in 2002 (revised in 2007 and 2021) when Heartbeat hired Carrie Abbott, an Evangelical leader active in the abstinence education movement, to create a program that would ring true to both Evangelicals and Catholics. Carrie based the program not only on the Bible but on what she learned from courses at Pope Paul VI Institute and from St. Pope John Paul II's *Theology of the Body* and his teachings on the dignity of women.

The program teaches women working in our centers—our foot soldiers—how to teach other women about sexual integrity and sexual wholeness: emotional, intellectual, physical, social, and spiritual. Sexual integrity is expressing the gift of female sexuality throughout life in a true, excellent, honest, and pure way. It is protection in childhood, direction in adolescence, and celebration in adulthood. It is based on several biblical pillars from the Old and New Testament.

The primary biblical teachings on which the program is based are first, Genesis 1:27–28: "God created man in his own image, in the image of God he created him; male and female he created them. And God blessed them, and God said to them, 'Be fruitful and multiply, and fill the earth and subdue it'"; and second, Ephesians 5:31–33: "'For this reason a man shall leave his father and mother and be joined to his wife, and the two shall become one flesh.' This mystery is a profound one, and I am saying that it refers to Christ and the church; however, let each one of you love his wife as himself, and let the wife see that she respects her husband."

One of the key concepts in the Sexual Integrity Program is that a woman's fertility—the ability to conceive a child, as evidenced in a healthy monthly cycle—is a gift (not a "curse" as it used to be called!), and it needs to be protected from disease and injury. Women need to know and appreciate how "beautifully and wonderfully made" their bodies are. Once a woman learns to appreciate this gift and its place in God's plan for the family, and indeed for the human race, she has a whole new concept of how special she is as a woman and how she deserves to be treated with respect.

The sexual integrity concepts can also be used effectively within the medical model, or pregnancy help medical clinic, in providing true reproductive healthcare for women. The term "reproductive healthcare" as used today—by Planned Parenthood and their allies such as the American College of Obstetricians and Gynecologists (ACOG), and even by the media at large—is simply a code term for contraceptives and abortion. Neither contraceptives nor abortion led to reproduction (their purpose is the opposite) or to good health; in fact, there are well-documented detrimental health effects associated with both contraceptives and abortion. True reproductive healthcare protects and enhances a woman's gift of fertility (and even helps heal infertility).

Pregnancy help medical clinics transcend Planned Parenthood (the main provider of "reproductive healthcare" for women; that is, contraception and abortion) and are the providers of true reproductive healthcare for women. Not only do we provide alternatives to abortion and offer life-giving pregnancy support, but we have been speaking about a new vision of the dignity of women for about thirty years now. Our PHCs are based on and explicitly share a new vision of women's true femininity, of their true sexual integrity—of God's Plan for Our Sexuality.

A handful of medical clinics, once part of our movement, have very recently decided that, in order to compete with Planned Parenthood for clients, they needed to go "head to head" and begin to provide contraceptives (since this is the "entry service" at most Planned Parenthoods). Sadly, these centers decided that to compete, they needed to duplicate services. Instead, what they need to do is transcend—by providing a life-giving new vision to the women the Lord sends their way: the vision of God's Plan for Our Sexuality.

This was confirmed for the entire pregnancy help movement when the leaders of the affiliation groups met in 2019 to consider an amendment to our Commitment of Care and Competence (CCC), the statement of values that unite all the pregnancy help organizations in the US. One statement in the CCC was amended by adding "contraceptives" to the list of what pregnancy help centers do not provide or refer for. The statement now reads: "We do not offer, recommend, or refer for abortions, abortifacients, or contraceptives. We are committed to offering accurate information about related risks and procedures." (See Appendix V for the complete CCC.)

Some of the innovative pregnancy help medical clinics have been experimenting with various models that incorporate sexual integrity education along with fertility appreciation and even some fertility care into their services. STD testing, in particular, is a medical service provided by many of our medical clinics that opens the door to follow-up services focusing on true reproductive health. Some of our affiliates in the forefront of these experimental programs are Guiding Star in Waterloo, Iowa; Silent Voices in Chula Vista, California; Thrive Women's Center in Charlottesville, Virginia; and Obria Clinics, based in Orange County, California.

There are also a handful of 100 percent pro-life OB/GYN medical clinics or family practice clinics emerging in a few states, headed by heroic physicians who feel compelled to leave the standard practice of medicine, dominated as it is by this ungodly view of reproductive healthcare. A few pregnancy help medical clinics have become full medical practices, such as Life Choices Family Medical in Lutz, Florida (formerly a Guiding Star pregnancy help medical clinic). Our pregnancy help center network and these full medical clinics are partnering wherever possible so clients can experience a full range of pro-life healthcare services. The original model for these faith-based healthcare clinics is Tepeyac Family Center in Fairfax, Virginia, founded by Dr. John Bruchalski. A recently founded consortium that is networking these providers is called Pro-Women's Health Care Centers (PWHC), and it has twelve certified centers in the country. It's goal is one in every state.

A recent development paralleling the pregnancy help movement, and a resource to pregnancy help center clients, is FEMM—Fertility Education and Medical Management. FEMM is a comprehensive women's health and wellness program using natural, science-based applications to identify a woman's health and cycle irregularities and provide the tools women need (many online) to seek advanced care and support. By helping women understand the central role of reproductive endocrinology in the management of their health, FEMM empowers women to achieve their health and fertility goals. Informed and empowered women will certainly be less subject to the predatory use of abortifacients masquerading as answers to reproductive challenges. In other words, the pill and implants are not the solution to all female health problems! An increasing number of pregnancy help healthcare professionals are FEMM-trained and informed by their extensive research.

There have been efforts in the United States throughout these last fifty years to limit the influence of Planned Parenthood and their version of reproductive health care—which is not at all healthy and is not at all reproductive. This culminated in a short-lived partial victory in 2020 when Planned Parenthood withdrew from Title X, thanks to Trump Administration rule changes. That is now reversed under the Biden Administration. The battle continues at the national and international level.

But meanwhile, Heartbeat continues to stand for, envision, and equip the pregnancy help movement to provide an inspiring and God-given alternative of true sexual health to women and families in their communities, and to keep God and God's plan at the core of who we are.

## At the Core: Our Mission

Part of our reframing process has been capturing the mission of Heartbeat's network in a way that is inspired by our call as Christians. Here it is, with the biblical verses that express the call:

> To Reach and Rescue as many lives as possible, around the world, through an effective network of life-affirming pregnancy help, and to Renew communities for LIFE.
>
> • REACH: "Reach down your hand from on high; deliver me . . ." (Psalm 144:7)
>
> • RESCUE: "Rescue me, O Lord, from evil men; protect me from men of violence." (Psalm 140:1)
>
> • RENEW: "He sent me to bind up the brokenhearted . . . to proclaim the year of the Lord's favor . . . They will renew the ruined cities that have been devastated for generations." (Isaiah 61:1–4)

Key to Heartbeat's reframing was clarifying that Jesus Christ is at Heartbeat's very core. We respect differences in doctrine and practice, but are unified in love of the Lord and serving Him. This is visible whenever we gather at our conference and other events. Our core training, The L.O.V.E. Approach™ (first published in 1994), teaches the Biblical basis for pregnancy help.

*Vice President of Ministry Services Betty McDowell leading a devotional at a Heartbeat Conference.*

*President Jor-El Godsey leading prayer at the Heartbeat Institute.*

*Board member Rev. John Wootton leading prayer with Vice President of Mission Advancement Cindi Boston-Bilotta in the Rotunda of the Russell Senate Office Building in Washington, DC, at Heartbeat's Babies Go To Congress® event.*

# CHAPTER 8

# PREVENTION, HEALING, AND LONG-TERM CARE

## Peggy Hartshorn

One of the aspects of the AAI Academy (now called the Heartbeat Conference) that intrigued me most when I first began attending in 1980 was the diversity of affiliates and the variety of programs they were providing. It was not just pregnancy testing and crisis intervention for women who were considering abortion, although this was the original and primary service of most centers. That's why they were called EPS centers, standing for Emergency Pregnancy Services. Of course, this was long before anyone had thought of using ultrasound in a center, which is now key to crisis intervention, as we will see in chapter 9.

The foot soldiers in the field during our first decade were already discussing and providing a wide range of help and support. Even the first AAI manual, written by Lore Maier in about 1975, included in the list of training needed for EPS center volunteers not only all issues surrounding pregnancy and abortion, but also "the importance of follow-up services . . . for the long-range benefit of the client and her baby; helping women who have had abortions; interviewing and counseling girls whose pregnancy test result is negative; assisting fathers-to-be and family members; helping families stay together . . ."

The original vision of pregnancy help was very comprehensive! How that vision developed throughout our history—spawning three additional movements with a "life of their own" outside the pregnancy help movement—is the subject of this chapter.

## From Negative Test Consultations in a PHC to Influence in Washington, DC

Our co-founder Sister Paula, especially, emphasized the importance of "counseling" sessions with women who had a negative pregnancy test (about 50 percent of all clients at that time). Today we would call that "consulting," since most of our foot soldiers are not professional counselors. We were not called into action to help the negative test clients choose life instead of abortion—they weren't pregnant! Instead, Sister Paula taught that we could help these women—especially those not yet fully committed to sexual activity outside marriage—discover through skillful questioning that sexual activity outside of marriage was not in tune with who they were as women (what she called the psychology of women). Negative test consultations were eventually seen as a "prevention" service, to complement the crisis intervention (consultations after the positive test) and the pregnancy support. If the woman captured the vision for abstinence until marriage, this would prevent abortions.

Soon, however, the epidemic of STDs was upon us, especially as HIV/AIDs (untreatable during the 1980s) became a scourge in the homosexual population and also spread into the heterosexual population. Our negative test consulting became more and more focused on the dire physical risks of sexual activity outside of marriage. The deeper psychological and spiritual dimensions of that activity began to take less prominence in our conversations with clients, and our training began to focus more on the physical, medical risks for women.

In the 1980s, some centers took their message out of the PHCs and began teaching in schools about abstinence until marriage in an effort to help prevent the kinds of cases they were seeing in their pregnancy centers. At our annual gathering of PHCs, abstinence education programs began to be highlighted and taught. Because programs in public schools must be secular, most of the programs were based on a medical model, teaching about the risks of sexually transmitted diseases in order to deter sexual activity. Many also added a relationship component. In addition to incorporating information and activities to teach young people about how to form lasting relationships, they explained that multiple sexual partners numbs that ability and endangers the "dream" of someday finding the person with whom they would spend the rest of their lives. Some abstinence programs were reluctant to discuss "marriage" per se (for fear of being ejected from the public schools), so they focused on a "lifetime monogamous relationship."

## Abstinence Education Takes on a Life of Its Own

In fact, the early "abstinence education movement" was really birthed out of AAI pregnancy help centers in the 1980s. And these years also included an important Supreme Court decision (*Bowen v. Kendrick*, 1988) that undergirded the extensive "faith-based initiatives" providing federal funding to abstinence, marriage, and fatherhood programs under George W. Bush and then Donald Trump.

Pregnancy Decision Health Centers in Columbus, Ohio ( PDHC), where I was board chair for twenty-three years, was the first center in the country to receive a federal grant for abstinence education in the schools through a "model program" initiative that was part of the 1981 Adolescent Family Life Act. It was administered by pro-life appointees in the US Department of Health and Human Services during the Reagan administration. This program was later challenged in the courts by our opponents as a violation of the separation of church and state, and PDHC was involved in depositions for the court case. It was eventually decided in our favor, with the Court determining that "faith-based" organizations can receive federal funding as long as those funded programs do not "proselytize" (in *Bowen v. Kendrick*).

After that first grant in 1984, I and other pro-lifers served on advisory boards for the US Department of Health and Human Services in the Office of Family Planning, and we were trained as grant readers on panels that rated proposals from all over the country for abstinence education grants. What a great learning experience! Presidents Bush and Trump continued to appoint pro-life leaders to key positions in HHS in subsequent years.

When I became president of Heartbeat in 1993, I called Leslee Unruh, a PHC pioneer and AAI affiliate in Sioux Falls, South Dakota, with whom I worked in the 1980s when both of our pregnancy centers were receiving abstinence funding. I suggested that perhaps she could help me identify for our Worldwide Directory all the centers with abstinence programs, along with the new "freestanding" abstinence education programs in the country. The phone call gave Leslee the vision, she later told me, to start the National Abstinence Clearinghouse to keep track of legitimate abstinence education programs (versus those that were called abstinence but, in fact, taught "comprehensive" sex education that promoted all types of birth control). The Clearinghouse became a major player in abstinence education throughout the country and around the world.

Another major ally that developed in the 1990s was the Medical Institute for Sexual Health (MISH), founded in Texas by OB/GYN Dr. Joe McIlhaney. MISH provided excellent, medically resourced, educational materials and great training programs for all of our programs and educators. Being secular and federally funded, these materials focused solely on sexual health and the medical risks associated with recreational sex, multiple sexual partners, and later, same sex relationships.

Now called The Medical Institute, it has recently been reframed by Dr. McIlhaney, and it is focusing on building strong collaborations with like-minded organizations (including Heartbeat International). Its first project has been to develop comprehensive educational standards that will provide a real alternative to the only other national standards—those promulgated by Planned Parenthood and their partners at SIECUS (Sexual Information and Education Council of the United States).

The career path of the Medical Institute's current director, Lori Kuykendall, shows the close connection between PHCs and the abstinence education movement. Lori's first job out of college was at the Women's Pregnancy Center in Southwest Houston, where she was hired to start an abstinence program. After then working in freestanding abstinence programs for many years, she was hired as the PHC director in Frisco, Texas, before joining the Medical Institute staff in 2020.

In 2019 Dr. McIlhaney and Institute board member Dr. Freda Bush, also an OB/GYN, updated Dr. Bush's groundbreaking book, now called *Hooked: The Brain Science on How Casual Sex Affects Human Development.* Dr. Bush is another example of how the abstinence movement and PHCs are connected: she has been the medical director of two PHCs in Mississippi.

Most recently, in the Trump Administration, Valerie Huber, founder of the National Abstinence Education Association, another ally formed in the 1990s (now Ascend), was appointed chief of staff to the assistant secretary for health (in HHS). She was able to finally orchestrate the defunding of Planned Parenthood from the Title X program that provides most of the family planning funds in the US; up to that point Planned Parenthood was receiving about $1M per day of our tax dollars to provide contraceptives in their clinics across the country). Planned Parenthood withdrew from Title X entirely rather than submit to the new rules. For the first time in history, a handful of life-affirming pregnancy help organizations received Title X funding to provide life-affirming family planning. With the new Biden administration, however, the pendulum has swung back. Planned Parenthood will again be the primary recipient of Title X family planning funds.

Most programs today have moved from a focus on the physical/medical risks of sexually transmitted diseases and multiple sexual partners to include building healthy, long-lasting relationships. They also focus secular, sociological, and economic research on the "success sequence": graduate from high school, get a full-time job, get married, have children.

Relatively small grants of our tax dollars, either directly from federal government grants or through block grants to states, have been available to abstinence programs since the Reagan administration. No comprehensive study of the total amount of these grants has been done. But the total is miniscule compared to our tax dollars granted to Planned Parenthood and its sex education partners for "comprehensive sex education" programs in our schools and communities.

## In PHCs, a More Complete Vision Than Abstinence

While PHCs first birthed abstinence education in their communities and rejoiced as these programs grew and developed, a desire for a fuller approach with clients who come into the centers continued to grow. We needed an approach that would allow us to fully share our Christian values with regard to sexuality.

What could we do to help the "negative test" clients (who were not pregnant yet) and clients who already had their babies and were in follow-up programs (who were being urged, after delivery, to be sterilized or go on long-term birth control)? Surely, there was a more life-affirming alternative. Heartbeat published our *Planting the Seed: The L.O.V.E. Approach* manual in 1994, and we urged volunteers and staff to provide a new V Step (Vision and Value) that would focus on the dignity of the woman, created in the image and likeness of God, and made for a purpose (not to be used by another person).

By the late 1990s Heartbeat materials were focusing on God's Plan for Our Sexuality: that sexual intimacy, marriage between one man and one woman, children, unselfish love or self-gift, and God all go together. By the early 2000s we introduced the Sexual Integrity Program with a totally new focus on women's gift of fertility. This is a vision that most of our clients (and even many of our own foot soldiers) find almost "revolutionary." It leads to reproductive healthcare that is truly healthy and reproductive—the alternative to "reproductive healthcare" as code words for contraception and abortion. A full discussion of this crucial step for Heartbeat and our movement is found in chapter 7.

Today, this new vision of who God created woman to be is desperately needed by those the Lord sends to us all over the world. And the pregnancy help movement is blessed to be able to provide such a redeeming message.

## Abortion Recovery Is Birthed and Takes on a Life of Its Own

Even in the 1970s there was a growing recognition that abortion not only killed unborn babies, but it had devastating effects on their mothers. Remember, Lore Maier, in AAI's first manual, lists "helping women who have had abortions" as one of the crucial topics for volunteer training. The very first woman I ever met who had an abortion was a woman who came to volunteer at Columbus Right to Life in about 1975. She would do anything she could, she said, to help prevent other women from making an abortion decision. I was stunned by her story and her emotional state. She seemed extremely nervous. She told me she had been a successful practicing attorney, contentedly married, when she discovered she had an unplanned pregnancy. Her husband told her he would leave her if she did not have an abortion. Her mother took her to the abortion clinic. When she experienced emotional "complications," her husband left her, and she could not forgive her mother for assisting in the abortion. It became obvious to me that abortion affected women deeply. Soon I came to realize that it also affected men, marriages, and entire families. In fact, I now know that abortion is a major factor (and perhaps a major cause) in the disintegration of the family that we see nearly fifty years after abortion was made legal in all fifty states as a result of the *Roe v. Wade* decision.

I still regret that in 1975 no one knew how to help this victim of abortion who came forward into the pro-life movement. She told her story publicly and was even featured in a very early pro-life educational film, but she soon disappeared. I often think about her and pray for her, hoping she finally found the healing so available today for anyone involved in abortion.

It is hard to imagine now, with the proliferation of research on the effects of abortion, but no one in the 1970s had yet recognized the existence of what in the 1980s came to be called "post-abortion syndrome" (a form of post-traumatic stress syndrome). There is some disagreement whether the first to use the term was by Counselor Terry L. Selby or Dr. Vincent M. Rue. Unfortunately trauma after abortion is still not recognized by secular counseling professionals—or by the American Psychological Association.

By the 1980s when I was regularly attending AAI Academies, pregnancy centers were sharing that some volunteers entering our movement had had abortions. How to help them? No programs existed within our centers at that time. There were no professional counselors doing post-abortion counseling, at least that we could find. The Christian counselors we knew actually warned against delving too deeply into the emotions of women who had abortions, surmising that this might unleash feelings that could even lead to suicide. They advised us that only licensed psychologists and psychiatrists should counsel with women who had had abortions, but none of these professionals had any experience in this area.

Our affiliate in Columbus, PDHC, launched a post-abortion recovery program in 1984, developed by volunteers within our center who had had abortions and based on the work being done in Cincinnati through WEBA, Women Exploited by Abortion—the first post-abortion organization, I believe, in the country. They called the program PAST (Post Abortion Support Team), and the main advisor for the project was Betty McDowell, LSW, the vice president of Ministry Services for Heartbeat, who was then a volunteer at PDHC.

In the 1990s, after I became president of Heartbeat, our PDHC in Columbus allowed Heartbeat International to take their groundbreaking program, renamed HEART (which stood for Healing the Effects of Abortion Related Trauma) to not only pregnancy help centers here in the US, but also around the world. It became a priority of Heartbeat, from the 1990s forward, to include healing from abortion in our training programs, whether at the Conferences or in our Academy.

I discovered that about the same time PDHC was developing the PAST support group model program, called *Forgiven and Set Free*, a Bible study model was being developed by Linda Cochrane, the director of a Care Net-affiliated PHC. This later became part of the Care Net's PACE (Post Abortion Counseling and Education) program. Another popular Evangelical program also grew out of a PHC about twenty years later, this one in Florida. It's called *Surrendering the Secret: Healing the Heartbreak of Abortion*, written by former PHC director Pat Layton.

Throughout the 1990s mental health professionals added to our understanding of the issues women face after abortion and provided various theories about how recovery is best achieved. Psychiatrist Philip Ney from Canada wrote extensively on the subject, his main work being *Deeply Damaged*, published in 1997, and he developed a months' long psychotherapy program called Hope Alive. There was controversy between those who advocated for nonprofessionals accompanying women through the healing process after abortion and those who advocated for professional counseling and therapy. Meanwhile, we were all learning from each other! Dr. Ney and many other experts in this field were often presenters at the Heartbeat conferences during these years.

It was a gigantic disappointment when the well-known Christian leader C. Everett Koop, the Surgeon General under President Reagan, wrote a letter to the president in January 1989 indicating that it would cost between $10M and $100M for the Public Health Service to do a study to prove whether or not post-abortion syndrome existed.

Having no recognition in the secular world has not stopped our movement from continuing to minister to those in need and to develop programs that bring healing and renewal to women, men, families, and even those who have been abortion providers and part of the abortion industry. In PHCs, abortion recovery is the second most "popular" program, with 80 percent of centers providing this service. (By comparison, about 73 percent provide ultrasounds.) Like the abstinence movement, after being birthed in pregnancy help centers, many abortion recovery programs have taken on a life of their own. Freestanding programs are listed in our Worldwide Directory. One such program that is gaining traction today is Support After Abortion, headed by Lisa Rowe.

## Programs Developed Outside PHCs

Many programs developed outside of PHCs have become great resources for our PHCs and their clients. For example, many PHCs refer clients to Rachel's Vineyard healing retreats, developed by Theresa Burke, PhD, and now a ministry of Priests for Life. Priests for Life also is the home for the Silent No More Awareness Campaign, founded by Janet Morana and Georgette Forney, which allows women and men to publicly share their stories about the devastation they've experienced due to abortion.

Janet Morana reminded me recently that Heartbeat International's network of centers played a key role in the founding of Silent No More. At the 2002 Heartbeat Conference, Janet and Georgette gathered a group of center directors to discuss whether there was a need for an organization such as they envisioned, and they got a very positive response. They officially launched the program at the 2004 Heartbeat Conference when actress Jennifer O'Neill, a celebrity spokesperson for

Silent No More, was the speaker for our closing banquet. A pregnancy center director (who had had an abortion) came up to the stage after Jennifer's talk and asked me if she could say something to those gathered. Taking the microphone, she confessed her abortion and her silence up to that point, and then she asked those pregnancy center directors and volunteers in the room who could say the same to stand up. Several women from every table in the room stood up. It was a powerful moment and confirmed the need for Silent No More. It also explains why abortion healing and support services are, after pregnancy tests, the most universal service offered in pregnancy help centers (see chapter 1).

Another resource for PHCs is the pioneering program Abortion Changes You, part of Life Perspectives, which was founded by Michaelene Fredenburg and is based in San Diego. This unique online program has recently expanded to include pregnancy loss through miscarriage, called Miscarriage Hurts. The goal of Life Perspectives is to develop a professionally acknowledged Standard of Care for those involved in grief therapy (for all types of reproductive loss) in the medical, social services, and counseling fields.

Churches have also pioneered abortion healing programs. In its 1975 Pastoral Plan for Pro-Life Activities, the United States Conference of Catholic Bishops (USCCB) called for an emphasis on ministering to those who had experienced abortion. Project Rachel was first developed in the Archdiocese of Milwaukee in 1984, and the USCCB adopted the name nationally in 2010, making it available to dioceses across the country. Project Rachel differs in form from one diocese to another, but all programs provide both spiritual as well as psychological resources.

Despite the origins of a particular abortion recovery program or its specific components, all of them implicitly recognize that in not following God's plan for our sexuality, especially God's plan for mothers to nurture and fathers to protect their children, great harm has resulted—sometimes physical, but especially emotional, psychological, and spiritual. Acknowledging this truth, along with healing, forgiveness, reconciliation, and naming and memorializing the child, are all part of the abortion recovery process.

Heartbeat International, like AAI in its early years, makes abortion recovery a priority in our training and at our conferences. Heartbeat has been networking closely with the relatively new Abortion Recovery Coalition, facilitated by Georgette Forney, which includes nearly forty abortion recovery programs ranging from Bible studies to twelve-step programs. Heartbeat's vice president of Ministry Services, Betty McDowell, participates in this group, whose purpose is to provide mutual support and encouragement to the members, assist one another in the development of best practices, and create an awareness regarding the impact of abortion. So many resources have developed over the past fifty years!

What a beautiful opportunity to help a woman or a man receive healing from the trauma of abortion, be at peace about their child (or children), and come into a relationship with the Lord who forgives, loves, and cares for them. Abortion healing is truly life-giving and is a crucial part of our mission to reach, rescue, and renew communities for life.

## Long-Term Comprehensive Care: Maternity Housing

Just as trauma is the driving factor in the need for abortion recovery within our movement, so is the need for long-term comprehensive care—specifically residential care—which has been a part of our pregnancy help movement since its founding fifty years ago. It has always been needed, and today it is needed more than ever before. In fact, a trend we are now seeing is that more PHCs are considering opening a residential care facility if one is not already available in their community.

Our residential programs today are based on "trauma-informed care." Many women who are pregnant and need help have experienced major traumas in their lives or in their families, including rape, incest, domestic violence, human trafficking, multiple sexual partners, addictions, and homelessness.

Needless to say, with such experiences, God's Plan for Our Sexuality has typically never been modeled—or even envisioned—by many of the women we serve in residential care. An understanding of God's plan for them and for their children is desperately needed, as is an environment of Christian love where they can experience forgiveness, healing, and restoration. Most often there is also an urgent need for professional medical and psychological care. But immersing women into an experience of Christianity is at the core of our residential care facilities today. These residential care facilities have grown in number and complexity since the early days to meet the needs of women and their children today.

Small, fledgling maternity homes were affiliated with and represented at the AAI Academies by the time I attended my first academy in 1980s. These organizations had been founded in the 1970s and were truly pioneering models. After *Roe v. Wade*, maternity homes needed to be "reinvented." The older models, most often part of a professional social service agency, such as Catholic, Lutheran, or Jewish Social Services, were large, somewhat institutionalized, and focused on adoption services. It was not uncommon for these homes to be connected to Christian hospitals where the young mothers even worked during their pregnancies. Most girls entered these institutionalized homes with plans to place their babies for adoption and keep their pregnancies confidential, in line with the adoption practices of the times, since this was the most common choice for single mothers before *Roe v. Wade*. Once abortions started becoming available state by state in the late 1960s and single motherhood lost much of its stigma, large maternity homes that were part of adoption agencies began closing. Not all girls and women who needed housing wanted to make adoption plans.

Both the second and third (volunteer) executive directors of

AAI started and led maternity homes (now closed) that grew from pregnancy help centers: Elinor Martin in White Plains, New York, and Judy Peterson in Orlando, Florida. The home in Orlando was founded as a Birthright pregnancy center but soon focused on housing and changed its name to BETA in 1972. (While Elinor and Judy served as the executive directors for AAI, the AAI office was located in their respective facilities.)

## Models of Care

Meanwhile, Anne and Jimmy Pierson from Lancaster, Pennsylvania, were developing a new model of maternity home. In response to a need in their church, they offered to house a teenage girl who also happened to be pregnant. That was the beginning of their family ministry. When they realized that housing pregnant girls was a call from the Lord, they bought a farm, complete with farm animals, and Anne and Jimmy and their two daughters began to model loving family life with girls and women who had never experienced it, especially those who had not experienced having a father in the home. They called it House of His Creation. They eventually housed two hundred girls over the years, about half of whom made adoption plans for their children.

Anne was a regular presenter at AAI Conferences, and soon the family model of housing, which generally accommodated only a few girls at one time, began to spread. Anne and Jimmy then founded Loving and Caring in 1984 as a national ministry to teach, provide resources, and help network the growing number of small, family-style maternity homes. I admired Anne's work and wisdom greatly and was happy that she became a member of the founding board of Heartbeat International.

Loving and Caring ceased operation (after Jimmy's death in 2012 and Anne's retirement in 2019), but Anne's series of workbooks for mothers, called *My Baby and Me,* are still part of the core resources available through Heartbeat International. Anne also had tremendous impact as an advocate for pre- and post-adoption services for women, and she pioneered the now familiar training on the biblical basis for adoption and the importance of strong and loving fatherhood (for which Jimmy was the role model!).

Our movement recognized Anne and Jimmy's impact with one of Heartbeat's Legacy Awards in 2011, and Heartbeat now awards a Jimmy Pierson scholarship each year to a foot soldier from one of our affiliated maternity homes.

Three other outstanding founders of maternity housing models were invited to speak on "best practices" at a conference funded by a family foundation in 2011. About ten organizations and about forty people were present. They found the discussion and relationships so stimulating that they agreed to meet again at the March for Life in January 2012 and form the National Maternity Housing Coalition. These leaders included long-time Heartbeat affiliate Gloria Lee of Our Lady's Inn in St. Louis (which pioneered the use of federal funding in a faith-based ministry); Chris Bell of Good Counsel Homes in New Jersey (which has always focused on women dealing with addiction, mental illness, and homelessness); and Mary Peterson of Maggie's Place in Phoenix, Arizona (which pioneered the model of faith-filled young women "mentors" living and working alongside the pregnant mothers).

## Heartbeat Central's Commitment

The Coalition joined Heartbeat International as an Affinity Group in 2012 and established an elected Leadership Council that same year. Heartbeat Central committed to learning more about housing challenges and providing even more services, as needed, to this affiliation group. To lead this effort, we hired Mary Peterson in the role of housing specialist and facilitator for these special ministries within our network.

Heartbeat currently identifies about four hundred housing programs in the US and 120 affiliated locations. Our services are available to all these groups.

Heartbeat has published several white papers on important and complex issues that housing ministries face, for example, white papers on post-residential programming. This highlights the trend in our housing ministries to focus on long-term change and meeting complex needs rather than just pregnancy. It is clear that our homes must focus on "whole person" issues—housing instability, education, employability, life skills, trauma, addictions, and mental illness—all with the goal of individual and family restoration and ultimately finding healing and peace in Christ.

Professional, ongoing services are crucial, but, as with all of our pregnancy help work, the real keys to the "successes" we hope for are the loving people who deliver the programs! As we are fond of saying in the crisis intervention part of pregnancy help, the best alternative to abortion is another person. The same is true in long-term care. The story of Aretha, which she shared in an interview, illustrates this beautifully.

Aretha arrived at Maggie's Place in Phoenix, Arizona, in March 2017, just eight weeks pregnant with her daughter Zoe. She arrived with more than twenty years of drug and alcohol use and a history of prostitution. "I came from chaos and darkness and stepped into a sanctuary of peace," she told us. "It was the love and sacrifice that the staff gave me that made me feel like I was part of a family."

During her time, she described running "home"—to the maternity home—when temptations for relapse were high. "I was given time to grow and heal, to be loved and encouraged," she said. "I loved just eating together and celebrating one another." One special memory involves watching one of the staff members read to a baby. Aretha had never seen that. She began collecting books and now reads to her daughter daily.

The ongoing services and post-residential programming she received after she moved out played a huge role in her sobriety, according to Aretha. After moving into a transitional apartment, she participated in parenting groups, ongoing therapy, Mommy & Me groups, and attachment groups, all offered as ongoing services by Maggie's Place to former residents. Aretha mentioned that the feeling of connection, the feeling of being a part of a family, was vital to her. The maternity home had become her family and leaving that home environment was tough. "I decided to take advantage of anything they offered. I needed it. In fact, as we would drive up to the outreach center, Zoe would say, 'We are home!'"

"At a Christmas event, I remember looking at the staff handing out gifts, and I thought to myself, *I want that.*" In November 2020, that dream was realized when Aretha became a full-time member of the outreach staff associated with the post-residential program of Maggie's Place. "It's a dream come true," she described. "I get to give back and be a part of what they are doing here. I know how important it was for me to feel celebrated; I loved watching my daughter be genuinely loved. Now, I mimic what I learned. I celebrate other women and encourage them to stay connected."

In describing the values that undergird maternity housing today and help explain the change in Aretha, Heartbeat's Maternity Housing Specialist, Mary Peterson, puts it this way:

> My own take on the work of maternity housing is summed up as "Belong, Believe, Behave." It's essentially Heartbeat's L.O.V.E. Approach in different words! Create a culture of belonging where a woman knows she is safe and welcome and a part of something—connect with her heart. Encourage new beliefs about who she is and what she is capable of—connect with her head. With those two as a strong foundation, invite her to build new behaviors and strategies through teaching and being a safe place to make mistakes.

There have been times in our movement's history when more maternity homes were closing than opening (primarily due to high cost of operation, difficulty of meeting client needs, and decisions to prioritize crisis intervention as abortion numbers skyrocketed). An interesting trend is emerging now with more and more pregnancy centers starting up homes in their communities. Heartbeat is currently working with several start-ups.

Heartbeat Central's plan is that our investment in leadership and programming, in partnership with the Maternity Housing Coalition, will continue to bear fruit, and that more and more women and families will find the love and support they want and need to embrace God's plan for their lives.

PHCs learn about key concepts and programs available, like abstinence education, at Heartbeat Conferences. Dr. Joe McIlhaney, Founder of the Medical Institute for Sexual Health (MISH), and his wife Marion (left), and Leslee Unruh, founder of the National Abstinence Clearinghouse, both still in leadership today, have been exhibitors and trainers for Heartbeat since the 1990s.

Pregnancy Decision Health Centers (PDHC) in Columbus, Ohio, was the first center to receive a federal grant for "prevention services" under a model program in 1984. Now called Common Sense Culture, it reaches thousands of students every year in Columbus schools.

A New Sexual Revolution Coalition, meeting at the Bush Library in 2019, recently formed to jumpstart efforts for true sexual health nationwide. Led by Dr. Joe McIlhaney (center back row) and ED Lori Kuykendall (back row, 2nd from right) of MISH, Heartbeat is represented here by Peggy (front row, 3rd from right) and Zeke Swift (front row, 3rd from left).

Abortion recovery was pioneered within PHCs in the 1980s. Now, 79% of PHCs offer this service, second only to pregnancy tests. Michaelene Friedenburg, founder of Abortion Changes You and Miscarriage Hurts, at a recent Conference. Silent No More, co-founded by Janet Morana, with Peggy above at a March for Life, traces its founding to a Heartbeat Conference (pp. 144–45).

Maternity housing, taking many forms, has been essential to pregnancy help since our founding. The National Maternity Housing Coalition, affiliated with Heartbeat, meets in Columbus in 2017. (L to R front): Mary Peterson, Susan Barrett, Kesha Franklin, Gloria Lee, Mark McDougal. (L to R back): Chris Bell, Randy James, Callie Neff, Stephen Wallace. Founders of the Coaliton are Mary from Arizona, Chris from New Jersey, and Gloria from Missouri, who each pioneered a different matenity housing model.

Anne and Jimmy Pierson, who pioneered the small home model with live-in house parents (mother and father) in the 1970's, received our Legacy Award in 2011. Mary Peterson, who pioneered a ministry model where pregnant mothers live in community with single women role models, received our Servant Leader Award from Vice President of Ministry Services Betty McDowell in 2021.

# CHAPTER 9

# GOING MEDICAL

## Jor-El Godsey

In the third decade of the history of our movement, a major shift began to occur in our service model, and Heartbeat is happy to have been part of the visioning and collaboration that helped make it possible. We refer to it informally as "going medical." It involved sonograms and ultrasound machines that gave us a window to the womb.

I've held many babies who were saved from abortion because of the powerful imagery available through a sonogram. Sure, ultrasounds show a mom her own child, creating a visual connection between that mom and the very child (sometimes children) who is at risk in the abortion decision. But a sonogram brings far more critical medical information to the moment. Is there really a pregnancy? Is that pregnancy viable?

One of the first ultrasound clients at my pregnancy help center in Colorado opened my eyes to the reality of how important ultrasound is, even beyond the obvious things mentioned above.

"I don't know, probably two to three months," is what this woman said to the client advocate who asked when her last period was. She was wearing a baggy sweatshirt and sweatpants. Life was rough, and she had been pretty much on the street, or couch-surfing, for a long time. Nothing in her life was normal, or regular, including her cycle. Of course, the pregnancy test was a bright blue positive.

"Can we give you an ultrasound? That way we'll know for sure." What our new client didn't know was that she would receive the first official ultrasound in our center. All the others had been of friends and family to get our nurses trained. She agreed, and the advocate introduced her to the nurse sonographer.

Once her sweatshirt came up to reveal her swollen belly, her pregnancy was very obvious. Soon the image on the screen confirmed what we already knew from the positive pregnancy test and the timing the client had given. But something was not quite as expected.

The nurse's eyes opened wide with surprise.

"Honey, according to the measurements I'm taking, you're actually about thirty weeks along," she said in that slightly raised tone that betrays a medical professional's level of concern.

The abortion she'd been seriously considering was no longer first-term—or even second-term. It had just become "late-term." Along with being a much more involved, multiday process, for this client it became one that was five to six times as expensive.

Ultrasound brought critical information to us so we could help her navigate the path ahead more clearly. She had not been sure about abortion before, and upon hearing that her child was so far along, she made the brave choice to say yes to her baby. As with most pregnancy centers, we kicked into gear—arranging healthcare, finding help for her housing needs, and so much more.

The technology tool of ultrasound was the source of key information for her decision-making process. Today, in 70 percent of pregnancy help centers across the United States, ultrasound technology is used regularly to confirm a "viable uterine pregnancy" and introduce the truth about the baby's development to the mom.

Knowing she has a viable uterine pregnancy is a crucial piece of information if a woman is considering an abortion. If the pregnancy is not viable, there is no "need" for an abortion, and there have even been documented cases of abortion clinics performing abortions on women who were not pregnant at all; tests of the "contents of the uterus" at labs had confirmed that there was no embryo in the uterus at the time of the abortion. Moreover, medical journal articles have documented that ultrasound examinations result in early bonding between mother and child. Clear recognition that the embryo or fetus is indeed real is also a vital piece of information for a person making a potential abortion decision.

Each of these "medicalized" pregnancy centers operates ultrasound under the guidance of an appropriately licensed physician and employs professionally trained nurses and sonographers to bring this powerful medical technology to each mother so she can make a fully informed decision about her baby.

In 2019 alone, US pregnancy help centers provided more than 430,000 ultrasounds, according to a Charlotte Lozier Institute report on pregnancy help. All of them were provided free of charge to the patient. Many of them were conducted by volunteer sonographers and nurses and read by volunteer physicians, each deploying their professional medical training and commitment to ethical healthcare.

While this is today's reality, thirty years ago it would have been very hard to find a pregnancy center with an ultrasound machine. The truth is, another thirty years before that, ultrasounds for obstetrics was only just gaining widespread access in full-size hospitals!

## Moving Pictures

In fact, ultrasound was first used for clinical obstetrical purposes in 1956 in Glasgow, Scotland. The National Center for Biotechnology Information credits obstetrician Ian Donald and engineer Tom Brown for developing "the first prototype systems based on an instrument used to detect industrial flaws in ships."[2]

---

2 https://(www.ncbi.nlm.nih.gov/pmc/articles/PMC3987368/.

Ian Donald is remembered as a "tall, red-haired charismatic Scottish obstetrician gynecologist with a brilliant mind and a quick temper." He was a devout Christian with a strong conviction of the sanctity of human life. While they never met, he was a contemporary of our own founder, Dr. John Hillabrand. They were only two years apart in age. Both men, as true of so many physicians in that era, were deeply principled in their practice and philosophy of care. Their deep faith resonated through the traditional Hippocratic Oath, long since abandoned by today's medical schools, for its truths, including "First, do no harm" and prohibition against helping "cause an abortion."

After developing "the world's first contact compound 2D ultrasound scanning machine called the Diasonograph," Dr. Ian Donald would be the very first to use such a tool exactly how we use them in pregnancy help centers today—namely, to reveal to the mom her own child that she was considering terminating. For Ian Donald, this anti-abortion stance, which also manifested in his vocal opposition to the 1967 Abortion Act, would eventually deny him honors (such as knighthood) in his own country. He saw this as an "attempt to eliminate an evil by substituting a different evil.[3]

In 1979, Ian Donald met with Pope St. John Paul II and found that the pontiff was well acquainted with ultrasound and the images it revealed. There can be little doubt that Ian Donald's work had an influence on the pope's encyclical, *Evangelium Vitae* (1995).[4]

Ian Donald, a man who changed the world of obstetrics and gynecology, said, "If I have done nothing else in my life, I have killed that dirty lie that the fetus is just a nondescript meaningless jelly, disposable at will, something to be got rid of."[5]

This is exactly the reason ultrasound was destined to be used in the life-saving work of pregnancy help centers.

---

3 https://www.ob-ultrasound.net/iandonaldbio.html.
4 https://www.rcpe.ac.uk/heritage/ian-donald-diagnostician-and-moralist.
5 https://www.rcpe.ac.uk/heritage/ian-donald-diagnostician-and-moralist.

## Medical Ministry

The latest edition in the Charlotte Lozier *A Legacy of Life and Love Report Series* (2020) traces the rise of the medical ministry in pregnancy help, and this chapter summarizes their findings in the following five paragraphs. The report notes the medical roots of the pregnancy help movement as evidenced by Heartbeat's founder Dr. John Hillabrand and other pro-life doctors (who often had early PHCs operating beside or even out of their medical offices in the 1970s.)

In 1984, a group of physicians and businessmen connected through a local Christian Action Council (now Care Net) prayer group in California and sought to open a new pregnancy center that would offer pregnancy confirmation ultrasounds and medical care. Dr. Geeta Swamidass, a member of that prayer group, became the first executive director of the new medical pregnancy center, the LivingWell Clinic, which opened in Orange, California, in April 1985. A physician of strong Christian faith, Dr. Swamidass went on to mentor staff at approximately nine existing pregnancy centers in California and Colorado, leading them to add medical services, including early obstetrical ultrasound under the direction of a licensed physician. First Resort in Berkeley, California, became just the second center to add ultrasound services (1989), and in 1991 the Pregnancy Help Clinic of Glendale in California implemented pregnancy confirmation ultrasound into their medical services.

A catalyst for medical pregnancy centers, especially in California, was the legal case, *Shanti Friend v. Pregnancy Counseling Center*, filed in during the late 1980s. Pregnancy centers, at that time, like doctors' offices, were sending client urine specimens to off-site labs. With the lab information in hand, the nonmedical staff would deliver the test result to the client. One client, likely planted by the abortion providers in the area, filed a lawsuit claiming this was a "diagnosis" and a violation of California state law. The local Superior Court judge ruled against the pregnancy center group, Right to Life League of Southern California, determining that reading the results constituted a "diagnosis" of pregnancy, which should be left only to licensed medical professionals. (Interestingly, Right to Life League was an affiliate of AAI at that time, and the results of this decision were reported and discussed at the 1987 AAI annual board meeting, the first AAI board meeting attended by new board member Peggy Hartshorn.)

This court decision inspired more California pregnancy centers to become licensed medical clinics under California law. But, about the time the case was making its way through the court system, pharmacy-type urine pregnancy tests started becoming widely available, allowing pregnancy centers to implement pregnancy self-testing by clients on-site rather than sending client specimens to labs (or becoming medical clinics). Nevertheless, the centers learned to adapt their methods and policies to meet the needs of those they served while defending against legal or legislative attacks.

The National Institute of Family and Life Advocates (NIFLA), helmed by former Care Net president and lawyer Tom Glessner, was established in 1993, to help with the legal issues concerning pregnancy centers. Soon the issues surrounding ultrasound and providing medical services became a major focus of NIFLA. (As previously mentioned, Heartbeat International was directly involved in seeding this new effort since Heartbeat and NIFLA had a formal collaboration agreement. Peggy served on Tom's founding NIFLA board, and Tom was on Heartbeat's board during that time as well.)

It was at an early NIFLA meeting when Tom first laid out a plan to help centers outside of California—especially the three operated by founding NIFLA board members—to become actual "medical clinics," under a (volunteer) physician medical director (where they did not need to be licensed by the state). These centers would provide "limited ultrasound"—an ultrasound exam for a limited purpose: to diagnose a viable uterine pregnancy (i.e., a pregnancy that appears to be proceeding normally, one that is not ectopic or in the process of a natural miscarriage). Three of the founding NIFLA board members took to the task of integrating medical services at their existing pregnancy centers—Care Net Pregnancy Clinic in Baton Rouge, Louisiana (1993), Life Choices of King County in Washington State (1994), and Pregnancy Decision Health Center in Columbus, Ohio (1995), where Peggy was the board chair.

To facilitate this on a national level, Tom compiled all the guidelines for the use of ultrasound from the FDA, professional associations of OB/GYNs, ultrasonographers, nurses, and others. He studied relevant laws and medical standards of care. He soon published the first PHC medical "conversion" manual, which Peggy helped edit. The new models and practices surrounding the addition of medical services were shared across the pregnancy center movement. By 1998, a total of fifty medical pregnancy centers or clinics were recorded. Then, by 1999, the first year Heartbeat International started a "medical" category of pregnancy centers in their Worldwide Directory of Pregnancy Help, there were over one hundred listings in the United States.

Migrating to medical services, especially ultrasound, was clearly a missional move.

## Stretching the Model

Heartbeat International soon sponsored recurring "Medical Clinic Symposiums" for a number of years to gather together pregnancy center leaders who were providing ultrasound services. We invited NIFLA and Care Net to join us as co-sponsors and invited all centers to attend. In keeping with Heartbeat values, we asked our entrepreneurial affiliates to share how they were expanding the medical vision, and we brought in other experts to stretch our thinking and help develop expanded models of medical services. These kinds of gatherings encouraged some of our affiliates to add additional services, such as STD testing and treatment, limited prenatal care, Napro-technology® (to teach patients about their reproductive health and treat certain medical conditions of the reproductive system), and perinatal hospice (support for families who chose life, not abortion, after their baby was diagnosed with a condition that would likely result in death in the womb or soon after birth). Even new revenue models were explored, with attention to Medicaid billing for reimbursement of medical services commonly covered by federal and state funding. This was no small thing, as we conducted detailed research and sponsored several trainings on the potential of, and the logistics necessary for, billing to Medicaid.

Continuing traction derived from those earlier meetings shows that today nearly 30 percent of pregnancy help centers are providing STI/STD testing, which continues to climb from 26 percent of centers in 2017. A majority of these—more than one in every five (21 percent) pregnancy help centers are providing both STI/STD testing *and* treatment services. This service seeks to meaningfully engage those who are sexually active prior to a potential unexpected, unintended pregnancy at-risk for an abortion.

Prenatal care is expanding in centers, with greater integration of obstetric-trained physicians and nurse practitioners into day-to-day staff positions. Yet ultrasound continues to be the number-one medical service found in pregnancy help centers in the US and globally.

As innovation and entrepreneurial efforts go, not everything "stuck." Medicaid billing was possible but quickly deemed not cost-effective for the limited medical services at the time. (This may be changing with the increased variety of medical services in the past decade.) Perinatal hospice remains a powerful and necessary service for those facing prenatal diagnosis. Unfortunately, though, the numbers of parents presenting with these needs have been insufficient to create standing programs in most PHCs.

Heartbeat adapted to the influx of medical personnel into the pregnancy help movement in several key ways. We created our own *Medical Essentials Manual* to assist affiliates with "going medical" (adding ultrasound) and helping assess the addition of other medical services. It also became clear that we needed a nurse on our staff to help guide centers through this manual and answer ongoing questions for healthcare professionals integrating into the pregnancy help ministry model. Lastly, and most widely used, are the specialized materials and trainings oriented toward the nurses, sonographers, and other medical personnel now working in PHCs. This includes our most-read monthly publication, *Medical Matters*, and authorized CEUs for nurses in their need for ongoing education. This helped pave the way for Heartbeat to expand and integrate a new team of nurses for abortion pill reversal (see chapter 13).

Two major contributors to expanding the model were Option Ultrasound Program (OUP) established by Focus on the Family's pregnancy help ministry in 2003, and the Knights of Columbus Ultrasound Initiative. Separately, these pro-life organizations have inspired hundreds of thousands to get involved in spreading the powerful life-revealing tool of ultrasound machines. Combined, they have placed more than 2,500 machines in PHCs across the country. In turn, this equipment has been used for more than a million ultrasounds championing the gift of life!

## Impacting Perspective

I first saw my own children through the power of ultrasound technology. For the oldest, it was a two-dimensional (2D) snapshot showing his grayish image against a black background, much like those pioneering pregnancy centers deployed in the eighties and nineties.

For my youngest (born ten years later), the technology had advanced to a 4D image that shows a rendered three-dimensional (3D) picture in motion (the fourth dimension). This is increasingly the most common choice for medical teams in pregnancy centers today—especially since the same tool can be toggled to 2D for key measurements the sonographer is pursuing.

Ultrasound images are so common now that they are almost every baby's first photograph. Certainly they provide an important perspective for a woman who is not at all certain she's ready for motherhood to confirm that she, in fact, already is a mother.

The earliest pioneers at the forefront of the pro-life movement—like Dr. Ian Donald and Dr. John Hillabrand—were often within the medical community. With ultrasound, the pregnancy help movement today takes up that same core ethic for life and welcomes principled professional competency to maximize its critical life-saving work.

Integrating medical professionals and medical services into the fabric of the pregnancy help network also paved the path for a new season of life-saving medical outreach: Abortion Pill Reversal, the subject of chapter 13.

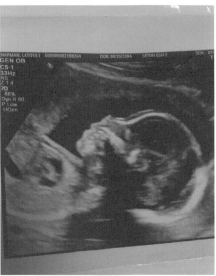

Tom Glessner, President of NIFLA, receives our Legacy Award in 2011 for his promotion in the US of PHCs "going medical" to diagnose a pregnancy using ultrasound. Seeing her baby in the womb helps a mom bond with her child, and sending the ultrasound picture home often moves a partner or grandparents to protect the new little life.

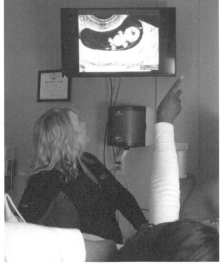

Heartbeat has long provided training and encouragement for Pregnancy Help Medical Clinics to add additional medical services such as STD testing and treatment, fertility care, and even pre-natal care. Pictured above is Holy Family Prenatal Care at Elizabeth's New Life Center in Dayton, Ohio.

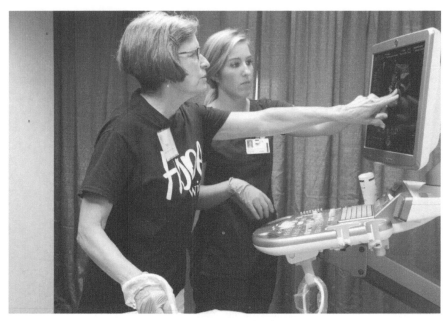

*Heartbeat trains nurses today in the use of ultrasound in Pregnancy Help Medical Clinics, and provides a range of courses through our Conferences and on-line Academy for the many nurses in our movement to obtain Continuing Education Units (CEUs).*

*Heartbeat's expanding medical staff responds to the growth of medical services in PHCs (74% provide ultrasound services) and recently to Abortion Pill Rescue now part of Heartbeat (chapter 13). Some of our Medical Impact team, in back row Christa Brown (far left), Lisa Searle (2nd from left) and Karen Lawrence (4th from left), are meeting with our nurses who respond to women seeking abortion pill reversal.*

# CHAPTER 10

# DEFENDING AGAINST ATTACK

### Jor-El Godsey

Compassion should be celebrated, not attacked.

Who would be against the work of pregnancy help centers that provide alternatives and support so that no woman ever feels that abortion is her only alternative? Who would attack those armed only with love? Even most pro-abortion leaders contend that no woman really wants to have an abortion—that those who do choose abortion have concluded that they have no other options. Former President Bill Clinton went so far as to declare that abortion should be "safe, legal, and rare."

The founders of Heartbeat International thought that even people who declared themselves "pro-choice" (once that term was coined) should and would want to support pregnancy help centers. After all, these are the places where a variety of choices can be considered as real alternatives to abortion, and these options—single parenting, marriage, adoption, foster care, community resources to help with finances, housing, prenatal care, and more—can be worked through with caring, loving, nonjudgmental help and support. Doesn't everyone agree that this is a good thing?

## Attacks Arise

Unfortunately, that has not been the case. "Big Abortion," headed by Planned Parenthood and NARAL Pro-Choice America, has orchestrated a number of attacks against pregnancy help centers and pregnancy help medical clinics, beginning in the early 1980s and continuing through today. They have attempted to smear the work of pregnancy help in the media, enact unconstitutionally restrictive laws at the local, state, and federal level, and file harassing lawsuits against us.

Their motives are partly financial, since every mother who chooses life for her baby will not be one who pays for an abortion. They are partly political, since many of the legislators and attorneys general who have led attacks on centers have made promises to pro-choice organizations that help elect them. And the motives are partly personal. No doubt, many of those who lead the fight against our centers have been involved in abortions for themselves or others and have an "emotional stake" in legitimizing that choice. We can't know all their motives for sure, but one thing we do know is that their public motive— to "protect" women from being hurt by our centers and clinics—is a false one. No woman has been hurt or injured in one of our pregnancy centers or clinics. Compare this to the many documented cases of women killed in "safe, legal" abortions in the United States.

As God would have it, these attacks that were meant for evil have actually strengthened pregnancy help centers in particular and our movement as a whole. The first example is the attacks in the 1980s that focused on the charge of "misleading advertising" and "fake clinics." In the early 1980s, Planned Parenthood of New York City hired Amy Sutnick for the specific purpose of finding a way to discredit pregnancy centers. Her efforts included charges of "deceptive advertising," alleged illegal practice of medicine, and the fact that because our centers are religiously based, they are not to be trusted.

Sending fake clients into our centers with hidden tape recorders and cameras in the 1980s was common. Both Ohio's Attorney General (who later became the Lt. Governor) and the New York Attorney General tried to restrict the most commonly used advertising for our centers, the Yellow Pages (a listing of all commercial businesses in a community delivered to every home, every year). New York was successful, resulting in restrictions in that city and intimidation in many other places.

Meanwhile, in California, Gloria Allred took legal action against the Right to Life League help centers in the Los Angeles area. The executive director of the Right to Life League during that time was Anne Kindt (who later would become a well-known national leader in the pregnancy help movement, Anne O'Connor). In 1989, a Superior Court in Los Angeles County ruled that nonmedical pregnancy center staff conducting "pregnancy testing"—first reading and then informing the client of the results of their pregnancy test— was considered by Judge Vogel tantamount to "practicing medicine without a license."

Eventually, in 1991, Chris Wallace, then with *ABC News*, conducted an undercover "hit piece" on our centers on *Prime Time Live*, painting them as unprofessional, deceptive, anti-woman, and calling them "fake clinics." In 1992, Congressman Ron Widen (D-OR) launched an investigation of pregnancy resource centers in the United States Congress, and he conducted a congressional hearing to document charges against our centers. As proof that this was a disingenuous effort, he would not allow one person from pregnancy help centers to testify!

## The Pain Becomes Gain

Feeling the pressure from Congress, the California court, and aggressive attorneys general in various states left us all frustrated, and even afraid for the future of our centers. How could we protect ourselves from more attack by abortion proponents? How could we avoid charges that we had false advertising, or that we harassed clients? How could we avoid the charge of practicing medicine without a license?

As noted previously, Heartbeat's intersection with NIFLA's Tom Glessner proved to be fortuitous. The two organizations, NIFLA and

Heartbeat International, partnered together with Peggy and Tom agreeing to serve on each other's boards. Joint affiliation with both groups was encouraged so centers would have the benefits of both Heartbeat's general expertise and NIFLA's specialized legal expertise. We partnered for about six years, as both organizations grew rapidly. Tom came to Heartbeat International conferences and taught our centers good legal practices and how to protect themselves to the greatest extent possible. This training eventually became the movement's first legal manual. NIFLA's focus on legal liabilities led them to enlist an insurance expert and pro-life advocate, Rick Renzi, to pioneer the first insurance program written specifically for the unique organizational and liability challenges of a local pregnancy help center.

The opposition charged us with being "fake clinics" (by which they meant, and still mean, fake *abortion* clinics). But ironically, we responded by becoming actual clinics—medical clinics that provide a medical diagnosis of pregnancy through the use of a limited ultrasound exam and more! This has made pregnancy help centers and clinics less vulnerable to legal scrutiny and stronger than ever in their missional outcomes.

## Attacks Abound

Attacks have continued, of course, even though many of our centers are now medical clinics operating under the license of a private physician (or licensed by their state where required, especially in Massachusetts and California). In the 2000s, NARAL, the major lobbying partner of Planned Parenthood, published a guide on how to close down your local pregnancy center, and five similar guides were published by various NARAL state coalitions. The National Abortion Federation also released a "report" on the evils of pregnancy centers in 2006. (In the years following, they released several state reports by repurposing this language and customizing the title to the state.)

Moreover, in 2006, Congressman Henry Waxman, then head of

the Committee of Government Reform, issued a "report" from the Special Investigations Division entitled "False and Misleading Health Information Provided by Federally Funded Pregnancy Resource Centers." By the way, the "federal funding" referred to in the title was based on the fact that about one hundred pregnancy centers in the nation had received a portion of a $50 million federal funding for abstinence education programs in the schools as part of the "faith-based" funding programs promoted under the Bush Administration; none of that funding was used in core center intervention programs that the Waxman report cited as using "false and misleading health information."

Nothing will satisfy our opponents on the subject of "accurate medical information," it seems, unless we are willing to proclaim that abortion has absolutely no negative physical or psychological effects and that there is absolutely no statistical connection between abortion and breast cancer. However, these statements are not true, and we are committed to truth and accuracy. Women deserve it. All medical information used by Heartbeat in our training and materials is referenced and approved by Heartbeat's Medical Advisory Board, consisting of nearly a dozen experts in the fields of obstetrics, gynecology, pharmacology, and radiology.

In 2002, New York's then Attorney General Eliot Spitzer (who fell from prominence as governor of New York due to a call girl scandal in 2008) orchestrated an attack all across New York, targeting twenty-four centers. In a major example of unity and cooperation, Heartbeat worked closely with our national partners and connected with outstanding local attorneys to unravel the strategy, and all charges were eventually dropped. This was miraculous, but also exhausting.

After New York, it was clear that Heartbeat needed its own attorney on staff to work with our centers on a regular basis, lead Heartbeat's center defense strategy, and work with our national partners when attacks occur. That position is now our general counsel (Danielle White, Esquire, a member of our executive team). Heartbeat partners with legal allies such as Alliance Defending Freedom, Thomas More Society, American Center for Law and Justice, Christian Legal Society, state Family Policy Councils, Catholic bishops' organizations, and specialized outside counsel as needed and appropriate, when and where attacks occur.

As we moved out of the 2000s, our opponents seized upon a strategy of introducing restrictive bills in cities and counties asserting, with no actual evidence, that our centers are "deceptive" and pose a threat to women. They quickly passed legislation between 2010 and 2011 in Austin, Baltimore, Montgomery County (outside Washington, DC), and New York City. The New York City bill, for example, required that a New York City commissioner promulgate rules for conspicuous signage for our centers, in English and Spanish, in a specific letter size and type, "warning" potential clients about what we do not do (for example, provide or refer for abortions or contraceptives). Penalties designated in the law were to be enforced by the New York City police department and involved fines, civil penalties, "sealing" the center, and even imprisonment! One of our center directors overheard then Mayor Bloomberg say, as he signed the NYC law, "It may be unconstitutional, but I'm signing it anyway." The harassment and smear campaign against us appears motivated not by any facts but by political pressure and paybacks spurred by allies of Big Abortion.

With the aforementioned pro-life legal and legislative partners and the strength of the First Amendment, we were fortunate that each of these laws, in turn, was found unconstitutional.

The United States District Court of Maryland led the way, with the court finding that the Baltimore ordinance "violates the Freedom of Speech Clause of Article I of the Constitution of the United States of America and is unenforceable" (decision handed down on January 28, 2011). The plaintiffs, Greater Baltimore Center for Pregnancy Concerns, a Heartbeat International affiliate, and St. Brigid's Roman Catholic Congregation, were victorious—but only momentarily.

Sadly, that plain interpretation was deemed less than acceptable by the City of Baltimore and its legal muscle, the Center for Reproductive Rights, and they appealed the decision. Moreover, they widened the scrutiny and subpoenaed Heartbeat International, Care Net, and NIFLA as affiliation partners of CPC Baltimore. Alliance Defending Freedom led the battle, which lasted until 2018. Fourth District Appellate Judge J. Harvie Wilkinson III refuted the vicious and frivolous attack by affirming the 2011 court's first ruling. "After seven years of litigation and a 1,295-page record before us, the City does not identify a single example of a woman who entered the Greater Baltimore Center's waiting room under the misimpression that she could obtain an abortion there. What the record does show is affirmative advocacy of abortion alternatives by a lawful nonprofit group."

The cost to the City of Baltimore, apart from the time lost, exceeded $1.5 million in taxpayer dollars.

## California Leads an Assault

In retrospect, the City of Baltimore was small compared to what the State of California would attempt.

In 2015 the California Assembly voted AB 775 into law. The California law, known among abortion advocates as the "Reproductive FACT Act," required pregnancy help centers to instruct their clients on how to obtain a state-funded abortion. This took the "deceptive" advertising attack to a whole new level in forcing pro-life pregnancy medical clinics to actively promote abortion services provided by the State of California.

The law also required nonmedical resource centers to post signage saying that the center was not licensed as a medical facility and did not have a licensed medical provider—even though being a nonmedical center did not require either. It then mandated that these disclosures be translated into as many as thirteen different languages. Moreover, the statute required the disclosure to appear in *any* advertisement for a given center (printed, posted, or digital), with the disclosure's text size even larger than the text of the advertisement itself.

NIFLA, with Alliance Defending Freedom, sued the State of California on behalf of its member organizations in California for an injunction on the law to keep it from being used against pregnancy help centers prior to evaluation by the court. The battle for injunction would be the proxy war for determining, at least in part, how the law itself would stand up under court scrutiny. Not unsurprisingly, the US District Court for the Southern District of California denied NIFLA's motion for preliminary injunction. Upon appeal, the Ninth Circuit affirmed the denial, and set the stage for an appeal to the Supreme Court of the United States in 2017.

For the first time ever, the work of the pregnancy help movement would be the focus at the highest court in the land. And the outcome would either embolden pro-abortion politicians and Big Abortion itself, or firmly protect pregnancy help against the same.

During oral arguments on a cold, wet day in March 2018, Supreme Court justices from across the ideological spectrum indicated major concerns with the California law. Even each of the reliably liberal Justices—Stephen Breyer, Elena Kagan, Ruth Bader Ginsburg, and Sonia Sotomayor—challenged California's burdensome and discriminatory requirements. "I mean, it is one thing just to say: 'We are not a licensed medical provider,'" said Justice Ginsburg. "But if you have to say those two sentences in thirteen different languages, it can be very burdensome." Other justices explored this point using Heartbeat International's amicus brief on this very topic (written by our General Counsel Danielle White), one of only two amici referenced that day.

Just three months later, in the final week of the SCOTUS calendar, our movement held its collective breath. Finally, the long-awaited decision, culminating a four-year journey of bruising losses, was handed down *against* the State of California's brazen attempt to compel pro-life pregnancy centers to promote abortions to their clients! The narrow 5–4 victory authored by Justice Clarence Thomas was met with thunderous celebration by NIFLA and their legal team, Alliance Defending Freedom (plus yours truly and Danielle White in the Chamber that day).

Justice Anthony Kennedy, known as the "swing" vote, joined the decision to reverse the lower court ruling, noting, "Governments must not be allowed to force persons to express a message contrary to their deepest convictions. Freedom of speech secures freedom of thought and belief. This law imperils those liberties."

Heartbeat's news outlet, *Pregnancy Help News*, providentially founded just weeks before California's AB 775, became a major source of news articles and commentary as the anti-PHC bill became first a law, then a multiyear court action. Jay Hobbs, the founding editor and chief writer, authored dozens of articles throughout the journey that became *NIFLA v. Becerra*. Many of Jay's articles at PregnancyHelpNews.com were reprinted by pro-life outlets and conservative news platforms. Some articles were used for source material for major, mainstream newspapers, magazines, and digital aggregators.

The words of Helen Keller express our hope that good will continue to prevail:

Although the world is full of suffering, it is full also of the overcoming of it. My optimism, then, does not rest on the absence of evil, but on a glad belief in the preponderance of good and a willing effort always to cooperate with the good, that it may prevail.[6]

By the grace of God, the attacks over the past several decades have led to a high level of professionalism in all that we do in our centers and medical clinics. The attacks resulted directly in the vision for "real

---

6 Helen Keller, *Optimism: My Key of Life* (New York: T.Y. Crowell Company, 1903), p. 17.

clinics" (with ultrasound) to counter the charge that we are "fake clinics." Even more lives have been saved and changed as a direct result of our response to these attacks.

And those attacks led, at least in the United States, to a reaffirming of the constitutional rights of those in the pregnancy help movement. Our standards of care and sincerity of mission are, at least for now, secure from intrusive meddling by those wielding government power.

## Fake News and Reviews

Far more common than bruising legal battles and elected officials abusing their power in order to punish the charitable work of compassionate pregnancy help outreach is the enduring public relations war waged by, and for, Big Abortion. Vicious claims are made in the public arena that would never survive scrutiny in a court of law (under oath) for lack of veracity, substance, or actual victims of crime.

One example is career congresswoman, Representative Carolyn Maloney (D-NY). In Congress since 1993, she has put forth a bill called "Stop Deceptive Advertising in Women's Services Act" (or something similar) a half-dozen times. Apparently, so the reasoning might go, because PHCs are not breaking the law now, we need a law so we can prosecute them for something.

In 2017 a group launched an "Expose Fake Clinics" campaign. Led by former comedienne Lizz Winstead and her group, "Lady Parts Justice League," it targeted pregnancy centers through a combination of in-person protests and online reputation smear tactics. The in-person protests involved undercover clients, sidewalk protests, and the "fake clinic" charge. Often the charge of "fake clinic" ignores the licensed professional healthcare nurses and doctors that are part of the pregnancy help outreach. While not every center includes medical personnel and medical services, every center is painted with the brush of being a "fake clinic" because they do not offer abortion services and contraception.

By their definition of "fake clinic," every clinic of any kind—urgent care, trauma center, cardiac care, etc.—would be fake since they don't provide abortions.

Fortunately, "Expose Fake Clinics" in-person protests were paltry in size. Ironically, some of the scant protestors donned medical lab coats to pose as medical people protesting the actual medical people at the PHCs who were not wearing lab coats. The fact that, year after year, 98-plus percent of all pregnancy help center clients report a positive experience is clear evidence why such campaigns gain little traction.

## When Activists Masquerade as Journalists

Because abortion is a worldwide product, Big Abortion has a worldwide reach. This includes abortion activists posing as journalists conducting "investigations" of pregnancy help, Heartbeat International, our affiliates, and our partnering networks.

Like their US counterparts, their allegations are far more fiction than fact and clearly are written with a bias for abortion and against anyone that would seek to simply provide an alternative. This is evidenced by how these same outlets, so concerned about "women's issues," are completely silent on the abuses by abortionists (Gosnell, for one), law-breaking by Planned Parenthood (selling baby body parts), and the related profiteering. Instead of using their funding and capabilities to further women's interests, they further abortion profits and ideology.

And there are plenty of willing friends in mainstream media outlets who will quickly pick up any headline that imagines impropriety among pro-lifers. Heartbeat International has addressed the bulk of these half-truths, misinformation, and falsehoods on a website called PregnancyCenterTruth.com.

## Responding Rightly

Heartbeat has always championed standards and woven them into all of the training and education for our foot soldiers and the centers and clinics where they carry out their mission. Heartbeat's leadership in expanding "Our Commitment of Care and Competence" (Appendix V) has already been discussed. We developed the first (and only) college-level, adult education, distance learning program for pregnancy consultants, called ConCert, through Project REACH (see chapter 11). We also established the first digital distance learning platform dedicated to the pregnancy help community. *The L.O.V.E. Approach* headlines what is now more than 350 courses and webinars within Heartbeat's Academy (an homage to the historical name of our AAI's education-focused conferences). These trainings feature a myriad of subject matter experts, including Heartbeat staff, from across several professional disciplines.

Heartbeat has developed a suite of training materials, in print and online, as companions to *The L.O.V.E. Approach:* a comprehensive board training manual called *GOVERN Essentials*, and a comprehensive director's manual called *DIRECT Essentials*. In addition, we have a medical manual for centers that want to add medical services, a legal manual, and an up-to-date staffing manual, among other resources. We also provide a comprehensive on-site center assessment, as well as strategic planning, peacemaking, and consultations personalized for special needs. Our unique Leadership Institute and our New Director Oasis are specialized, intensive training opportunities for special groups of leaders within our movement.

In 2008 Heartbeat launched a one-of-its-kind certification program for our foot soldiers called the LAS certification, which stands for Life Affirming Specialist. After core training requirements, someone working in a center or clinic can obtain an LAS certification. By attending Heartbeat International-approved training and workshops that meet certain standards, consultants in our pregnancy help community can obtain continuing education credits and keep up their certification as Life Affirming Specialists. Every conference and several online courses and webinars have also been approved for continuing education credits for nurses as well.

Attacks or no attacks, we believe it is important to do everything to the best of our ability with excellence and integrity. And this is what we provide in all our training and support for our affiliates. Our main "weapon" in the battle continues to be communicating truth in love. We provide love and support, in ways that are above reproach, to women and families every day. As a result, communities are stronger, and our ministry is more effective.

**Proactive Portrayal**

While defensive reactions have made us stronger, we've also gone on the offense. Rather than letting those dedicated to our demise define who we are and what we do, it is increasingly important to carry our message to where it matters.

The message that "pregnancy centers are great for America" is one that Heartbeat takes to Washington, DC, every year in our proactive effort to influence influencers in our nation's capital. At the national level we call this woman-centered, service-minded outreach Babies Go to Congress®; it has also been the model for state and local outreach. BGTC, as we know it, has also served as a model for other countries to intentionally spotlight the missional impact of pregnancy help on the client outcomes we celebrate. We highlight what we should all agree with—that every woman should be loved and supported during her pregnancy.

In our Babies Go to Congress® program, Heartbeat makes an appointment with a member of Congress or their Washington office staff, and we bring a mother and baby (or mother, father, and baby) who have been helped by a pregnancy center in their district. Also coming to the congressional office with the constituent mother and her baby is the director of the local center and a representative from Heartbeat International. Each mother tells her story of how the center has helped her, confirming that without the center's help, this baby would likely have been aborted. Sometimes the babies, in strollers and carriers, chime in with their thanks too! The center director explains all the services provided at their center. Thus we all make friends for local pregnancy centers that provide a wide range of vital community services in their congressional districts, all at virtually no cost to the taxpayers!

Over the past few years, Heartbeat has been able to visit some four hundred congressional offices (Senate and House of Representatives) and has brought seventy moms and babies to Congress. We try to focus on pro-choice or noncommittal congressional representatives and senators, and we have almost invariably gotten a positive response. Legislators and their aides find it almost impossible to argue, once they have a mother and baby—who are their own constituents—in front of them, that the work of their local pregnancy center is anything other than a very good thing.

## Communities of Compassion

While Big Abortion is driven by profits and bolstered by raw political power, the work of pregnancy help is fueled by local people doing good things for those in their own community at no cost to them. The political table has long been tilted in favor of Big Abortion and its allies. But the compassion of the pregnancy help community is empowered by the good heart of the grassroots people and by no less than the God of the Universe (see Psalm 139 and 1 Corinthians 13) who called the great work of pregnancy help into existence. And it is He who continues to protect us!

### Psalm 124
*If it had not been the Lord who was on our side,*
*let Israel now say—*
*if it had not been the Lord who was on our side,*
*when men rose up against us,*
*then they would have swallowed us up alive,*
*when their anger was kindled against us;*

*then the flood would have swept us away,*
  *the torrent would have gone over us;*
*then over us would have gone*
  *the raging waters.*
*Blessed be the LORD,*
  *who has not given us*
    *as prey to their teeth!*
*We have escaped as a bird*
  *from the snare of the fowlers;*
*the snare is broken,*
  *and we have escaped!*
*Our help is in the name of the LORD,*
  *who made heaven and earth.*

"Thumbs up" from Tom Glessner, President of NIFLA, as the legal team exits the Supreme Court, signals the waiting crowd that our free speech rights are re-affirmed in the NIFLA vs. Becerra decision. Heartbeat President Jor-El Godsey and Legal Counsel Danielle White (above left and in the center right) were in the Supreme Court Chamber when the decision was handed down.

*Heartbeat has responded to attacks on PHC's as "fake clinics" by pro-actively reaffirming our Commitment of Care and Competence (Appendix V), certifying the special training and expertise of pregnancy center staff and volunteers through our Life Affirming Specialist certification, and highlighting the truth in Congress that "Pregnancy Centers are Great for America!"*

*Each year, clients from PHCs throughout the U.S. join Heartbeat as we meet with federal lawmakers to share their stories at our Babies Go to Congress® event and as we join the March for Life.*

# CHAPTER 11

## STEERING INTO AREAS OF GREATEST NEED

### Peggy Hartshorn and Jor-El Godsey

One of our major challenges in this battle for the sanctity of human life, this epic struggle to save the most innocent and vulnerable among us and their mothers from abortion, is that the prime battlegrounds, the abortion clinics, are most often located in the areas where the army, the foot soldiers armed with love, are most in need of reinforcements, training, encouragement, and even new battle plans. In the United States, most abortions are performed where populations are concentrated, in the heart of our major cities. But most PHCs are located in the metropolitan suburbs, mid-sized cities, small towns, and rural areas.

Let's be clear that the PHCs in small towns and rural areas are also areas of great need. The women and families they serve are not being offered discount coupons on the street for the nearby abortion clinic (as happens in Los Angeles), but they are at risk for abortion, especially as telemedicine expands and abortion pills are available (still illegally) on the internet. And they are at risk for all of the consequences of casual sexual intimacy—physical, emotional, psychological, and spiritual— plus abandonment, abuse, and more.

The centers located outside our metropolitan areas do great work in helping women change their lives (and those of their families) and in creating a culture of life in their communities. An example is Dinah Monahan's work, for which she received our Legacy Award in 2021. Dinah and her husband Mike started housing girls in their home in the 1980s, then founded three PHCs and a maternity home in their rural area. The ministries, three hours from the closest abortion clinic, are in Show Low, Springerville, and in Arizona's White Mountains— our only affiliate on a Native American reservation (Apache). All these PHCs have ultrasound, and tiny lives are being saved, but their major impact is in relationship building and mentoring their clients. Dinah designed the "Earn While You Learn" program that provides videos and other materials that keep clients coming back to earn points for items that they and their babies need. It is now one of the most popular programs in the country for PHCs who are called to impact their clients with long-term follow-up and care. The three small-town centers saw 14,983 clients visits in one year! (Three of Dinah's grandchildren, from Ethiopia through adoption, led the Monahans to also establish a pro-life outreach to single pregnant mothers in that country.)

However, the large numbers of abortion providers and historic numbers of abortions in our largest metropolitan areas—going on for nearly fifty years—have created major challenges, not the least of which is a "culture of death" that is the source of discouragement and attack against our foot soldiers. During the 1970s and 1980s, there were few efforts by our movement as a whole to bring strategic help to the foot soldiers in these areas of greatest need. But that changed in the next three decades, with Heartbeat leading the way in the 1990s. Not all of the efforts of Heartbeat and others to steer more pregnancy help into these areas have borne lasting fruit. But there have been some powerful successes by heroic foot soldiers based in some cities. The lessons learned have led to exciting innovations today. This chapter will tell that story.

## Big Apple and Big Abortion

Heartbeat realized this "distribution problem" early on—pregnancy help was not located where most abortion clinics were. One of our early outreaches in 1993, when Peggy first became president, was to schedule a series of regional conferences around the country. We wanted to meet the foot soldiers in our army, find out more about their needs and what they were doing, and bring Heartbeat resources to them. We used our Worldwide Directory, which listed all the United States pregancy help service providers by state, to send invitations to the leaders when we were going to be in their region. Once we got to the northeastern states, we realized that there was a glaring problem. A vast number of abortions were being performed in that region of the country, but there was a very small number of pregnancy help service providers.

New York City was the prime example. In the mid 1990s, there were about one hundred known abortion providers in the city (including clinics, hospitals, and private doctors who advertised abortions) with barely a handful of small pregnancy help centers, none of them with ultrasound services.

Peggy has always had a heart for New York City, not just because it's the Big Apple and a cultural phenomenon, but because it is where the abortion industry in the US first grew and thrived. Brooklyn was the home of Margaret Sanger, where the first Planned Parenthood opened its doors and is still operating. Dr. Bernard Nathanson, a founder of NARAL, operated what he called "the world's largest abortion clinic" there (before he became a pro-life convert).

So Peggy called all the centers in the New York City area listed in Heartbeat's Worldwide Directory to arrange a small gathering to introduce them to Heartbeat. Our initial offer of help (training, manuals, consultation, advice, networking, and prayer support) seemed small, considering the fact that New York City performed then (and still does) about one-fourth of all the abortions in the United States and is sometimes called the "abortion capital" of the US.

Some center directors in New York City, fearful of attack from pro-abortion opponents, kept their home phone numbers secret (even from their office staff and volunteers), so it was very difficult to contact everyone. Finally, one of the center directors offered to have the gathering at her parish church. Eight centers were represented when we met on September 25, 1997, at Immaculate Conception Church on East 14th Street. Most representatives there did not even know one another. Unlike other regions of the country, they had no coalition or regular networking.

In our frank and honest meeting, it became clear how difficult it was (and still is) to do pregnancy help work in New York City, and how much courage and stamina these foot soldiers had. Some centers indicated that their staff and volunteers had to commute over an hour to get to the centers, the cost of office rental space was exorbitant, advertising (in the Yellow Pages at that time) was so costly that only a couple of the centers had one-line ads amidst the pages of large abortion clinic ads. Most importantly, the work was difficult and exhausting. Almost every woman who called or came in wanted an abortion. New York paid for abortions, so it was the primary option that nearly every woman considered. This is still true today.

The Church around them seemed almost oblivious to their situation and need. A few Evangelical churches supported two small centers—one in Manhattan, and one on Long Island. The famous and beloved pro-life hero Cardinal John J. O'Connor of New York City had proclaimed that any woman who needed help with a crisis pregnancy could come to the Church, so many Catholics presumed that the need for alternatives to abortion was already being met. However, that was not at all the case. Abortion percentages were very high in all the boroughs, with about half of all pregnancies ending in abortion in Brooklyn. Sadly, this is still the case today.

The centers present at that meeting welcomed the help of Heartbeat. We eventually gave our work in NYC a name: Project REACH. The acronym stood for the following: R – Reach those at Risk for abortion; E – Educate them about their options; A – Advertise abortion alternative services; C – Develop Centers to strengthen their services and foundations; and H – Add Health and Healing services, especially ultrasound, to save more lives and post-abortion recovery programs to reduce repeat abortions (because 50 percent of all abortions are performed on someone who has already had an abortion but has not been healed).

A New York center board member introduced Peggy to Jim Manning who had an interest in Project REACH. He had just sold his business and, for the first time in many years, had the time to get involved in something he cared deeply about: pro-life. He got involved wholeheartedly, donating space in his midtown Manhattan town house (which had been his office hub) for a Project REACH office and training center, and providing major funding for the project, pledged over five years. We conducted bimonthly trainings in Midtown for all foot soldiers, bringing in experts in various fields of organizational growth and development as well as programming.

Every NYC center (ten organizations in fourteen locations) participated in a joint advertising campaign. We took out a full-page ad in every NYC Yellow Pages Directory, putting them in competition, for the first time, with the NYC abortion clinics. Because the heading Abortion Alternatives came before Abortion Services, our centers were listed in front of every abortion clinic in the city.

Project REACH also funded the first ever distance learning program in our movement, the ConCert (Consultant Certificate) program of Heartbeat International. Many of the NYC foot soldiers took this adult-education, college-level course in pregnancy center consulting. In 2010, the effort to transition ConCert into an online course would lead to Heartbeat's Academy, the digital training platform accessed by more than seven thousand students across the US and around the globe.

Eventually, we hired New York attorney John Margand to head up the project. He later applied for and received a federal grant for

Project REACH that funded the first abstinence education program in New York City schools, called Healthy Respect. Federal grants funded abstinence education in the Yonkers school district through Project REACH for nearly a decade.

After about five years, Heartbeat turned over leadership of the project in NYC to Program REACH, a newly formed New York nonprofit that worked with the growing coalition of the pregnancy centers in all five boroughs. Heartbeat has continued our relationships with the pregnancy centers there, many of whom became and are still Heartbeat affiliates.

Despite all these efforts and some major successes, twenty years later the PHCs in New York City are still facing major challenges. The hurdles for PHCs to become medical clinics in order to provide ultrasounds are still too great. During Project REACH, NIFLA collaborated with Heartbeat to study the options, eventually concluding that the centers in NYC could legally follow the model used elsewhere in the country— to operate medical services, such as ultrasound, under the license of a private physician. Shockingly, no pro-life physician has been willing to allow a center to operate under his or her license, so NYC centers have tried innovative ways to provide ultrasounds. For example, Expectant Mother's Care for a time rented space in their offices to physicians who could bill ultrasounds to New York's generous PCAP program (that pays for services to low-income pregnant women). One PHC had a partnership with a NYC Catholic resource, the Giana Center, which provides fertility care and has ultrasound services. These efforts provide only a tiny fraction of the number of ultrasounds needed to potentially reduce the number of abortions in the city.

New York City leaders have continued to be biased toward the abortion industry and against the good work of pregnancy help. The pro-abortion culture there is as strong as ever. New York City centers faced a major attack with restrictive regulations passed by the New York City Council, as discussed in chapter 10.

## Where Abortion Clinics Abound

In 2004, Heartbeat explored other parts of the country with too many abortion clinics and too few pregnancy help centers. Using the limited technology available, websites, online Yellow Pages, and a web mapping system, we manually developed a list of all of the abortion clinics in the United States, city by city, and then listed the closest center(s), indicating how many miles they were from the abortion clinics. It was a very revealing spreadsheet, showing that many clusters of abortion clinics have only one or two pregnancy help centers nearby, and some of the abortion clinics did not have a pregnancy center within twenty miles or more!

Peggy took this study to a meeting of all of the pregnancy help center organization leadership, now called LAPCO, and revealed the findings. It was clear that up to this time, we had been trying to keep up with the growth of our movement wherever it was occurring, as the Holy Spirit was raising up people around the world to do this great work. Could we help steer our movement into areas of greatest need—by going into our major cities, where there were few, if any, pregnancy help centers—and "wake up" the Church to start them?

It was also clear that abortion clinics were disproportionately located in African American and Latino American neighborhoods, and abortion providers were targeting other immigrant neighborhoods as well. In fact, at that time, the African American and Latino American populations combined were only about 24 percent of the population, but they represented some 60 percent of all abortions performed. Sadly, those percentages have remained about the same today.

Other organizations got into the effort. Focus on the Family, headed at that time by Dr. James Dobson, already had a Sanctity of Life department that served pregnancy help centers. They held a series of meetings to discuss the shocking disparity between abortion clinics and pregnancy centers in metropolitan areas; they called these discussions "Impacting High Abortion Communities." Care Net was Heartbeat's partner in a joint venture called Option Line (see chapter 12). Peggy and the president of Care Net, Kurt Entsminger, agreed to institute projects that both would call "Urban Initiatives." We would choose key cities and take the lead in helping start centers, working in conjunction with one another where we could.

Heartbeat decided to focus on Miami, Florida. Miami had thirty-seven abortion clinics and not one pregnancy help medical clinic—that is, a pregnancy center with ultrasound services under the direction of a physician medical director.

Rev. John Ensor, from Boston, also an abortion hub, led the successful development of A Woman's Concern there in the 1990s. It had become a multicenter medical clinic and the first PHC to hire a physician as its full time medical director. It was a model "urban center," operating with a diverse staff and helping reduce the number of abortions in that city. John felt called to resign from the Heartbeat board, join the staff, and lead the Heartbeat project in Miami. He visited the area several times to understand the situation more fully, setting up a temporary "office" each time, with his laptop, in a local Panera Bread. Finally, John and his wife, Kristen, decided that the only way to be successful in "waking up" the Church would be for them to move to Miami and become a part of the community for at least two years, which they did. John discovered that the Catholic Church in the Miami area, well aware of the abortion problem, had been struggling to keep several help centers functioning for years. They provided primarily material aid and referrals for community help. The Evangelical churches were largely unaware, so John spoke at one or more churches in Miami every weekend, and sometimes during the week, calling attention to the problem and challenging Christians to answer the call.

Early on, John connected with an outstanding leader, Martha Avila, who gave up a lucrative business position to answer the call to serve in Heartbeat of Miami. At one of the churches where John spoke, a woman named Jeannie Pernia told him, "I was part of the problem—my mother and I ran one of the abortion clinics in Miami for several years—now I want to be part of the solution." Jeannie helped Martha found Heartbeat of Miami and served for many years as the director of their first location, Hialeah Pregnancy Help Clinic, which opened in 2007. When the site for the clinic was chosen, Jeannie told us that the abortion clinic she operated had been directly next door! How God heals and restores!

Today Heartbeat of Miami, still led by Martha Avila, operates four pregnancy help medical clinics, three of which are in Latin communities (Hialeah, Kendall, and Miami) and one in North Miami which serves an African American community. The clinics employ sixteen full and part time employees, including five sonographers, plus fourteen volunteers. Martha's strategically located clinics now see thousands of women at risk for abortion every year (most years the clinics do well over 3,000 ultrasounds) and most of these women decide to continue their pregnancies.

The women who come to Heartbeat of Miami are enveloped in love and support, medical care (such as ultrasounds) and provided with follow-up, hope, practical help, and prayer—the formidable "weapons" of the army of foot soldiers armed with love.

## Minority Leadership

Martha's long-term commitment and visionary and passionate leadership in serving those most targeted by the abortion industry have been recognized by Heartbeat through our Legacy Award, given to her in 2021. The impact of Heartbeat of Miami also drew the attention of the White House in 2019, where Martha Avila, a Cuban-American, stood with President Trump and Vice President Mike Pence during Hispanic Heritage Month and decried the fact that "Hispanics and African Americans, even though we're a minority . . . we form the majority of abortions in our country." She went on to say, "Pregnancy centers are good for America," echoing the motto of Heartbeat International's Babies Go to Congress®, which Martha had been involved in for many years prior to her national recognition.

The reality of abortion's inversely proportional impact on US minorities reveals that the key to the development of pregnancy help centers in areas of greatest need—and perhaps the key to ultimate victory in the pro-life cause here in the US—is the leadership of the African American and Latino American community. While others can provide a catalyst, resources, and vital support, pregnancy help centers in African American and Latino American communities must be led by and "owned" by members of those communities. Dr. Alveda King, a former member of the Heartbeat International board who has dedicated her life to awakening the African American community to the harsh reality of abortion, illustrates the need for this when she says, "You can't go into someone's house, tell him he has a problem, and that you know how to solve it better than he does."

Like Martha Avila in Miami, another outstanding urban pregnancy help leader in our movement today is Sylvia Johnson-Matthews of Houston, Texas. Heartbeat honored Sylvia with a Legacy Award in 2011 for her courage and professionalism in leading pregnancy help ministry in a major urban abortion "hot zone." Sylvia directed a pregnancy help center in Orlando, and then, in 2001, was motivated to start the first urban center in what Houston's mayor described as the "forgotten part of the city." Houston Pregnancy Help Center has two locations (Fifth Ward and downtown Houston), just a few miles from the largest abortion facility in the US, the 78,000-square foot Planned Parenthood abortion clinic, complete with a surgical wing for later-term abortions. In recent years, the Houston PHC added a medical mobile unit to their outreach into underserved areas of Houston. Sylvia Johnson-Matthews is a Spirit-led, indomitable foot soldier, and she has raised up hundreds of others to fight alongside her, loving thousands of women into choices for LIFE.

## Pregnancy Help Hits the Road

Sylvia Johnson-Matthews' medical mobile unit in Houston is one of well over one hundred like it on the road today across the United States, and the mobile clinic model has recently spread to other countries.

Mobile units, as we call them, are recreational vehicles, vans, and the like, rigged with an ultrasound machine and the basic accoutrements of an ultrasound room in a PHC. Powered by a dedicated crew, including a sonographer or a licensed nurse trained in obstetric sonography, mobile units carry vital pregnancy help to underserved areas. This is often where no brick-and-mortar location exists, or a mobile unit can augment a nonmedical pregnancy resource location with medical services.

The idea of these rolling clinics that extend pregnancy help outreach for greater accessibility to those at risk for abortion has been floating around since the early 1990s. But it was not until 2003 that they were given focused attention and molded into a powerful model for ministry impact.

Sylvia Slifko, a long-time pro-life advocate, was directing a pregnancy help center in Akron, Ohio. Concerned that her center wasn't seeing as many women at risk for abortion as she knew needed their help, she spent dedicated time praying about the situation. Out of that season of prayer, she felt providentially impressed to "go where the women are." And, in her mind, she could see a mobile medical clinic able to take the message of life, and life everlasting, where the women at risk for abortion were. She gathered a team around her, and that mobile unit became a real outreach in 2004.

Over the next few years, the power of the mobile unit to "reveal life at the crossroads of decision" became evident as Sylvia and her team worked out the kinks and refined this model of pregnancy help. In 2007, she stepped away from local PHC ministry to incorporate ICU ("I See You") Mobile, which partners with and serves PHCs and other life-affirming ministries to help them reach women in crisis. Adding a fleet brand, Image Clear Ultrasound, the ICU Mobile team continues to provide a full turnkey approach that includes all the equipment, pre-deployment consulting, comprehensive training, and ongoing coaching. Sylvia's vision, now under the leadership of CEO Greg Van Buskirk, has helped launch seventy mobile units across the country.

A second national mobile unit group called Save the Storks launched their version in 2013: a high-end Mercedes Sprinter. These are smaller and more maneuverable—especially for parking—than the larger RVs, but the units come at a greater cost. Save the Storks has sought grants to aid PHCs in adding this type of mobile unit and has seen steady growth, deploying more than sixty medical mobile units on the road.

## Pregnancy Help on the Sidewalk

But pregnancy help does not occur only within the walls of a PHC or in a mobile unit.

The sidewalk in front of, or near, abortion clinics has been a battleground of sorts for those against abortions. Operation Rescue, in the late 1980s and early 1990s even took to peaceful sit-ins that blocked the entrances to abortion clinics. These "rescues" intentionally violated trespass laws, which often created confrontations with law enforcement and led to arrests and trials. While they turned away abortion clients temporarily, they were not a sustainable outreach to the women seeking answers for their unintended pregnancies.

Sidewalk outreach to women has been part of the pro-life movement for decades with well-known groups such as Pro-Life Action Ministries (Brian Gibson, St. Paul, Minnesota) and Pro-Life Action League (Eric Scheidler, Chicago, Illinois). Yet it was four members of the Brazos Valley Coalition for Life in central Texas who would ignite a worldwide movement of sidewalk impact in 2004. They gathered for an hour of prayer and found themselves drawn to the time frame of forty days—a time frame God consistently has used throughout salvation history to transform His people.

The prayer, around an old wooden table, led them to launch a forty-day campaign of prayer and fasting, a community outreach, and a constant, peaceful vigil in front of the Planned Parenthood facility that had opened in their community just a few years earlier. The four—David, Shawn, Marilisa, and Emily—vowed to cover the entire *forty-day, 960-hour, around-the-clock vigil,* even if no one else joined them. They gave their new project a name: 40 Days for Life. In less than six weeks, this first 40 Days for Life campaign saw more than one thousand volunteers cover all 960 hours of the vigil. The grassroots, door-to-door effort reached more than 25,000 households. The campaign made local, state, and even national news. And the local abortion rate dropped by 28 percent.

The next year, inspired by Brazos Valley Coalition for Life's success, communities across the United States launched their own campaigns: Houston, Texas; Dallas, Texas; Green Bay, Wisconsin; Kitsap County, Washington; Charlotte, North Carolina. In 2007, the original 40 Days for Life leaders launched the first ever nationally coordinated 40 Days for Life campaign, spanning eighty-nine cities in thirty-three states. Before long, campaigns were hosted in all fifty states. Now, led by Shawn Carney, 40 Days for Life campaigns happen in hundreds of cities and dozens of countries across all six populated continents—in places like Houston, Manhattan, Indianapolis, Toronto, London, Sydney, Mexico City, Cape Town, Bogota, Moscow, and Hong Kong.

### Grace Places

A calling to pregnancy help often arises from the pain of experience. Amy Ford faced an unplanned pregnancy in her teens. Friends pulled away, and she felt uncomfortable, even unwelcome, at her home church. A few years later, in 2008, after she had married and settled in Dallas, that experience fueled a passion and desire to help her new church to extend grace to young women with unplanned pregnancies. Amy and her friend Salina started a weekly small group at her church to minister to young pregnant moms with support, friendship, guidance, and love.

The word spread among churches who sought to duplicate Amy's outreach. In 2012, Embrace Grace was established as a national nonprofit to equip churches all around the nation to have a pro-love focus and to help women be brave and choose life. Their discipleship programs have grown to more than seven hundred active support groups impacting more than six thousand women within the loving, grace-filled compassion of a local church prepared to help through other challenges of life. Churches are already established in places of greatest need, and Embrace Grace can bring pregnancy help into the church community.

## Catalyzing a New Season of Growth

Pregnancy help centers saw a super-charged growth in the mid-1980s. When plotting "Years Services Began" on a graph, an obvious spike appears in 1984, 1985, and 1986. This was the second decade of Heartbeat history (and pregnancy help history). "Urban Initiatives"— which helped some major cities like Miami establish PHCs—was initiated in the 2000s, the fourth decade. And in our fifth decade, Heartbeat committed to inspire a new season of new pregnancy help centers to increase life-affirming outreach in underserved communities. New centers mean more at-risk clients reached with life-saving ministry.

Originally envisioned as "50 in 5"—fifty new PHCs in five years—the program sought to catalyze locally developing efforts with stronger, more comprehensive foundations that can translate to stronger and sustained impact sooner: more clients, more quickly, with more positive outcomes. It soon became clear that limiting the idea to just fifty, and to only five years, would shortchange the opportunity for saving even more lives.

Thus, Heartbeat's "Life Launch" was born in 2018, spearheaded by a $500,000 leadership gift matched by several donors. The program itself creates a matching grant to leverage community funding and supercharge local efforts to get started quicker and get founded better. Heartbeat matches $30K raised locally with $30K in a mix of direct funding and direct services for intensive and comprehensive guidance to start up a PHC.

These Life Launch start-ups are catalyzed by leveraging our PHC starter manual called *Built by Design* accompanied with guided implementation, core training, and key leader coaching. Added to that is digital marketing expertise via our Extend Web Services and our PHC operations software called Next Level Center Management Solutions. These core resources and more provide a quicker path to pregnancy help impact in targeted communities.

Now in only its third year, Life Launch has partnered with more than two dozen local communities to launch new organizations that have opened PHCs in seventeen states. Many "Life Launchers" quickly grow their services from initial care—including pregnancy tests, consultations, and material assistance—to medical services such as ultrasounds, STI testing, and even the Abortion Pill Rescue Network. Life Launch is well on its way to fulfill that original vision for "50 in 5" and hopefully, many more!

## Truly a Movement

The pregnancy help movement has been just that—a movement:

- Moving from intermittent response to the rising abortion culture to a connected network of compassionate care.

- Moving beyond the method of pregnancy centers to incorporate adaptive outreach on sidewalks and mobile units.

- Moving to include underserved areas in urban communities and remote rural outposts in every state in the US and in most countries around the world.

We are a movement steering toward greater impact and better help for women.

*Project REACH in New York City, 1997-2002, was our pioneering effort to advance pregnancy help in an area where, in one borough, abortions outnumbered live births (see pp. 187–90). The first distance learning program in our field, ConCert, was launched there. The first ConCert graduates are pictured with Peggy (first row far left) in the Manhattan townhouse where the Project was headquartered.*

*Heartbeat coordinated with other organizations in an effort known as the "Urban Initiatives" in the 2000s. Staff member John Ensor, his wife Kristen, and Peggy are with Martha Avila, David Behar, and Jeannie Pernia, staff members of Heartbeat of Miami, the first PHC in Miami with ultrasound (pp. 192–93).*

*Heartbeat also helped in Pittsburgh, where existing Pregnancy Help Centers collaborated to open an urban center in an underserved area of the city.*

*Life Launch, that supercharges local efforts, is Heartbeat's new approach to steering pregnancy help where it's needed (pp. 198–99). Born in 2018, it is already a great success!*

*Powerful pro-life leaders have brought life saving pregnancy help to urban, ethnic areas targeted by abortionists. Sylvia Johnson-Matthews (left) receives our Legacy Award in 2011 for her work in Houston. Martha Avila (right) receives our Legacy Award in 2021 for her work in Miami.*

*Mobile units let PHCs expand their service areas. The ICU (Image Clear Ultrasound) fleet, founded in 2007, currently has 70 units on the road, and the Save the Storks fleet, founded in 2013, numbers over 60 units.*

# CHAPTER 12

## REACHING AND RESCUING THROUGH OPTION LINE

### Peggy Hartshorn

Heartbeat's Option Line connects a person vulnerable to abortion in the US or Canada—in real time through a direct voice connection—to a person ready to help in a pregnancy center in her own community. This happens, person to person, about 1,100 times per day! Since its first call was answered in 2003, Option Line has handled over four million contacts! Option Line even makes appointments for women in need in many local centers and clinics when their offices are closed, so a woman only makes one call for help. Additional visitors to the Option Line website can, with a center locator system, find their closest pregnancy centers, its hours and services, by entering the caller's zip code.

Why is this important? The Holy Spirit has raised up thousands of pregnancy help organizations in our nation and around the world, but until Option Line, there was nothing linking this network together in an effective, professional way and making it so easy for women to find and access life-saving help. Now that's just a click away!

The battle rages on between what abortionists offer and what our centers and clinics offer. It calls to mind Deuteronomy 30:19—"I call heaven and earth to witness against you this day, that I have set before you life and death, blessing and curse; therefore choose life, that you and your descendants may live."

We know, for example, that if a woman is considering abortion or is vulnerable to abortion (facing pressure from parents, boyfriend, financial concerns, and other issues), and she comes into a pregnancy help medical clinic and sees her baby on the ultrasound screen, there is an 80 percent chance (or higher) that she will choose life for her baby. The bonding begins to take place between mother and child, and her maternal instinct helps the mother protect her baby and not be overcome with fears and other pressures. The same often holds true for a father, who, when he sees the image of his child on the ultrasound screen, often begins to fight to protect his child. In 2019, the Charlotte Lozier Pregnancy Center report indicated that 486,213 ultrasounds were performed in pregnancy help medical clinics in the US. With 80 percent of mothers choosing life, that means that nearly 400,000 lives were saved!

But if the mother gets to an abortion provider first, we estimate that 80 percent of the time the mother will go through with the abortion, the baby will be killed, and chances are that the mother and family will be left with physical, emotional, and/or spiritual scars. The Guttmacher Institute report for 2017 indicated that about 800,000 abortions were performed that year in the US.

Who will get to the woman first? Option Line's key role in reaching and rescuing babies and women from abortion, and how its cutting-edge services have come to be, are the subjects of this chapter.

## An Original Vision Becomes a Reality

A national toll-free 800 number was one of the original five goals of our founders. A hotline was near and dear to their hearts; it was a key element of the safety net they envisioned. In Los Angeles, Sister Paula was involved in the first ever pregnancy help hotline in 1971, one of the first outreaches for providing alternatives to abortion in the United

States. But the goal of an AAI national hotline was still unachieved when I became president in in 1993 and we changed our name to Heartbeat International.

In the 1990s there were three other national hotlines for life-affirming pregnancy help. One, operated by Birthright USA, referred primarily to Birthright centers, and only to other centers when a Birthright center was not available. The Birthright office (later the First Way office, under the leadership of Denise Coccioloni in New Jersey) operated the hotline, and it advertised primarily in New Jersey, New York, and on the East Coast. Care Net started a national 800 number in the mid-1990s that referred callers to Care Net centers. Advertised primarily on billboards and through Care Net centers, the phone system automatically routed a caller to a center in her area code. If the center was closed, the caller received a message or might be connected to the home of a volunteer who was covering the center's phone. If there was no Care Net center in that area code, the call was sent to the Care Net administrative office where the caller received an automated message.

America's Pregnancy Helpline operated the third hotline from a call center in Dallas. It was originally founded to help connect families who wanted to adopt with women wanting to make adoption plans for their babies, but the Helpline had broadened its mission to become a general information line (and website) for any pregnancy-related question or issue. The staff at the call center answered callers' questions as fully as possible, and then they ended the call. They referred only about 50 percent of their callers to a local pregnancy help center.

Heartbeat was being urged to join, support, and or advertise one of the existing toll-free numbers. No one had to convince me of the necessity of a pregnancy help hotline. In 1980 my husband and I had the hotline for our Columbus pregnancy help center installed in our bedroom until the office was officially opened. We had to have a phone installed someplace by a certain date in order to get the number in the phone book. Unbeknownst to us, once installed, the number was accessible by operators when anyone called Information and asked about abortion! For several months, Mike and I learned "on the job" and answered many a desperate caller considering abortion. My resolve became firm that every call from a woman (or other person) vulnerable to abortion, at any hour of day or night, must be answered by a trained person who could provide help. If a woman has the courage to call, we must be there to answer.

Our leadership (board and staff) agreed that Heartbeat's mission was to reach and rescue as many lives as possible through an effective pregnancy help center network, so two features were indispensable for an 800 number. First, it must be answered by a well-trained, loving person 24/7, never by a machine. If a woman calls for help and does not receive it immediately, her next call might be to an abortion clinic. Second, the best alternative to abortion is another person. Ideally that person should be in the caller's own community (not on a phone line)—if possible, within her local pregnancy help center. Every caller should be referred to the pregnancy help network of care.

Eventually, Heartbeat made a proposal to Care Net, and they accepted it. Together we would develop a legal joint venture and open a call center for the 800 number. We would hire and train our own staff, and we would make sure every caller was referred to her local Heartbeat International or Care Net pregnancy help center. Because of higher operating costs in Virginia, where Care Net was and is located, they proposed that the call center be opened in Columbus, Ohio—and it remains there today, in the same building with Heartbeat headquarters.

We founded Option Line during a period when our pregnancy help movement was exploring many ways that we could be more unified. LAPCO recently had been founded to bring leaders of the national service providers closer together, and Heartbeat, Care Net, and NIFLA were all urging pregnancy centers to consider joining more than one affiliation group. So, the centers that are part of the Option Line referral network, both then and now, represent about 85 percent of all the centers in the US and Canada. It was a great example of unity and collaboration during that period.

## Cutting-Edge Technology

In its first ten years under the joint venture, Option Line made use of the latest technology, so it was the first-ever internet-based pregnancy helpline. That is, it used VOIP technology, not phone lines, and call center employees not only answered phone calls but also emails and soon added a messenger-type chat. They also used email to answer calls for help outside North America, referring those in need to a resource in Heartbeat's Worldwide Directory. People could reach help through the 800 number or at optionline.org or pregnancy centers.org. The website featured a cutting-edge MapQuest function so that when a zip code was entered, the ten closest pregnancy help organizations appeared with their programs and hours and directions to those locations.

The innovations achieved in Option Line's first ten years were due in great part to the creative, risk-taking, entrepreneurial staff, mostly composed of recent young college graduates. They were led by Kelle Berry, who had a brand new IT degree, experience working in pregnancy help centers with her mother when she was a teenager, and a great passion for our mission. When Kelle transitioned out of leadership, another young woman, Bri Laycock, with the same can-do attitude (who was hired one month after Option Line opened in 2003) continued that culture within Option Line up to the present time. Bri is now leading Heartbeat's Ministry Solutions department, which includes Option Line. And the Option Line director is Nafisa Kennedy, who has personally handled 230,000 contacts—by phone, email, and chat! Nafisa knows the women we serve, how we reach and communicate with them, and how to make a smooth transition to our pregnancy help network!

## Unity in the Movement

Option Line has created unity in many ways in the movement besides between Heartbeat and Care Net. It has always been promoted by almost all other pro-life organizations, including advertisers at the local, state, and national levels (who add the Option Line number to their ads). Option Line contact information is found on websites, billboards, in church bulletins, and everywhere a woman might be looking for help. Now, of course, that is primarily on her cell phone! Through the years, Option Line has agreed to answer many other crucial pro-life numbers. These include the Safe Haven number (that women can call to find a safe place to surrender their babies after they are born, no questions asked), numbers attached to media campaigns to reach women (for Virtue Media in Georgia, Michigan Right to Life, and others), state coalitions that do advertising campaigns (Florida and North Carolina), plus about seven hundred maternity homes and other help centers who roll over their phone numbers to Option Line at certain times so no cry for help goes unanswered! Most recently, Option Line started answering the Abortion Pill Reversal number that appears on the internet and in other advertising, sending callers to the nurse on duty who can connect the woman to the life-saving abortion pill reversal protocol (see chapter 13).

After ten years, when Care Net changed their strategic plan, the partners decided to end the joint venture. Heartbeat had the first option to "purchase the assets." This was a major decision for Heartbeat, since we had been sharing the operating costs equally with Care Net, and advertising costs would also fall solely to Heartbeat. We knew that if we committed to taking on the mantle of leadership, we would immediately double the cost of operations. Could we do this and continue to operate at the highest level of excellence? Lives could be at stake if we failed. But we were still passionate about the mission, envisioned thirty years before by our founders, and Option Line was sending so many women to the pregnancy help network and saving so many lives. After great study and prayer, the Heartbeat leadership took a gigantic step of faith. Option Line became solely an outreach of Heartbeat International in 2011. Honoring our ten-year collaboration, Heartbeat still includes the Care Net service centers as part of the Option Line referral network.

## Major Advances This Decade

When we took sole leadership of Option Line in 2011, Heartbeat leaders did not imagine the great strides that would be made from that point on in the history of Option Line! In its first eight years, under the joint venture, Option Line served one million contacts. In the next ten years (2011 to 2021) we have served three million more! Option Line has made advances not only in numbers of those reached but also in services Option Line provides to the worldwide pregnancy help network to strengthen the care provided. Much of this has been accomplished through creative adoption of the latest in technology by Option Line's still young and passionate staff and leadership team, and their constant question: Who and where are the women in need and how can we reach even more of them and connect them centers?

Several examples illustrate the giant leaps and bounds Option Line has made in the last ten years. For example, the Option Line website now includes links to center websites (through our Extend program). All medical information on these websites is standardized and medically referenced so centers and visitors can be assured that all information is accurate; this is a great service to the centers and to the website visitors.

In 2015 Option Line adopted technology that allows some of our phone consultants to answer calls from outside the call center (maintaining oversight of all calls for training purposes can still take place). This allowed us to transition to 24/7 coverage in Spanish as well as English for phone calls, emails, and chats. An Option Line Spanish website was added as well as Spanish language advertising, allowing us to reach and rescue many additional Spanish speakers.

Innovations to draw even more women to Option Line are constant. One is the recent "Online Pregnancy Test." Over 90 percent of those who click it on the Option Line site take the test. It is so engaging that many women want to chat with an Option Line consultant, which is our first step in inviting them to their local pregnancy help center or clinic. Planned Parenthood has a similar test online that leads right into making an abortion appointment. When our staff saw the Planned Parenthood online pregnancy test, they thought, *We can do that!*—and they did it!

Heartbeat's Abortion Pill Rescue Network, APRN (see chapter 13), has made great strides since 2018 when Option Line created a web presence (through Extend) and began advertising abortion pill reversal, thus getting ads in front of many "shoppers" even before they take the first abortion pill. Option Line connects women in need with an APRN nurse who can explain the reversal process and get the caller to a doctor or nurse practitioner who can write the prescription. Option Line consultants are a direct part of saving a life when the reversal process is a success, which only adds to their passion for the lifesaving work they are called to do!

Option Line even found a pro-life doctor in India who was willing to prescribe the APR protocol to an Indian woman who found the APR website after looking desperately online when she changed her mind about aborting her baby. This leads to the question: What are the possibilities for Option Line in Heartbeat's international mission? Option Line has always had a special appeal to our international affiliates, since nothing like it exists in any other country in the world. Option Line consultants already train people (who answer their own phones around the world) through online courses in Heartbeat's Academy. But there are many other unique opportunities for international collaboration.

In Italy's *Movimento per la Vita* (MPV), for example, one of Heartbeat's joint affiliation partners, a hotline called SOS Vita existed for many years and was answered by women on cell phones around the country. The Italians saw the Option Line model and asked for our assistance in training their staff to use a centralized, web-based communications system. They jumped immediately into chats that led to pregnancy help center appointments. In 2015, Option Line Director Bri Laycock taught them Heartbeat's *The L.O.V.E. Approach*, which they translated into *The 5 A's*, and this is now the core training for SOS hotline workers.

Option Line currently takes chats from around the world. An Option Line live chat widget sits on a PHC website in fifteen different countries. Option Line answers the chats and refers women to a phone number in each of these countries. The technology exists for the next step: someone from each of those countries could have a "seat" and chat directly from those countries. Then Option Line would be truly international!

At the beginning of Option Line's eighteenth year (2021), it has transitioned to an "omni-channel" phone system, making it possible to port numbers from around the world—so Option Line could literally also answer phones from around the world. Phone technologies are catching up with technologies like email. The possibilities are mind-boggling!

We are now "an internet world." In the not so distant old days, someone had to "do" the advertising and choose the media. The internet has become the new Yellow Pages and billboards, and the internet itself does the advertising. Because many pregnancy help center websites and other websites aim at Option Line, and since Option Line itself has run ads since 2013, over 100 million "impressions" of Option Line have appeared on a screen—creating awareness that life-affirming pregnancy help exists.

No other organization in the world reaches more women!

When our founders envisioned an 800 number as one of their five original goals in 1971, they could never had imagined the "internet world" of today. Kelle, Bri, and Nafisa, part of the young team noted in this chapter who have run with the technology over the past twenty years, were not even born at the time the original vision was articulated in 1971. Yet it is the same Holy Spirit who has been at work inspiring and empowering "behind the scenes" throughout Heartbeat's fifty years—and He will continue to be in the future. We can't even imagine the possibilities ahead for reaching and rescuing even more lives if we continue our culture of seeing what the Lord is doing and stepping out in faith.

*Option Line opened in 2003 as the first ever web-based, 365 days per year, 24/7, fully staffed call center, having the goal to connect every person in need to her local PHC. It is now answered in English and Spanish. Kelle Berry, front center, founding Director, with the original Option Line staff.*

*Second Director of Option Line, Bri Laycock (2nd from left), now Heartbeat's Senior Director of Ministry Solutions, has brought the Option Line vision and operations worldwide. In 2014 she taught Heartbeat's L.O.V.E. Approach (the basis for Option Line consultations with people in need) to consultants on Italy's hotline "SOS Vita."*

*Nafisa Kennedy joined Option Line in 2006 and personally handled about 230,000 phone calls, emails, and chats before she became Option Line Director in 2017. Other staff—who are answering cries for help and connecting callers to the life-saving centers in their own communities—also bring years of experience on the line!*

*Option Line hosts Father Frank Pavone, with Priests for Life, in 2008, before the latest technology (left). Option Line call center today (right) has the technology for our US consultants to take chats from around the world! It will soon be possible for women on the Option Line platform to chat directly with other women in their own countries!*

*Option Line and Heartbeat staff informally mark Option Line's 2 millionth call in 2014, eleven years after its founding. Six years later, Option Line had doubled its reach to 4 million calls for help.*

# CHAPTER 13

## ABORTION PILL RESCUE

### Jor-El Godsey

Surviving an actual abortion happens so rarely that it is, statistically speaking, nonexistent. Until this past decade, that is. Now it is happening with increasing frequency—at least for the increasing number who select the option of a chemical abortion process (often referred to as a medical, or medication abortion or RU-486, the abortion pill).

Usually it seems true that "there is nothing new under the sun." But the truth here is that abortion pill rescue is indeed something new in our pregnancy help movement. Pro-life medical personnel, especially heroic doctors along with a network of PHCs, make the rescue possible, as they made pregnancy help possible in first place fifty years ago. By the grace of God and these heroic pioneers, there is a new frontier of hope for women who choose abortion in desperation. This chapter tells that story.

### New Chemical to Abort Babies

In the early 1980s, the French pharmaceutical company Roussel Uclaf, seeking to control high blood sugar levels, found that their new compound, mifepristone, worked by blocking the effects of cortisol.

They also found that mifepristone blocked the effects of progesterone, a hormone produced by pregnant women critical to a healthy pregnancy. Rouseff-Uclaf's internal designation for mifepristone was RU-486. Abortion proponents immediately began to position the product as a "new birth control" rather than an abortion-inducing drug.

The French government approved mifepristone as an abortion drug in 1988. The new chemical abortion was approved by the United Kingdom in 1990, Sweden in 1991, and other European countries followed. The Bush (41) administration raised concerns, through the US Federal Drug Administration, about the safety of mifepristone for abortion, and that kept it from gaining a quick foothold in America. But in 1993 the new Clinton administration forced a review of the FDA's findings. Prior to Clinton leaving office in 2000, the FDA approved mifepristone for abortions in pregnancies up to seven weeks.

At the time of the approval of mifepristone (marketed as Mifeprex), the FDA required that prescribers comply with a rarely used protocol known as Risk Evaluation and Mitigation Strategy (REMS). Among the tens of thousands of drugs approved by the FDA, only sixty are currently subject to REMS guidance. In 2016 the FDA expanded the window of use from forty-nine days (seven weeks) to seventy days (ten weeks). The FDA requirement states, "Mifeprex must be ordered, prescribed and . . . may only be dispensed in clinics, medical offices, and hospitals by or under the supervision of a certified healthcare provider."[7]

The abortion industry, through direct action and via proxies, has been challenging this restriction for several years. During the recent COVID-19 crisis, a federal judge lifted the requirement that Mifeprex be dispensed under the supervision of a certified healthcare provider in one of the physical settings described above; he allowed it to be dispensed via tele-med services.

---

7 www.accessdata.fda.gov/scripts/cder/rems/index.cfm?event=RemsData.page, accessed 3/24/2021.

Mifepristone is paired with misoprostol (approved by the FDA for treating ulcers) to create the two-pill abortion pill regimen. Mifepristone, the first pill, works to block the progesterone that sustains the developing baby in the womb. The second pill, misoprostol, is to be taken approximately twenty-four hours after the first pill, often at home, to expel the baby. This is described in abortion pill marketing as a "heavy period." Many women, unfortunately, describe this as a horrendous, bloody experience occurring in their own bathroom, or dorm room. Some report that they even see the tiny baby they are aborting.

Sometimes the first thing a woman feels after taking the first pill, mifepristone, is regret.

## Changing Her Mind

That very thing occurred in 2006 when a young woman phoned Dr. Matt Harrison, a family physician in North Carolina. After taking the first pill, mifepristone, she expressed deep regret to Dr. Harrison and asked if there was anything she could do. Knowing that mifepristone was designed to outcompete the mother's naturally produced progesterone, he prescribed a high dose of prometrium (synthetic progesterone) to try to outcompete the foreign abortion pill.

It worked. Baby Kaylie was seen healthy on the ultrasound just a few weeks later. She was born in 2007 and is the first known successful abortion pill reversal.

Across the country in California, in 2009 Dr. George Delgado was connected to a woman in El Paso, Texas, who had similar regrets about taking the first pill. He quickly devised a protocol similar to Dr. Harrison's to reverse the effects, and the baby was saved. Dr. Delgado, convinced this was happening to many women who were being told there was nothing they could do, began to invite other doctors and nurses to help.

In 2012, the Abortion Pill Reversal Network was created and became an official program of Dr. Delgado's Culture of Life Family

Services, which included his private practice and a PHC. Dr. Delgado established a website on the reversal process and provided a phone number, believing that more women were probably regretting taking that first pill and might seek help to reverse its effects.

He was right.

Rebekah Hagan took the mifepristone pill in the abortion clinic. Upon returning to her car, she looked into the bag containing the second pill, misoprostol (along with some pain medication and an antibiotic). As Rebekah tells it, "Looking through that bag made it real. All of a sudden, that kind of hit me, and I thought, 'Oh, my gosh, what did I just do?'" Right there in her car, she closed her eyes and prayed and looked online for help. She found the new website, Abortion Pill Reversal Network, and called the number. She was referred to a nurse in a PHC who explained how the chemical abortion and the reversal process worked. Then she was referred to a physician. And sixteen hours after taking the first abortion pill, she received progesterone. She continued on progesterone for almost five weeks. It was the first time that particular doctor (whom she later found out was the brother of Dr. Delgado) had prescribed progesterone to counteract mifepristone. In fact, Rebekah recalls, "We had no idea if it was going to work."

In October 2013, Rebekah gave birth to a healthy son. The fledgling network worked for Rebekah. And it was working for women across the country.

As pro-life doctors heard about the need and understood how simple and safe the progesterone protocol was, they jumped on board. Soon there were several hundred doctors dotting the US map. By 2018, several hundred babies had been born healthy.

In fact, Dr. Delgado invited the women contacting his hotline from 2012–2016 to allow their experience to be compiled into a medical study. The resulting "observational case series" included 754 patients who attempted to reverse the chemical abortion process. Published in the medical journal *Issues in Law and Medicine* in 2018, the study showed effective reversal rates of 64 percent (P < 0.001) for intrauterine muscular injection and 68 percent (P <0.001) for oral ingestion.[8] The study also confirmed that there was no apparent increased risk of birth defects. The overwhelming conclusion? Reversing the effects of mifepristone using progesterone is safe and effective.

But Rebekah already knew that. And so did hundreds of other women by that time.

## Big Abortion Shifts to Chemical

Although approved in 2000 for use in the Unites States, the abortion industry was slow to adopt the abortion pill protocol at first.

By 2011, it was used for only 11 percent of all abortions. The FDA expansion of its use to seventy days (ten weeks) in 2016 increase dits use among abortion providers. Coupled with growing telehealth technologies, "tele-abortions" became more and more popular in permissive states. By 2017, more than 30 percent of all abortions were from the abortion pill. It is projected that in 2020, some 50 percent of abortions were by the mifepristone/misoprostol combination. (Actual studies confirming the 2020 numbers will not be available until 2022 or 2023.)

## Heartbeat Gets Involved

Delgado's small but tenacious Abortion Pill Reversal Network (APR Network) was being outpaced by the increasing inquiries for the reversal protocol. Calls were coming in around the clock, a pace that was greater than Delgado's team could handle.

Enter Heartbeat International.

I took that call from Dr. Delgado in 2017 and talked with him about the growing needs.

---

8 https://pubmed.ncbi.nlm.nih.gov/30831017/; see also https://www.researchgate.net/publication/327249344_A_case_series_detailing_the_successful_reversal_of_the_effects_of_mifepristone_using_progesterone.

We were not only big fans of his work in building the APR Network but also had hosted him several times at our annual conferences, where he informed our affiliates and others of the life-saving APR protocol. We have featured his work and several of the powerful success stories in *Pregnancy Help News*.

Dr. Delgado needed help answering the phone in order to address the growing interest in APR. Our Option Line was perfectly positioned to help triage calls for the APR Network. But he also needed some additional website heft for greater outreach, a training platform for the growing team of healthcare professionals, and client-intake and tracking software to facilitate better handoffs to APR providers.

On that call we talked about how, in addition to Option Line, Heartbeat's website and digital marketing team at Extend Web Services could be a help. Our Academy learning platform could be the answer for training tools to onboard providers and pregnancy help centers seeking to get involved. And our just released Next Level Center Management Solution could be adapted for a specific APR client-intake tool and bring much-needed efficiency to the nurses engaging APR prospective patients. Heartbeat International's affiliate network, core products, and new initiatives were the right match to build on Dr. Delgado's pioneering effort.

After a few months of due diligence and board review, Dr. Delgado and I stood on the stage at the Heartbeat International 47th Annual Conference, held providentially in Anaheim, California, Delgado's home state, and we announced that Heartbeat would be assuming operations of the Abortion Pill Reversal Network. We all felt honored and humbled that Dr. Delgado would trust Heartbeat International to adopt his "baby."

That same day, Option Line officially took its very first APR Network call. Such an appropriate opportunity for an organization once known as Alternatives to Abortion International! Who would have ever imagined that an alternative could be provided right in the very midst of an abortion?

It took us a few months to get oriented to the new dynamics. One dynamic was adjusting to the necessary speed of service. For nearly fifty years we've been helping women on their way toward an abortion decision to make a different choice. While there is a general immediacy to that, a woman's decision often takes days, or even weeks.

But the abortion pill reversal had to happen as soon as possible for maximum success.

And, as Rebekah's narrative highlights, women were calling usually within hours of the first pill. Instead of days or a couple of weeks, while a decision is being made or researched, we suddenly only had hours to connect her with life-saving help. We were able to adopt Dr. Delgado's processes and immediately begin to work to refine them.

Moreover, we knew we needed to increase the impact of the APR Network not by addition but by multiplication—by an exponential increase, in fact. With the numbers of chemical abortions already into the hundreds of thousands, we knew we needed to be more efficient, more effective, and scale APR Network in a big way. Fortunately, some key financial partners saw the same need in the same way and gave us a significant grant to ramp up our efforts.

To create more clarity between the Abortion Pill Reversal (APR) medical protocol itself and the team members and myriad of components that were part of the effort, we shifted our branding to the Abortion Pill Rescue Network. There are a number of people at Heartbeat International and in the APR Network that help each woman, from those that create and maintain an effective website and digital marketing to those that answer the initial call at Option Line. From the forty nurses (now) who man the hotline each and every day, including overnight, to the hundreds of doctors and pregnancy help centers that prescribe and follow through, the team is vast.

In truth, the APR Network leverages nearly every department of Heartbeat International. The gracious and gifted leader who oversees the hotline is Christa Brown, BSN, RN. Christa joined Heartbeat

International as a part-time nurse, just a handful of months before APR Network came our way. Having been a veteran of pregnancy help center ministry and leadership in northern Indiana, she took up the full-time challenge (and then some) to strengthen and scale the APR Network.

At the end of 2019 we were able to double the number of lives saved to a total of one thousand—from around 450 between 2012–2017 to more than 550 between 2018–2019! And then, by the end of 2020, even with the coronavirus impact and related lockdowns, we celebrated an additional 1,000 reversals, now counting a total of 2,000 babies saved by the APR Network! Twice as many, in just one-sixth the time.

Just recently, Dr. Brent Boles, a practicing, board-certified OG/GYN for nearly three decades, joined the Heartbeat International team as medical director of APR Network. He has been an integral part of the APR Network Medical Advisory Team since its inception and will provide the guidance and expertise needed to grow the network even further. He will also work with Heartbeat leadership to implement medical impact strategies that serve the pregnancy help movement in even greater ways.

Pregnancy help centers are a vital part of the growing APR service model. Whether an APR mom is connected with the physician first or through a prescribing PHC, there is a critical need for her ongoing support. So often choosing life, even that "last chance" through APR, can be a hotly contested matter by those that encouraged (or coerced) her to abort in the first place. PHCs realize that her decision likely needs love and support beyond just taking the prescription for progesterone. But that's what pregnancy help is: care, compassion, and loving a woman through her pregnancy and beyond. And that's why PHCs are crucial components of the APR Network.

It's no wonder that the APR stories are now abounding.

## Countering the Narrative

And Big Abortion and its allies are not happy.

Even as they make themselves champions of "choice," they actively work to discount the successes and attempt to discredit the obvious effectiveness of progesterone. APR is countering the narrative that a woman can't do anything once she's started an abortion. (In fact, Big Abortion's own research shows that if a woman simply does not take the second pill, depending on her circumstances, 8 to 25 percent of the time the first pill will not "work," allowing the pregnancy to continue.)

In truth, abortion pill reversal is making abortion statistics wrong!

For most abortionists, there is rarely a follow-up call or visit. Most states require abortions to be reported to the Department of Health. This means that each chemical abortion pill they dispensed to a patient are being relayed as an abortion accomplished. Yet APR has helped at least two thousand babies to be born (and counting). If any of those two thousand were reported as abortions, they're wrong! Those abortions were not accomplished. To the contrary, they resulted in lives saved.

There are many children alive today that the CDC, or Guttmacher Institute, still have recorded as abortions.

We need to make more of those statistics wrong. Abortion Pill Reversal and the Abortion Pill Rescue Network will continue to offer women one last chance to choose life! Heartbeat sees the Abortion Pill Rescue Network as a key component of our life-saving and life-changing services in the future.

*These are a few of the thankful mothers who found Abortion Pill Reversal and saved their beautiful babies with the help of the Abortion Pill Rescue Network. To learn more, go to AbortionPillReversal.com.*

*Statistics show that more than 2,000 lives have been saved thanks to Abortion Pill Reversal, including these beautiful babies.*

*Introduced by Vice President of Development Cindi Boston-Bilotta at our 2021 Conference, two heroic mothers who saved their babies through Abortion Pill Reversal tell their stories to the pregnancy help community. On Cindi's right are Sarah Hurm and Rebekah Hagan, with Heartbeat medical team member Lisa Searle.*

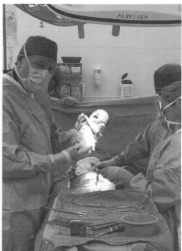

*Providers of Abortion Pill Reversal (APR). Clockwise from left: Dr. George Delgado, developer of the APR protocol and founder of the Abortion Pill Rescue Network, with Jor-El when the network became part of Heartbeat in 2018. Heartbeat APR Medical Director Dr. Brent Boles delivering the first baby he helped save with the APR protocol. Dr. Boles without his medical mask! Christa Brown, BSN, R.N. (right), Heartbeat's Director of Medical Impact, with Dr. William Lile, APR provider, and two doctors (left) in Ireland being trained in APR.*

# CHAPTER 14

# ADVANCING GLOBALLY

## Jor-El Godsey

The international mission of Heartbeat International was near and dear to the heart of our co-founder Lore Maier, that passion was passed on to Peggy, and now it has been passed on to me. In my twenty years on the staff of Heartbeat, one of the most challenging and also rewarding things the Lord has allowed me to do is to get to know and become inspired by the foot soldiers the Lord is calling up around the world.

I have been blessed to host them here in the US and also to "walk with them" them right where they minister. I've been in forty countries on all six continents, marveling at what the Lord is doing in pregnancy help through his humble servants around the globe! Other Heartbeat staff also travel, train, mentor, and marvel. We started keeping track of our miles in 2008. They now total two million (an average of 175,000 miles per year over the last ten years).

But the total number of miles is not the really amazing thing—it is God's people responding to His call. The story of these heroic foot soldiers is the subject of this chapter.

## Where Sin Increased

Russia was the first country in modern history to legalize abortion. That was more than a century ago.

Once legalized, abortion access was then super-charged by Communist policies and decades of socialized medicine. With an abortion rate that averaged twice the birth rate over several decades, some reports suggest the *average* Russian woman has personally endured seven abortions!

In 1979 Comminist China began to require (read that "force") abortions as part of its macabre population control-oriented "one-child policy."

The number of abortions globally is staggering. Conservative estimates place the number exceeding one billion since Russia's legalization. A conservative estimate is 40 to 50 million every year. According to the World Health Organization (WHO), abortion is the leading cause of death each year.

This is true in the US as well, with nearly 900,000 recorded surgical and chemical abortions (primarily via RU-486, part of the "abortion pill" regimen) yearly. About 25 percent of all pregnancies end in abortion. That rate is much higher in some major cities and among African Americans, Latino Americans, and some immigrant groups. According to US CDC statistics, in 2017 abortions exceeded the next leading cause of death, heart disease, by more than 30 percent. In 2020 the estimated number of abortions will certainly exceed all deaths from cancer *and* COVID combined.

In recent years, even traditionally pro-life countries that have withstood the international encroachment of abortion on demand—specifically Ireland and Argentina—have yielded to abortion activism, either by popular vote or political pandering.

This is bad news for the core building block of the civilization: the family. It's even worse news for demography, as many countries fall well below the replacement rate for their indigenous population. Unfortunately, it is good news to the global profiteers of abortion ideology and persistent purveyors of the culture of death.

The sin of abortion abounds globally.

The Apostle Paul, in his letter to the Romans, gave us some hope in reflecting, "Where sin increased, grace abounded all the more" (Romans 5:20).

## Grace Abounds through Pregnancy Help

The abounding grace today is the good news that the Holy Spirit is working mightily and raising up hundreds of thousands of people worldwide who are aware of the problem and are answering the call to help. Our best estimate (a conservative one) is that there are nearly two thousand pregnancy help locations outside the US (which has itself close to three thousand). It is difficult to keep track of the specifics of where and how the Holy Spirit is working, but when it comes to pregnancy help around the world, Heartbeat invests in the effort to keep up-to-date on the global landscape.

From the very beginning, Heartbeat has maintained the Worldwide Directory of pregnancy help, listing what we know of, or knew of at one time, locations of pregnancy help centers/clinics, maternity homes, and other life-affirming pregnancy service providers by country and city.

Fifty years ago, our founders, especially Lore Maier, had a worldwide vision for the pregnancy help movement. As the first executive director, she wrote hundreds of letters to contacts around the world, sharing the vision. She and Dr. John traveled extensively, at their own expense, inviting others to start pregnancy help centers in their own nations and become part of the federation of AAI (now Heartbeat International). These emerging leaders were invited to the annual AAI Academy and encouraged to participate fully as affiliates. As a result international leaders joined the AAI board in the mid-1970s.

It became one of the missional imperatives of AAI to keep track of all the emerging pregnancy help service providers, whether or not they became official affiliates. AAI published this Worldwide Directory each year to be the most complete list of life-affirming pregnancy help, including provider locations around the globe, for the purpose of connecting those looking for help with those looking to help.

Heartbeat International invests key resources to fulfill this task. This year's Worldwide Directory (2021) contains more than four thousand entries for the US (including pregnancy help centers/clinics, medical providers, maternity support organizations, maternity homes and other residential programs, professional social service agencies, nonprofit adoption agencies, and abortion recovery programs), plus 2,849 service locations in 113 other countries. HBI has identified life-affirming programs in more than half the countries of the world.

PHCs use the Worldwide Directory to refer clients for help, when needed, outside their own service area or for a specific help they do not provide themselves (such as housing). They also use it to identify like-minded organizations for networking. Our Option Line (see chapter 12) uses the Worldwide Directory for referrals to centers outside the US and Canada when requests for help are received through the Option Line website (www.optionline.org).

## Equipping and Encouraging

Heartbeat International today, as we have done from the beginning of our history, responds to the growing global abortion threat by equipping and encouraging local and missionary efforts of reach and rescue. We invest time, talent, and treasure into leadership training, resources, and individualized support whenever we are contacted by current—or emerging—pregnancy help efforts outside the United States. We also work proactively to network and support the growing pregnancy help movement worldwide.

Today, indigenous groups are starting most of these new centers, often called to action when Planned Parenthood or a United Nations-sponsored program comes into their region to liberalize abortion laws—ostensibly to take care of "hard cases" (such as rape or incest) or under the guise of "women's reproductive healthcare," much as they did in the US in the late 1960s and 1970s. The real intention of most of these groups is to radically change the sexual mores of the culture, taking away that culture's traditional moral and religious underpinning for marriage and the family. It is heartbreaking to see other countries fall for the same lies that made abortion legal as a "last resort" in the US (during all nine months of pregnancy) almost fifty years ago and is now being promoted as something actually "good."

Heartbeat has been providing leadership training and mentoring for international pregnancy help leaders partly through our annual international training conference since the 1970s. Our current scholarship program provides support to cover part of the expenses for selected international leaders to train at our conference and then visit and network with centers in the United States; international delegates raise support in their own countries for the other part of their expenses.

## Sowing into Emerging Leadership

In 1999, Barbra Mwansa of Zambia came with one of the first groups of ten or so international leaders we invited to join us for the US Heartbeat Conference and stay for intensive training afterward. She or her husband, Pastor Edward Mwansa, has attended almost every conference since, and they have become close partners with Heartbeat. A capable pastoral couple, they caught the vision and have developed over the years a ministry that encompasses a "traditional" pregnancy help center with pregnancy testing and ultrasound services, an abstinence education program in the schools, and a post-abortion program. But the ministry also has a maternity home (built with cement blocks made on site by Barbra and Edward and their many volunteers and added on to when they had the resources to make more blocks); an orphanage, where some of the children are HIV-positive but, because of excellent care, cannot be distinguished from the other children; a feeding program for children that also teaches natural family planning for the mothers;

and a boys' ranch to teach skills to street kids. The Mwansa's work is supported by a for-profit business in Kitwe, local community support, church sponsorship, and individual donors, including pregnancy help centers, from the United States.

In 2000, Lily Perez, along with her husband, Rene, came to the Heartbeat International conference from the Philippines for the first time. They had housed homeless pregnant girls in their own small home. Their first girl had been brought to their home by a local police officer who found the girl wandering in the streets after a major hurricane. He knew that Lily and Rene loved children, so he asked them if they would take her in. They did, and their ministry started that day.

After being trained at the Heartbeat headquarters, Lily left with a passion to do even more in her homeland and her region of the world, along with the knowledge and tools to get started. Eventually, these formalized into the vision for the NGO (Non-Governmental Organization) that they started, calling it Pregnancy Services of Southeast Asia (PSSA). After years of pioneering leadership, PSSA now has six centers, and Lily has contacts in several other regions of the Philippines and elsewhere in Southeast Asia who want to help start pregnancy help centers.

Even though abortion is still illegal in the Philippines, many desperate women can purchase mifepristone on the streets. We learned that a group of Filipino foot soldiers armed with love was formed to visit hospital emergency rooms and minister to women bleeding there (in the midst of abortions caused by mifepristone). These foot soldiers call themselves "Veronicas" after the woman who, in the tradition of the early church, wiped the face of Jesus as He carried His cross on the way to Calvary. Jesus left the image of His face on her cloth (*Vera iconica* means "true image"). They see Jesus' face in the suffering faces of the women who succumb to abortion out of desperation. People in the Philippines are responding with the message of love and hope in community pregnancy centers, so no woman will ever feel that abortion is her only alternative.

The Philippines, Latin America, South Korea, and parts of Africa are in the crosshairs of Planned Parenthood and other pro-abortion forces (who partner with the United Nations) since these countries are among the last remaining distinctly Christian countries in the world. In these places, abortion has almost always been viewed as an abomination. Sex education in the schools and free contraceptives are not yet the norm, as they are in many Western and other developing countries. Generally, children and large family-size are still welcomed and valued. However, these values are eroding at an alarming rate, and pro-life people are fighting desperately in these regions to preserve the legal protections still provided to human life in the womb.

To stand against this tide, and for many other valiant reasons, hundreds of individual leaders have come to the United States to be trained by Heartbeat International over the past decades, from every inhabited continent and more than fifty countries.

Just like in the United States, however, Heartbeat has found that it is not enough to simply respond to those who initiate the contact and come to us for help in establishing pregnancy help centers. We must also go proactively to areas of greatest need, as we have here at home, to help the local church, the Body of Christ, understand the need and catch the vision. Then Heartbeat can provide or facilitate help and support on-site to those who answer the call to champion life.

## Networking and Nurturing

Following the missionary-style travels of our founders in the 1970s and early 1980s, Heartbeat International has continued to travel extensively to create and support pregnancy help networking opportunities across the globe. Oftentimes these are in direct partnership with sister organizations and regional networks.

We have had several successful experiences with Heartbeat-sponsored conferences overseas, creating long-lasting connections and inspiring new pregnancy help leaders and locations. In the first decade of the new millennium, in partnership with LIFE International, we hosted key gatherings in Eastern Europe—in Budapest and Ukraine. We have also supported long-standing pregnancy help networks in Australia and new ones in Africa by sending our staff to provide key trainings at multiple conferences on those continents.

In 2010, when I served as vice president of Affiliate Services for Heartbeat, we began to formalize our relationships with groups that were networking with emerging PHCs in their own countries and regions. We proposed Joint Affiliation Partnerships with these networks, thus creating a global federation of existing and emerging networks. In these special relationships, the centers in other countries, as members of their own network, have membership also in Heartbeat International. Along with joint affiliation of the centers with Heartbeat, we often license our core training materials to the partnering organizations in those regions so they can be translated or modified to better suit the culture and serve their communities. The regions where we currently have Joint Affiliation Partnerships include Canada, Australia, Africa, South Africa, Israel, Italy, Latin America, Spain, and the Philippines.

## European Networks

The largest network of pregnancy help outside the US is that of *Movimento Per la Vita* (MPV), established by renowned Italian pro-life champion Carlo Casini in 1975. A visionary and acclaimed judge and politician, Mr. Casini opened the very first pregnancy help center in all of Italy in his hometown of Florence. His tireless efforts and impassioned eloquence inspired more Italian foot-soldiers to help those facing unplanned and unexpected pregnancies with alternatives to abortion. Mr. Casini (now deceased) was honored with Heartbeat's Legacy Award in 2015.

Today, MPV has more than four hundred pregnancy help locations (*Centri o Servizi di aiuto alla vita* or CAVs) including more than forty maternity homes! Like Heartbeat, they operate a nationwide call/

contact center, known as SOS Vita. The Secretary General of MPV, Dr. Giuseppe Grande, honors Heartbeat and our long-standing collaboration, by referring to SOS Vita as "the Italian Option Line"!

In nearby Spain, *ProVida* (Spanish Federation of Pro Life Associations) originated from the first Pro Life Association of Spain in 1977. Like so many international PHCs, *ProVida* accomplishes its work through the volunteers of its associations in various Spanish cities. *ProVida* promotes respect for all human life through personalized assistance to single mothers, free medical and psychological care for women faced with an unplanned pregnancy, food and housing aid, educational courses, organization of conferences, seminars, and conferences promoting a culture of life. Current president Alicia Latorre organizes this network of nearly forty pregnancy help locations from Barcelona to Sevilla and Bilbao to Madrid.

## Advancing in Africa

Africa Cares for Life was the vision of Gail Schreiner, who started a pregnancy help center in Durban, South Africa, around thirty years ago. Hers was the first pregnancy help center in Africa, as far as we know. Her example spread all over South Africa and nearby countries. The level of personal sacrifice needed to do this work outside the US, such as in Africa, is moving and inspiring. Gail almost had an abortion almost thirty years ago, when her boyfriend took her from Africa to England for the "procedure." But she got off the abortionist's table and refused to kill her child, knowing that she would face the loss of her boyfriend, her job, and the support of her family. And that's exactly what happened because of her choice for life. One woman, a Good Samaritan, however, took Gail into her own home and helped her through her pregnancy. That's how Gail knew there was a need for pregnancy centers. God finally moved her to start one, and she stepped out in faith and said "yes."

In 2000, to unite and support the PHCs that had emerged in South Africa (and some of the neighboring countries of southern Africa),

Gail helped birth the network Africa Cares for Life. After more than twenty years of leadership, Gail handed the reins of leadership to Daniele Gradwell. She has led the network, renamed the Pregnancy Help Network in 2019, into a new season of fruitfulness and faith-filled outreach. She is guiding the vision for "a healthy pregnancy help organization in every community in South Africa," which now numbers just shy of eighty locations.

Barbra Mwansa, mentioned previously, was similarly inspired to start a pregnancy help network after she and her husband Pastor Edward founded their first center in Kitwe, Zambia. Years earlier, Barbra's mother, who feared her teenaged daughter might be pregnant, gave her a commonly used "remedy" to start her period. Barbra attributed her problems in later pregnancies to this abortifacient. The same "remedy" given to Barbra's sister by their mother resulted in her sister's death. Barbra had a calling to save other African girls from this fate. From the Mwansa's home and ministry in Zambia, they have selflessly crisscrossed the African continent envisioning and equipping Christian pastors and lay leaders to establish and support the vital life-saving work in their own cities and countries. This effort has become the Association for the Life of Africa (AFLA), which has blossomed to more than 150 pregnancy help service providers in thirteen different countries across Sub-Saharan Africa.

### And in the Americas . . .

In 1989, while Jorge Serrano Limón was president of the Pro-Life Committee in Mexico, he attended a Human Life International (HLI) conference in New Orleans, where he met Magaly Llaguno, executive director of *Vida Humana Internacional* (VHI), the Hispanic outreach of HLI. Laura Nelson, founder of the Women's Help Centers in Chicago, shared her own personal abortion story at that conference, saying, "If someone had explained to me what was going to happen and what the abortion consisted of, I would never have done it." Jorge, stirred by

Laura's compelling statement, opened the first known Latin American pregnancy help center in Mexico City on August 15, 1989. Known as a Center for Help for Women, or *Centro de Ayuda para la Mujer* (CAM), it became the prototype for other centers. There are currently seventy CAMs in the Republic of Mexico.

Five years later, during a pro-life congress in Guadalajara, Jorge Serrano spoke again with VHI's Magaly Llaguno, this time about establishing a Latin American network of CAMs like those in Mexico. Now in eighteen other countries, there are an additional 130 CAMs that have served more than 300,000 women. Many Latin American countries have not yet succumbed to the pressure to officially legalize abortion in any form. However, laws against abortion providers are neither routinely nor consistently enforced, making chemical and surgical abortions possible and making the need for the pregnancy help outreach, provided by CAMs, acute.

Pregnancy Care Canada (PCC) represents the fulfillment of a long-standing vision for a national organization to serve as a comprehensive Canadian source of expertise and mentoring to equip and empower pregnancy care centers from coast to coast. Beginning in 1989 and through the mid-1990s, several seasoned directors from across Canada met regularly at US conferences (such as Heartbeat's) to encourage one another in their work. Out of these times, what was known as CAPSS (Canadian Association of Pregnancy Support Services) was birthed. More recently, in 2019, Pregnancy Care Canada became the official name and today serves and supports the work of over eighty Canadian pregnancy care centers under the leadership of Laura Lewis, MD.

## Down Under Steps Up

Australia is a country vast enough to be its own continent, yet it has a population concentrated mostly on the coasts. Slightly larger geographically than the US contiguous forty-eight states, the Australian population is less than 8 percent of that of the US.

Rev. Dr. Daniel Overduin, pastor of Redeemer Lutheran Church at Albert Park from 1964 to 1977, had studied the emerging field of bioethics and became a spiritual and scientific champion of the sanctity of life. In response to liberalization of abortion laws, in 1972 Overduin founded Birthline, a South Australian pregnancy help center, the first of its kind in Australia. Next came centers in Brisbane, Newcastle, Hobart, and the Australian Capitol Territory (ACT). In just a handful of years, pregnancy help centers stretched from Cairns to Hobart, Sydney to Perth, and Melbourne to Darwin. Dr. Overduin was a colleague of Heartbeat founders Dr. John Hillabrand and Lore Maier.

In 1979 he was a driving force among seventy-eight people from fourteen agencies who formed the Australian Federation of Pregnancy Support Services. In 2007 the "Federation" changed its corporate structure and began trading as Pregnancy Help Australia Ltd (PHA). For several years, PHA operated a national hotline for pregnancy-related concerns. Today, under a new season of energetic leadership, led by Lara Malin Wynyard, PHA is building upon the national hotline era with greater outreach and connectivity. PHA consists of a network of twenty-two pregnancy help centers that span the continent.

### Israel—A Crossroads of Cultures

The ancient land of Israel is a crossroads of Jewish, Muslim, and Christian heritage. The small nation, comparable to the size of New Jersey, has residents steeped in all of these faiths and the many Middle Eastern cultures of the surrounding region. In the early 1980s, a small group of pro-life individuals learned that approximately one-quarter of pregnancies in Israel were terminated by abortion. After much prayer, the *Be'ad Chaim* ("For Life") Association was formed. It was officially recognized by the Israeli government in 1988, and the first crisis pregnancy center opened that year in Jerusalem. The goal of *Be'ad Chaim* is to offer women new hope, practical help, and healing.

Today, Sandy Shoshoni, national director, oversees various centers throughout the country that provides hotline services, counseling, and practical assistance. Like other networks and PHCs, they provide abortion recovery ministry for women who have aborted and are dealing with reproductive loss. Women from all faiths, as well as the tourists who travel to the Holy Land each year, are helped to choose life. In 2016 *Be'ad Chaim* was recognized with an award from the Israeli Knesset (Parliament) for their faithful contribution to women's health in Israel.

## Outposts of Hope

In Eastern Europe, where Communism all but destroyed the family, the entire region struggles with major demographic issues due to the ravages of abortion. Russia, Ukraine, Hungary, along with many Western European countries, have only a token few pregnancy help outreach efforts.

Influencers in Russia are now trying to reverse the damage done, and they are uniting to try to reconstitute the Russian family and confront the "demographic winter" that is so evident there. Leaders among the Orthodox, such as Fr. Maxim Obukhov, have been laboring for decades to provide pregnancy help and establish local PHCs.

In the Ukraine, long-time Heartbeat affiliate Kharkov Pregnancy Assistance Center, led for nineteen years by Lena Batina, has been a source of faith-filled compassion and courage, yet nearly alone as a service provider amidst a population of more than 40 million.

In Serbia, Vesna Radeka has been a long-serving director of a pregnancy help center in Novi Sad. Despite age-old ethnic tensions, she has traveled across the Balkans, training and encouraging other pregnancy help leaders in their local outreaches. Only in recent years have other Serbian PHCs opened to join Vesna, like the Pro Baby Centre in Belgrade run by Mila Todorovic. Neighboring Croatia now has a pregnancy help center in Daruvar, founded by Anita Jovanović.

Macedonia finally opened its first pregnancy center, Lydia: A Beating

Heart, in 2012 in the capital of Skopje under the visionary leadership of Svetlana Jovanova.

Poland and Malta are the only European countries to hold the line against the encroaching abortion culture. Despite a largely pro-life population, Poland only has a handful of pregnancy help centers, although it has a network of maternity homes supported by the state.

Life Line Malta is a pregnancy support center with a nonprofit helpline operated by Life Network Foundation Malta, a registered NGO whose mission is the endorsement of every human life from conception to natural death. Like every PHC, they provide a warm, friendly interface to help empower people to make life-affirming choices.

Romania has been able to support a number of pregnancy help efforts in the wake of being released from the grip of Communism. A vibrant new leader in Romania is Alexandra Nadane, executive director of *Asociația pentru sprijinirea femeii însărcinate și a familiei* ("The Association for Pregnant Women and Family Support"). Alexandra received "The Heart of the Future" award from Heartbeat, as a young, energetic, tireless champion for life who has spearheaded pro-life efforts from nationwide vigils to opening pregnancy help centers.

Many countries and leaders that space does not allow us to mention in this book are tirelessly laboring in vineyards around the world.

## More to Do in Asia . . . and Beyond

India is a country with more than a billion people and a staggering 15.8 million abortions each year, dominated by sex-selection abortions that especially targets girl babies in the womb. Currently a handful of stalwart pro-life leaders are raising up pregnancy help centers to meet the challenge of helping Indian women access alternatives to the ever-present pressure to abort.

Life for All (LFA) was founded in 2009 by Simon Durairaj and his wife, Johanna, who directs the ministry. They have labored to be a voice for the voiceless in the subcontinent of India. Not only do they operate a maternity home next to their family home, they have been steadily building a national hotline outreach with but a few phone counselors available. LFA has also facilitated national summits each year, often with one in the north and another in the south of this vast country.

Another group of Heartbeat affiliates is known as Bethel House India, which provides life-affirming alternatives to abortion and female infanticide. Bethel House India was founded and run by long-time Canadian missionaries to India, Doug and Anna Roth, who sought to spread the message of life with the disadvantaged. They are raising up and empowering local Indian leadership, such as the national director Godfrey Rajkumar, based in Bangalore, to open a network of pregnancy help centers. In just a few short years of dedicated work, they've successfully opened five PHCs they call Resource Life Centers.

In other parts of Asia, besides the Philippines and India, Heartbeat, in conjunction with our friends at Passion Life led by John Ensor (formerly a board member and staff member of Heartbeat International) is working strategically in areas that must be kept confidential due to the persecution of Christians going on there. We have found that the dedicated Christians in "underground churches" are often totally ignorant of the facts of human development, and they have no concept of what abortion actually is—that is truly destroys a living, growing, human being in the earliest stages of development. They have almost no understanding of what the Bible teaches on the sanctity of every human life. When they learn these truths, they are deeply repentant for their silence on abortion. Despite the risk to themselves, they are keenly motivated to become involved and provide shelter and support for women who, often in ignorance, are being emotionally or physically coerced into abortions.

The need internationally is great. It is estimated that about 55 million abortions occur worldwide every year, and 98 percent of them occur outside the United States.

By some estimates, 98 percent of spending on the pro-life mission is dedicated to 2 percent of the abortion problem found in the United States. That means that a mere 2 percent of such life-saving funding is being spent on 98 percent of the problem in the rest of the world.

In the United States, with the vast amount of resources that we have been blessed with, we must make even greater efforts to share these resources with those overseas who are heroically stepping forward as foot soldiers armed with love. The challenges are daunting, but the Lord is great, and the opportunities are limitless for Christians, including our pregnancy help network here in the US, to become involved with financial investment, prayers, and partnerships around the globe.

Heartbeat reconstituted our World Council in 2019 to help advance our shared mission. The World Council was first formed by our founders, Lore Maier and Dr. John. It calls together foot soldiers around the world for prayer, relationship building, encouragement, support, and wisdom. Its core members are the leaders of Heartbeat's joint affiliation partners in Canada, Australia, Africa, Israel, Italy, Latin America, Spain, and the Philippines. We are committed to work together to reach and rescue as many lives as possible around the world to renew our cultures for life!

Abortion is a global problem that requires even more foot soldiers armed with love to rise up and advance. Heartbeat will do that in solidarity with our brothers and sisters in Christ!

We have celebrated our International mission and trained leaders from around the world at our US Conference since 1999. After the exciting "Parade of Nations," showcasing national flags and traditional costumes, International leaders gather in 2020.

Only Italy and Zambia are close to the US in numbers of PHCs "per capita" (4 per 500,000). Left, with Peggy, is the founder of Italy's Movimento per la Vita, Carlo Casini (with his wife Maria) who received our Legacy Award in 2015. Right, with Jor-El, is Zambia's Barbra Mwansa, founder of Association for Life of Africa. Barbra and husband Pastor Edward Mwansa received our Servant Leader Awards in 2008.

Heartbeat's World Council, leaders of our joint affiliation partners. In first row, beside Heartbeat's President Jor-El Godsey, Ellen Foell, International Coordinator, and Annette Evans, translator, are: Alicia La Torre, Spain; Barbra Mwansa, Africa; Lily Perez, Southeast Asia; Dr. Giuseppe Grande, Italy; second row (L to R): Melissa Heiland (guest); Lara Malin Wynyard, Australia; Sandy Shoshani, Israel; Dr. Laura Lewis, Canada; Danielle Gradwell, South Africa; Magda Hernandez, Latin America.

*Heartbeat has trained international pregnancy help centers and leaders on site for nearly 40 years. In Russia, led by Jor-El (far right), Heartbeat collaborators included leaders from Life International in the US, Russia, the Netherlands, Ukraine, and Georgia. Bri Laycock, Director of Center Solutions for Heartbeat, at the PHC (CAV) in Florence, Italy, and training PHC leaders in St. Lucia.*

*Heartbeat recently initiated bi-annual Leadership Summits in Europe. Heartbeat staff Bri (4th from R), Jor-El, Peggy, and International Coordinator Ellen Foell (8th, 9th and 10th from R) are pictured with some of the participants of the first Summit in Brataslava, Slovakia, 2014. Others were in Bibione, Italy, and Belgrade, Serbia.*

*Jor-El trains on-site in Australia and Peggy trains on site in Zambia. Heartbeat International literally has trained in countries from A-Z.*

# CHAPTER 15

# THE HEART OF THE FUTURE

## Jor-El Godsey

Pregnancy help is not new to the last fifty years—not even close.

The Bible recounts a form of pregnancy help in ancient times when the nation of Israel was under the captivity of Egypt (see Exodus 1:15–20). Pharaoh feared the population increase of the People of God and ordered Hebrew midwives Shiphrah and Puah to kill baby Hebrew boys at birth. Fearing God more than Pharaoh, the midwives still tended to births but refused the ghastly decree, even at their own personal peril.

The midwives were preserved, but Pharaoh was not deterred. His next move was to deputize all "his people" to complete what the midwives would not do. They were commanded to throw every newborn boy into the Nile. One of those newborn Hebrew boys was set adrift in a basket and rescued by Pharaoh's own daughter, who named him Moses (see Exodus 2:1–10). Moses, being a newborn boy, was meant for destruction. But God intervened with His own special kind of pregnancy help.

Fast-forward to the New Testament.

Although far from unplanned by God the Father who sent Him (see John 3:16), many things surrounding Jesus' birth looked very much like an unplanned pregnancy encountered in PHCs today (except the angelic appearance, of course). The pregnant girl was only in her teens, not yet married, and the man with her was not the father of the baby. At one point, they were even temporarily homeless, hence the stable and the manger. Fortunately, we know that God provided for this family in special ways— shelter, resources (gold, frankincense, and myrrh), rescue (flight to Egypt)— in order for Jesus to be able to fulfill His grand plan of redemption.

The pregnancy help community seeks to surround and support women in their pregnancy and even beyond. Pregnancy help is anchored in two powerful biblical truths. The first is God's creative power, promise, and potential for each human life (see Psalm 139). The second is based on the intrinsic value that each and every life should be given the chance to live and be "rescued [from] being taken away to death" (Proverbs 24:11).

While this book has been a celebration of the last half-century of pregnancy help, we are also eagerly looking forward to the next half-century and beyond.

## Getting to the Core, the Heart

The way forward must be informed by the journey taken to get here.

Whether the methods are direct or digital, through counseling rooms or classrooms, in a seat in a building or on the sidewalk outside a building, the core of the mission is love. Love for the woman who is at risk for an abortion, and love for the child who is in danger. Love for the future that God has signaled, and love in the face of fear that cannot see His Hand.

The international symbol of love is a heart. Indeed, the heart is more than a symbol of our love and affections; it is also something that helps indicate health and life.

Since the beginning as AAI in 1971, Heartbeat International has featured the heart symbol as part of our logo. Our current logo, first introduced in 2013, is affectionately, missionally, and even prophetically called the "Heart of the Future." The heart of the movement it reflects is to connect that desperate heart in need with care and compassion, hope and help, truth and trust.

Fifty years from now this will still be the heart of the pregnancy help movement and the community of faithful foot-soldiers that fill its ranks.

## As Many *Lives* as Possible

Heartbeat's mission is "To Reach and Rescue as many lives as possible, around the world, through an effective network of life-affirming pregnancy help, to Renew communities for LIFE." This is Heartbeat's pathway to fulfill our life-saving vision of "making abortion unwanted today and unthinkable for future generations." To make it "unwanted today," we must work to make it an unnecessary path for those in life-and-death decisions about abortion.

"Where will women go for help in unexpected or distressful pregnancies?" This has been a key question people who care about the dignity of every human life have asked, long before 1973. They knew then and know now that most women who "choose" abortion, legal or illegal, do it as a last resort, often because of fear, pressures, or coercion.

While the wheels of politics continue to turn, this avenue has not been and can never be successful in protecting the value and sanctity of all human life. Even in light of improving scientific knowledge through ultrasound or the public revelations of the abortion industry's unthinkable actions, a lasting change in abortion's political machinery has yet to break free from the whims of legislators and the twisting tides of elections.

Meanwhile, for more than fifty years—even before *Roe v. Wade*—the burning question of "where will women go" has propelled the pioneering work of the pregnancy help community. Their efforts manifest in the three thousand pregnancy help organizations across the US, plus an additional two thousand around the globe.

## As Many *People* as Possible

At the core of pregnancy help is our shared understanding that the very best alternative to abortion is another person. It is another person, offering help, hope, compassion, and information, that makes the difference. That difference is found in one-on-one intervention inside the pregnancy centers, or on a mobile unit, and one-to-many in prevention assemblies at the middle school or high school nearby. That difference is one-to-a few in reconciliation groups dealing with regret over a past abortion, or one-to-a classroom of pro-lifers learning to bring life-saving skills more fully into their own daily lives.

Now stepping into our sixth decade, Heartbeat International has found that the strength of our network is precisely in the diverse, localized, proactive, and responsive approach of our organizations— and more importantly, in the pioneering, creative, and entrepreneurial spirit of those who lead and serve in them. As you see in our history, Heartbeat International has always championed the diversity of grassroots approaches to deliver local life-affirming help to women who desperately need it.

The largest network in the world, and the first network founded in the US, Heartbeat International accomplishes our mission through committed, compassionate people. Heartbeat International equips and encourages those currently in the pregnancy help community, inspiring and equipping new members of the compassion arm of the pro-life movement.

For each person we count actively involved in the movement this year, our analysis shows that nearly four times that number of babies are saved from the risk of abortion each year. We envision at least a hundredfold increase into the life-saving work of pregnancy help in the next half-century. That would mean approximately one million people would be actively engaged in championing pregnancy help! That's what it will take to address the 40 to 50 million abortions around the globe each year.

We can see this happening, especially as together we inspire each new generation to show up for the most vulnerable. The generations arising now are already oriented toward a deep sense of social justice. We just need them to engage the greatest social injustice of our time: the intentional killing of innocent human children in the womb.

A necessary part of that hundredfold increase is inviting more multicultural and multinational involvement in leadership and active outreach. Whole countries and cultures are nearly bereft of the power of pregnancy help. But all should be beneficiaries of this life-saving work that counters the culture of death and its population-control mindset. Every continent has at least some real examples to follow of this selfless, almost always, sacrificial service—examples of the kind of life-changing love that will help rescue millions from abortion regret, or worse.

## As Many *Places* as Possible

As we've seen, since the early years of our movement, pregnancy help people quickly found that the strongest services were provided through dedicated locations uniquely positioned to serve at-risk populations. Innovation and entrepreneurial improvements have empowered pregnancy help centers to put to use powerful new technologies, including ultrasound and specialized internet marketing.

In the first five decades of our movement, the number of locations has grown exponentially—from outpacing abortion facilities in the mid 1990s to eventually growing to the current four-to-one ratio of pregnancy help center and clinic locations to abortion clinics in the US. Even the traditional business life cycle curve, with the movement maturing and sometimes consolidating, we've been able to focus on both entrepreneurial and intrapreneural (in-house entrepreneur) improvements, new methodologies, and the strengthening of services and standards of care.

Heartbeat International has already begun to catalyze a new season of growth in service provider locations in the US with our Pregnancy Help

Center Life Launch Program. The average number of at-risk moms choosing life for their babies (which we often call "life decisions") at any one US location is approximately 250 each year. Heartbeat's Life Launch Program alone, adding just ten PHCs a year, will soon result in an added 2,500 life decisions annually. Over the next fifty years, those first fifty Life Launch PHCs (in total) could add 125,000 lives saved just in the US!

Looking at the locations per capita, the US currently has more than four PHC locations (4.126 using 2019 population estimates) per 500,000 people. Zambia's number is similar, with Italy's not far behind. Sadly, for almost all other countries the number (per 500K) is well below one. That means we have a lot of work to do to achieve even one PHC for every half-million people.

Our vision is to see underserved countries and cultures gain the ability to open up new PHC locations for rescue opportunities and increased life decisions. Surprisingly, there are several "underserved" countries which are economically "developed," such as in Western Europe. We see the clear need for every country below one PHC per 500K to strive to reach at least that level. But even reaching one PHC per *million*, outside the US, would add some 6,500 PHCs to the worldwide life-saving effort. If each could see just 150 life decisions, we'd be *saving almost one million more lives every year.*

Even if it took all fifty years just to get to that level of locations, we'd likely see 20 to 30 million more lives saved around the globe. By itself, that's not enough against the death-dealing of Big Abortion. But it would be a significant step up from where we are today.

Some countries that are facing a "demographic winter" (below-zero population growth) will likely have their eyes opened to this critical need. Such a realization should cause them to quickly rethink their liberal abortion laws and move to restrain the demolition of their own demography. Moreover, they should also see how important it is to protect families and precious babies in the womb. When they do, it will bring the revelation that supporting pregnancy help efforts will support their own country's people!

## As Many *Paths* as Possible

However, just adding people and locations will not be enough. To expand the nature of compassionate pregnancy help beyond the traditional structures of service providers, we are going to need new paths, new methods, of deploying pregnancy help people.

These paths must include continued variations of existing models and improvement of recent innovations. Some of these are already finding footing. Some PHCs are expanding into new medical services, while others are going "lean" with an "express" model with simplified services for expedited ministry efforts in busy, high-population areas. Mobile units will scale up in services and down in size to create greater capacities and accessibility. Some "mobile" units are not vehicles, but people who act like field agents and travel to where the need is. The "house calls" of old may have new life in this increasingly disconnected social structure.

The global pandemic has opened up the whole world to virtual outreach. As industry and economies shift in this direction, so must ministries like ours. This virtual outreach method, a modernization of the age-old hotline, opens up larger and larger service areas for meaningful, life-saving ministry. As noted previously, Option Line and Abortion Pill Rescue Network are already reaching around the globe with pregnancy help impact. Like others, we're figuring out the way forward to reach where we can't yet go.

Telehealth is becoming a way of life for millions, and soon even billions. This is one key adaptation that pregnancy help is, only now, beginning to learn how to leverage. It will be a necessity if we are to maximize our ministry metrics for success. This will foster stronger ministry reach and missional outcomes overall by increasing the number of lives saved.

## Renewing Communities for Life

Finally, Heartbeat International's consistent dedication and fortitude in fifty years of advancing life-affirming pregnancy help worldwide reflects our deep commitment and capability to fulfill this mission into the future. It is hard to estimate just how many individuals have been trained, as staff or volunteers, to show and share love to those facing an abortion decision over the past fifty years. How many others have heard the presentations in churches, online, through sermons, and through social media?

Such individuals, equipped with greater knowledge and compassionate clarity to help, have certainly made a difference in, at least, their own families. These families, joined with local pro-life efforts like PHCs, have exerted life-minded influence in their community. Communities with a core value for life, bolstered by churches preaching the gospel of life, make stronger decisions in their policies and protections. This renews communities for life.

Despite the dark political stranglehold abortion has on our culture, there are growing points of light shining with hope. The actual abortion numbers—at least, in the US and a few other countries—have been declining for thirty years. The US abortion rate is the lowest it's been since *Roe v. Wade* (1973).

And that's the good news, such as it is, on the "abortion" side. The decline of abortions has been inversely related to the growth of the pregnancy help movement, its community, and its work.

Over our fifty years, we can estimate, conservatively, that more than five million moms at-risk for abortion were helped to make a choice for life. And that's just in the US! That means more than five million families were blessed by the birth of a child that could have otherwise been lost to abortion. This is the equivalent of saving the population of whole countries like New Zealand or Norway. Or that of US states Tennessee and Alabama. Or cities the size of Atlanta or Washington, DC.

Babies change families. Families change communities. Communities change countries. All of these change culture. Our impact for the culture of life ultimately works on many levels: for the family, with the church, within the community, and within our countries to affect the culture.

The last fifty years prove that good people can network together to accomplish great things!

The next fifty years promise to be more of the same as the ranks of pregnancy help swell each year. The pregnancy help movement will continue to reach and rescue lives. We will continue to renew families and friends, communities and countries, lifetimes and lineage because the heart of the future is love and life! We will continue to be faithful, faith-filled champions until abortion is unwanted today— and unthinkable in future generations!

The "Heart of the Future" is saving and changing as many Lives as possible, with as many People as possible, in as many Places as possible. This map shows where Heartbeat affiliated pregnancy help organizations were located in 2020, just going into Heartbeat's 50th year. And it shows where pregnancy help will be going and growing in Heartbeat's next 50 years!

Track how pregnancy help expands each year—to make abortion unwanted now and unthinkable in future generations—with the most current Life Trends report on heartbeatinternational.org/lifetrends.

# APPENDIX I

## HEARTBEAT INTERNATIONAL SERVANT LEADERS (1996–2021)

Servant Leader Awards are given to recognize special people who have given of themselves sacrificially in the service of life, as both servants of others and leaders in their own right.

Jesus is our model of Servant Leadership. The Son of God, the most powerful person to ever live on this earth, was also the Good Shepherd who gave up his life for His sheep. The night before He died, He washed the feet of His disciples, telling them:

> "You call me Teacher and Lord; and you are right, for so I am. If I then, your Lord and Teacher, have washed your feet, you also ought to wash one another's feet. For I have given you an example, that you should do what I have done to you." (John 13: 13–15)

The Servant Leader Awards were inaugurated at Heartbeat International's 25th Anniversary Conference (1996) and given to individuals and couples who were some of the "giants" in the first two decades of Heartbeat's history when we were called Alternatives to Abortion International.

On the occasion of Heartbeat International's 50th Anniversary Conference (2021), the award was renamed The Peggy Hartshorn Servant Leader Award to recognize the first president of Heartbeat International, who served in leadership from 1993 though 2015.

## Servant Leader Award Recipients

| | | | |
|---|---|---|---|
| 1996 | Esther Applegate | 2003 | Dr. John C. Willke, MD |
| 1996 | Alice and Dr. Frank Brown | 2004 | Kurt Entsminger, JD |
| 1996 | Dr. John Hillabrand, MD | 2004 | Vivian Koob |
| 1996 | Annette Krycinski | 2004 | Gail Schreiner |
| 1996 | Lore Maier | 2005 | Kelle Berry |
| 1996 | Anne and Jimmy Pierson | 2005 | Vicky Botsford |
| 1996 | Ursula and Ed Slaggert | 2005 | Susan Brown |
| 1996 | Sister Paula Vandegaer | 2005 | Father Frank Pavone |
| 1997 | Carol Aronis | 2006 | Russ Amerling |
| 1997 | Margaret Lee | 2006 | Linda Augspurger |
| 1998 | Rev. John Ensor | 2006 | Beth Diemert |
| 1998 | Dr. Pam Smith | 2007 | Anne Foster |
| 1999 | Molly Kelly | 2007 | Sam and Gloria Lee |
| 1999 | Pat Lassen | 2007 | Dinah Monahan |
| 1999 | Imre Teglasy | 2008 | Dr. Alveda King |
| 2000 | Jim Manning | 2008 | Pat Layton |
| 2000 | Juergen Severloh | 2008 | Edward & Barbra Mwansa |
| 2000 | Julie Wilson | 2008 | Julie Parton, PhD |
| 2000 | Curt Young | 2009 | Pauline & George Economon |
| 2001 | Sheila Boyle | 2009 | John Tabor |
| 2001 | Kurt Dillinger | 2009 | Janet Trenda |
| 2001 | Rev. Johnny and Pat Hunter | 2009 | Dr. Levon Yuille |
| 2001 | Bethany Woodcock | 2010 | Marianne Casagranda |
| 2002 | Dr. Elaine Eng | 2010 | Sandy Epperson |
| 2002 | Olusegun Famure | 2010 | Jorge Serrano |
| 2002 | Tom Glessner, JD | 2010 | Charles & Barbara Thomas |
| 2002 | Mike Hartshorn, JD | 2011 | Lola French |
| 2003 | Rev. David Bentley | 2011 | Patricia Lindley |
| 2003 | Dr. Eric Keroack, MD | 2011 | Elaine Ham |
| 2003 | Mary Suarez Hamm | 2011 | Cindi Boston |

| | | | |
|---|---|---|---|
| 2012 | George & Louise Eusterman | 2020 | Kim Triller |
| 2012 | Jeannette Kuipoff | 2020 | Judy Vasquez |
| 2012 | Pat Sween | 2020 | Robyn Chambers |
| 2012 | Lily Perez | 2020 | Amy Scheuring |
| 2013 | Amy Jones | 2021 | Robert Foust |
| 2013 | Ann Carruth | 2021 | Brenda Newport |
| 2013 | Beverly Kline | 2021 | Mary Peterson |
| 2013 | Becky Coggin Hyde | 2021 | Michael Spencer |
| 2014 | Paula Grimsley | 2021 | Margaret (Peggy) Hartshorn, PhD |
| 2014 | Kirk Walden | | |
| 2014 | Kim Warburton | | |
| 2014 | Bobbie Meyer | | |
| 2015 | Sol Pitchon | | |
| 2015 | Debbie Nieport | | |
| 2015 | Chuck Donovan | | |
| 2015 | Carlo Casini | | |
| 2016 | Phil Holsinger | | |
| 2016 | Rev. Andy Merritt | | |
| 2016 | Lena Batina | | |
| 2016 | Joy Pinto | | |
| 2017 | Tom Lothamer | | |
| 2017 | John McCastle | | |
| 2017 | Susan Barrett | | |
| 2018 | Dr. George Delgado, M.D. | | |
| 2018 | Sharon Pearce | | |
| 2018 | Kerry Jepson | | |
| 2018 | Ken & Cathy Clark | | |
| 2019 | Giuseppe Grande, MD, PhD | | |
| 2019 | Mark McDougal | | |
| 2019 | Martha Avila | | |
| 2019 | Timothy Jaccard | | |
| 2019 | Alexandra Nadane | | |

# APPENDIX II:

## HEARTBEAT INTERNATIONAL LEGACY AWARD RECIPIENTS (2011–2021)

Heartbeat International Legacy Awards recognize people and organizations whose contributions represent a major and lasting impact in the pregnancy help movement, affecting generations to come.

Heartbeat International Legacy Awards were inaugurated on our 40th Anniversary (2011).

### John Hillabrand, MD, 2011

Founder of Alternatives to Abortion Incorporated (AAI) in 1971, "Dr. John" provided strong medical roots, values of professionalism and collegiality, and an emphasis on love and service to both mothers and babies, foundational to Heartbeat International and our movement.

### Lore Maier, 2011

Founder of Alternatives to Abortion Incorporated (AAI) in 1971, Lore provided a passionate call to defend the dignity of every human life, through a service of acceptance and love, that "knows no boundary to origin, country, religion, education, political persuasion, or social standing," foundational to Heartbeat International and our movement.

### Sister Paula Vandegaer, SSS, 2011

Founder of Alternatives to Abortion International (AAI) in 1971, Sister Paula, an early proponent of the dignity and unique "psychology" of women, wrote the first "Counseling Manual" for pregnancy help whose principles are found in almost every subsequent pregnancy help training course.

### Anne and Jimmy Pierson, 2011

Founders, in the 1970s, of the "family model" maternity home, housing a small group of pregnant mothers with a Christian family of mother, father, and children to model and demonstrate the strong family unit and especially the value of fatherhood and beauty of the adoption option.

### Thomas Glessner, JD, 2011

Founder of National Institute of Family and Life Advocates (1993), and the leading proponent in the 1990s of the medical use of ultrasound within pregnancy help centers.

### Sylvia Johnson-Matthews, 2011

Founding visionary and executive director of Fifth Ward Pregnancy Center in Houston, Texas, in 2004, a model pregnancy help ministry located in an abortion "hot spot" and led primarily by and for African American women and families who are targeted by the abortion industry.

### Carlo Casini, 2015

Italian judge, and later a member of the European Union Parliament, who founded the first pregnancy help center in Italy (Florence) and then created and led *Movimento per la Vita*, with the plan for a pregnancy help ministry in every region of Italy, making it the largest group of centers in any one country outside of the US.

### Right to Life League of Southern California, 2018

Founded in 1968, the League started the first pregnancy help hotline in 1971, was one of the first affiliates of AAI, and was the first regional network of pregnancy help ministries.

### Birthright International, 2018

Creator of the first "pregnancy center" and first affiliation group for pregnancy help centers, characterized by a focus on volunteerism, a single name, and an operations charter; started in Canada by Louise Summerhill who opened the first Birthright center in Toronto in 1968.

### Pastor Andy Merritt, 2021

Andy served Edgewood Baptist Church in Columbus, Georgia, for over forty years, where he pioneered the nation's first Evangelical church-sponsored Pregnancy Help Center (1981) and the New Beginnings Adoption Agency (1984).

### Heartbeat of Toledo, 2021

One of the first pregnancy centers in the US, opened in 1971 by Heartbeat founder Dr. John Hillabrand and located in the same building as his medical office in Toledo, Ohio. Heartbeat of Toledo exemplifies the pro-life medical roots of pregnancy help. Lore Maier, Heartbeat founder, and Dr. John's nurse, Esther Applegate, RN, pioneered "pregnancy help" at this center.

### George Delgado, MD, 2021

The medical director of Culture of Life Foundation in San Diego, George pioneered the medical protocol that became Abortion Pill Reversal (in 2009) and founded the Abortion Pill Rescue Network, adopted by Heartbeat International in 2018.

### Dinah Monahan, 2021

Dinah hosted women in her own home until founding Living Hope Women's Centers and Hope House Maternity Home in 1999 and the first Native American-led pregnancy help center (all in Arizona), along the way creating *Earn While You Learn (Bright Course),* a program used by pregnancy help organizations worldwide.

**Martha Avila, 2021**

Founding executive director of Heartbeat of Miami, a model pregnancy help medical clinic group, opened in 2007, located in an abortion "hot spot" and led primarily by and for Hispanic women and families who are targeted by the abortion industry.

**Margaret "Peggy" Hartshorn, PhD, 2021**

First president of Heartbeat International (1993-2015) who clarified Heartbeat's Christ-centered identity, prioritized Christian unity within the movement, wrote *The L.O.V.E. Approach* (1994) and other seminal training materials, and co-founded Option Line (2003).

# APPENDIX III

## HEARTBEAT INTERNATIONAL
## BOARD MEMBERS (1971–2021)

Diane Abernathy, West Chester, OH

Barbara Williamson Adams, Dallas, TX

A.G. Ladd Alexander, Shreveport, LA

Florina Alexander, Shreveport, LA

Esther Applegate, Toledo, OH

Carol Aronis, Loveland, OH

Keith Armato, Park Ridge, IL

Dr. Conrad W. Baars, San Antonio, TX

Peggy Becker, Cincinnati, OH

Fred Bein, Columbus, OH

Alejandro Bermúdez, Englewood, CO

Ron Blake, Galena, IL

Cindi Boston, Springfield, MO

Ann Boyle, Glasgow, Scotland

Alice Brown, St. Cloud, MN

Dr. Frank Brown, St. Cloud, MN

Judie Brown, Washington DC

Dorothy Butcher, Palos Verdes, CA

Rev. Charles Patrick Carroll, Collegeville, PA

Shiney Cherian Daniel, Mesquite, TX

Pat Chumbley, Phoenix, AZ

John Cissel, Lynnfield, MA

Cathy Clark, Yorba Linda, CA

Msgr. Eugene V. Clark, Crestwood, NY

Ken Clark, Yorba Linda, CA

Gary Crum, Washington DC

Paula Salsedo Cullen, Spokane, WA

Chris Dattilo, Bluffton, SC

Joe Dattilo, Bluffton, SC

Mercedes R. de Martinez, Bogota, Columbia

Pia de Solenni, Del Mar, CA

Nancy Donner, Columbus, OH

Chuck Donovan, Cincinnati, OH

Msgr. Michael J. Doyle, Toledo, OH

Jim Dundas, Dover, DE

Grit Ebner, Vienna, Austria

Randy Engel, Export, PA

Rev. John Ensor, Boston, MA

Diana Escobar, Pensacola, FL

Maria Fitzpatrick, Phoenix, AZ

Dr. James Ford, Downey, CA

Thomas Glessner, Fredericksburg, VA

Jor-El Godsey, Lewis Center, OH

Felicia Goeken, Alton, IL

Rev. Gilberto Gomez, Bogota, Columbia

Doug Grane, Wilmette, IL

Karen Gregoire, Great Falls, MT

Marion V. Grimes, Lackawanna, NY

Rev. Richard Groshek, Lansing, MI

Mari Anne Hamilton-Cotter, Chicago, IL

John E. Harrington, Peterborough, ON, Canada

Thomas Hajdukiewicz, Sewickley, PA

Mary Suarez Hamm, Silver Spring, MD

Nola Hanes, Ann Arbor, MI

Bente V. Hansen, Oslo, Norway

Jane Hanzel, Detroit, MI

Margaret Hartshorn, Columbus, OH

Michael Hartshorn, Columbus, OH

Jackie Henry, Glen Ellyn, IL

Marie Hern, Milwaukee, WI

Dr. John Hillabrand, Todedo, OH

Mary Anne Hughes, South Bend, IN

Chris Humphrey, Pittsburgh, PA

Patricia Hunter, Fayetteville, NC

Larry Jacobs, Rockford, IL

Rosemary Hamilton Jandron, East Lansing, MI

Marie Karbus, Granada Hills, CA

Garza Kelly, Arlington, VA

Alveda King, Atlanta, GA

Annette Krycinski, Dimondale, MI

Ann Laird, Houston, TX

Charles Lamar, Frisco, CO

Jeremiah Leary, Cincinnati, OH

Margaret Leary, Cincinnati, OH

Rev. Stephen Letourneau, Hayes, KS

Ceil Levatino, Las Cruces, NM

Anthony Levatino, Las Cruces, NM

Lorna Lincke, Whittier, CA

Dyxie Lincoln, Colorado Springs, CO

Gregory Loesch, Columbus, OH

Betty Loescher, Minneapolis, MN

Anthony Logan, Indianapolis, IN

Peg Luksik, Johnstown, PA

Barbara Lund, Fargo, ND

Dr. William A. Lynch, Boston, MA

Lore Maier, Toledo, OH

Jim Manning, New York, NY

Rita Marker, Snohomish, WA

Elinor Martin, Yonkers, NY

Derek McCoy, Seabrook, MD

Brandon McCrary, Dallas, TX

Anne McDonald, Fort Wayne, IN

Carol McMahon, Pittsburgh, PA

Marie Meaney, Front Royal, VA

Dr. Patricia Mena, Santiago, Chili

Pastor Oscar Mendoza, Bethlehem, PA

Ancil Mitchell, Oxnard, CA

Dr. John F. Monagle, Toledo, OH

Elizabeth Mullins, St. Louis, MO

John Murphy, San Martin, CA

Anne Murray, LaHabra, CA

Rev. Denis O'Brien, Mexico City, Mexico

Bodil B. Oftestad, Oslo, Norway

Joseph Orr, Toledo, OH

Rev. Prof. Daniel Ch. Overduin, S. Australia

Julie Parton, Garland, TX

Robert Pearson, Honolulu, HI

Steven J. Perrin, Wichita, KS

Judy Peterson, Orlando, FL

Anne Pierson, Lancaster, PA

Rev. Pierre Primeau, Bogota, Columbia

Robbie Randolph, Greer, SC

Sister Maryann Regensburger, Waukegan, IL

Victor G. Rosenblum, Chicago, IL

David Rudolph, Los Angeles, CA

Richard L. Schleicher, Huntington Beach, CA

Dr. Edward Sheridan, Washington, DC

Andy Show, Columbus, OH

Zeke Swift, Cincinnati, OH

Marilyn Szewczyk, Baltimore, MD

John Tabor, Tucson, AZ

Thome, Gary, Houston, TX

Janet Trenda, Ontario, CA

Patrick Trueman, Chicago, IL

Sister Paula Vandegaer, Los Angeles, CA

Joseph G. M. Vidoli, Perrysburg, OH

John Wasserman, Toledo, OH

Mary Weyrick, Paso Robles, CA

Margaret White, Croyden, England

Rev. Carey C. Womble, MD, Tucson, AZ

Pastor John Wootton, Galena, OH

Sherry Wright, Cisco, TX

Rev. Curtis J. Young, Washington, DC

George Zallie, Clementon, NJ

# APPENDIX IV

## HEARTBEAT INTERNATIONAL CONFERENCE HOST CITIES (1972–2021)

| | | | |
|---|---|---|---|
| 1972 | Collegeville, Minnesota | 1997 | Orlando, Florida |
| 1973 | Kenosha, Wisconsin | 1998 | St. Louis, Missouri |
| 1974 | Toledo, Ohio | 1999 | Baltimore, Maryland |
| 1975 | Los Angeles, California | 2000 | Columbus, Ohio |
| 1976 | New Orleans, Louisiana | 2001 | Glendale, California |
| 1977 | Pittsburgh, Pennsylvania | 2002 | Pittsburgh, Pennsylvania |
| 1978 | St. Louis, Missouri | 2003 | Omaha, Nebraska |
| 1979 | Washington, DC | 2004 | Charlotte, North Carolina |
| 1980 | Chicago, Illinois | 2005 | Chicago, Illinois |
| 1981 | Phoenix, Arizona | 2006 | Orlando, Florida |
| 1982 | New York, New York | 2007 | St. Louis, Missouri |
| 1983 | Lansing, Michigan | 2008 | Dallas, Texas |
| 1984 | Baltimore, Maryland | 2009 | Richmond, Virginia |
| 1985 | Denver, Colorado | 2010 | Orlando, Florida |
| 1986 | Columbus, Ohio | 2011 | Columbus, Ohio |
| 1987 | Baltimore, Maryland | 2012 | Los Angeles, California |
| 1988 | Detroit, Michigan | 2013 | Dallas, Texas |
| 1989 | Lake Buena Vista, Florida | 2014 | Charleston, South Carolina |
| 1990 | Pittsburgh, Pennsylvania | 2015 | St. Louis, Missouri |
| 1991 | Toledo, Ohio | 2016 | Atlanta, Georgia |
| 1992 | Cincinnati, Ohio | 2017 | Chicago, Illinois |
| 1993 | St. Paul, Minnesota | 2018 | Anaheim, California |
| 1994 | Columbus, Ohio | 2019 | Dallas, Texas |
| 1995 | Pittsburgh, Pennsylvania | 2020 | Virtual Conference ("Covid Year") |
| 1996 | Chicago, Illinois | 2021 | Columbus, Ohio, plus Virtual |

# APPENDIX V

## OUR COMMITMENT OF CARE
## AND COMPETENCE

Originating in the early 1990s and inspired by Heartbeat's original Affiliation Principles from the 1970s, the "Commitment of Care" focused on client care. It was formally adopted by major US pregnancy help affiliation organizations in January 2001. This ethical code of practice dispelled abortion activists' false accusations and formed the basis for strong client service approval ratings.

Robust growth of pregnancy help efforts brought additional scrutiny. In response, the Leadership Alliance of Pregnancy Care Organizations (LAPCO) added new basic standards for organizational competency. This expanded "Commitment of Care and Competence" was introduced in 2009 and updated in 2019.

This commitment to ethical practices is the core standard for affiliation for all major life-affirming pregnancy help affiliate groups.

- Clients are served without regard to age, race, income, nationality, religious affiliation, disability, or other arbitrary circumstances.

- Clients are treated with kindness, compassion and in a caring manner.

- Clients always receive honest and open answers.

- Client pregnancy tests are distributed and administered in accordance with all applicable laws.

- Client information is held in strict and absolute confidence. Releases and permissions are obtained appropriately. Client information is only disclosed as required by law and when necessary to protect the client or others against imminent harm.

- Clients receive accurate information about pregnancy, fetal development, lifestyle issues, and related concerns.

- We do not offer, recommend, or refer for abortions, abortifacients, or contraceptives. We are committed to offering accurate information about related risks and procedures.

- All of our advertising and communication are truthful and honest and accurately describe the services we offer.

- We provide a safe environment by screening all volunteers and staff interacting with clients.

- We are governed by a board of directors and operate in accordance with our articles of incorporation, by-laws, and stated purpose and mission.

- We comply with applicable legal and regulatory requirements regarding employment, fundraising, financial management, taxation, and public disclosure, including the filing of all applicable government reports in a timely manner.

- Medical services are provided in accordance with all applicable laws, and in accordance with pertinent medical standards, under the supervision and direction of a licensed physician.

- All of our staff, board members, and volunteers receive appropriate training to uphold these standards.

# ABOUT THE AUTHORS

**Margaret (Peggy) H. Hartshorn, PhD**, became involved in the pro-life movement soon after the Supreme Court decision *Roe v. Wade* on January 22, 1973. Peggy and her husband, Mike, joined the local Right to Life group, and they began housing pregnant women in their home in 1975. They first learned about Heartbeat, then called AAI, in 1978, and Peggy joined the AAI board in 1986. Peggy and Mike opened Pregnancy Decision Health Centers in Columbus, Ohio, on January 22, 1981, where Peggy served as chairman of the board for over twenty years.

In 1993 Peggy resigned from her job as a professor of English at Franklin University in Columbus, Ohio, to become the first full-time president of Heartbeat International. She served in this position for twenty-three years, leading the organization during a period of major growth and expansion. She has served Heartbeat as chairman of the board since 2016.

Peggy has been married to Mike for fifty-two years. They have two adopted children, now married, and five grandchildren.

**Jor-El Godsey** has been actively involved in the pro-life movement since 1987. From board work with a start-up pregnancy help center in South Florida (1991) to an executive director role in Colorado (1999), Jor-El has been involved with various aspects of local pregnancy help leadership and ministry. Jor-El joined Heartbeat International in 2006 as vice president of Ministry Services and became vice president of the organization in 2013.

Jor-El became president of Heartbeat International in 2016. He leads "Heartbeat Central," which offers extensive training opportunities worldwide in our Academy, practical tools for center operations in our Center Solutions division, and far-reaching programs such as Option Line and Abortion Pill Rescue Network.

Jor-El met his wife, Karen, while attending a pregnancy help training, and they were married in 1994. They have three adult children and make their home in Columbus, Ohio.

# ACKNOWLEDGMENTS

Thanks are due especially to our passionate partners around the world—the pregnancy help community "on the ground" that is continuing to create the history of this amazing movement. It is these foot soldiers armed with love who are living the stories told in this book and those that will be told in years to come. I thank the mothers and families who have allowed us to share their experiences, their beautiful faces, and those of their children—who are here because of a courageous choice for LIFE.

I also thank those who created Alternatives to Abortion International (AAI) in 1971 and with whom we are blessed to be in contact with during our fiftieth birthday year!

Sister Paula Vandegaer, one of our three founders, spoke with me, offered great encouragement, and, despite her failing health, she sent a personal video message to our 2021 conference participants. Sister Paula will always be one of my personal heroes and role models, and I thank the Lord for allowing her to celebrate Heartbeat's 50th birthday, part of the fruit of her labors here on earth, before He welcomed her into eternal life.

Also, thanks to Esther Applegate, Dr. Hillabrand's nurse, AAI "consultant" for new pregnancy help centers, and first volunteer at Heartbeat of Toledo (one of the first pregnancy help centers in the US), who sent us touching pictures of founder Lore Maier. Alice Brown, first AAI board chair, and her husband, Dr. Frank Brown, also an early board member, and Dr. Charles Hermes, a colleague of Dr. Hillabrand who attended many of the early organizational meetings, are still in contract with us. It is these heroes and their contemporaries to whom we owe such a debt of gratitude for the strong foundation they built.

Heartbeat's president Jor-El Godsey helped envision the project from the very beginning as a history of the entire pregnancy help movement through the lens of Heartbeat International, and he made an excellent co-author every step of the way!

Andrea Trudden designed the cover and picture layout. For picture selections, I had great assistance from Andrea and Lauren Bell who searched our photo archives, and NIFLA allowed us to use their photos related to the *NIFLA v Becerra* decision. Several Heartbeat staff members helped by reading drafts of chapters and offering feedback, searching personal pictures (and memories) at my request to help tell the stories, and doing fact-checking: Betty McDowell, Beth Diemert, Ellen Foell, Bri Laycock, and Mary Peterson. Karen Hartman helped with printed and electronic archives. Final proofreading was done by Karen Ingle. Copyeditor Claudia Volkman, who shares our passion for LIFE, worked faithfully to improve the style and readability of this book and offered crucial feedback.

Thank you all!

Errors and omissions (and there must be many in this fifty-year history of such a powerful and diverse movement!) are my responsibility.

—Peggy Hartshorn